FAIRY FILMS

ACKNOWLEDGEMENTS

The road to making *Fairy Films* has been a long and winding one, with plenty of unanticipated complications along the way. Now that it is finally realized, I would like to express my deepest gratitude towards those who helped bring this collection to life:

All of the essayists, not only for their insightful contributions, but also for their enthusiasm and unwavering patience in seeing this collection to completion;

Natania Barron, for the lovely cover;

For everyone who triple-checked my double-checks and still found bits that slipped under the radar;

And my friends, family, and those who endorsed this collection.

Finally, special appreciation for the intervention of Hope & Patrick Dugan, Jim Nettles, and everyone at Educated Dragon, without whom this project might have endlessly lingered in limbo.

INTRODUCTION

Joshua Cutchin

We act like the world is modern.

Don't get me wrong—in many respects, it is, with quite a bit to like. Within twenty-four hours, I can be on the other side of the planet if I choose to do so, riding in an automated vehicle with self-heated seats, all while carrying the Library of Alexandria in my pocket. Contemporary advancements deserve all the accolades heaped upon them, from trivial matters of convenience to lifesaving medical treatments.

With this comes hubris, however. We are the pinnacle of human evolution (we think). Every technological advance sweeps away the detritus of superstition (we think). Each new wave of scientific understanding casts light into the darkest recesses of existence (we think). But our current environment—at the very least, the way its inhabitants think—is not modern.

Modernity is a story we repeat because it comforts us. It grants us the *veneer* of sophistication, the *appearance* that our superstitions have been stripped away... but scratch the surface, and you will find that the old ways never truly left. We just hid them. Our silly world has covered ancient beliefs in a sophisticated *glamour* no less potent than the most convincing magical illusion.

What, pray tell, do I mean by this? For illustration, consider—a predictable example, given the book you hold in your hands—the Good Neighbors, the Fair Folk, the Gentry. The fairies. Few people believe in their existence, and that small handful is often hard-pressed to admit as much in mixed company. Modernity has obliterated the fairies from serious thought and discussion entirely. Nothing remains of them, save the amusements of children.

Or so we are told. But remember: *the old ways never truly left.* The Wee Folk retreated from the hills and dales of our landscape into our culture, where they yet remain.

Simply take a look at language. The small mouth noises that we make are poor placeholders for the actual, ineffable nature of reality. Even if we ignore this fundamental truth, we find superstition clinging to our vocabulary like morning dew (at least in English—I'm sure readers may find similar examples in their own native tongues). The words we choose betray how deeply our superstitions run.

Glamourous. Stroke. Bug. Cobalt. Nymph. Ghillie suit. These words and terms—there exist many others—all, to some degree, originate in fairy belief, yet remain with us today. Contemporary culture's insistence that fairies hold no sway over us is a fallacy. Denying their influence is to yield to the glamour of modernity.

Even more evident is the appearance of fairies across practically every industry. A trip down the supermarket aisle reveals all manner of mermaids, pixies, leprechauns, tommyknockers, and elves hawking processed foodstuffs. Pay attention, the next time you find yourself sitting at a stoplight; odds are, there's a gnome staring back at you from the logo of the landscaper's pickup truck.

These niches offer a fine refuge for fairy belief, but none substantively change or shape culture. They don't need to, because the Gentry long ago captured the true levers of power: our media landscape. Fiction furnishes fairies with fertile fields to flourish, both overtly and covertly.

I have long been fascinated by how the "hidden hand" of fairy belief influences our most popular modern media, namely motion pictures and television programming. *Fairy Films: Wee Folk on the Big Screen* delves into how, against all odds, these ancient beliefs persist from the depths of time, only to seep through the most unlikely of places, the glowing screens that have captured our collective imagination for over a century.

The original vision for *Fairy Films* only encompassed motion pictures without direct ties to fairy folklore—in other words, media where no fairies were literally depicted onscreen but rather where fairy belief nonetheless bubbled to the surface of its own accord. Such is the true power behind these archetypes.

Several of these essays employ this strategy, tackling films where fairies never appear, but where their influence is nonetheless palpable: my own essay on the 2013 Dutch thriller *Borgman*; Mark Anthony Wyatt's whimsical approach to the cult classic television series *Twin Peaks*; Dr. David Floyd's Jungian examination of the science-fiction classic *Close Encounters of the Third Kind*; Wren Collier's masterful take on J-Horror. Even the 1984 adaptation of *Dune* and the 1975 version of *The Rocky Horror Picture Show* find their way into the mix, thanks to those rascals James P. Nettles and Patrick Dugan.

On the other hand, the remaining essayists picked films that either explicitly described fairies or where their presence was so obvious that it left little doubt as to what inspiration the filmmakers were drawing upon. This was not my original vision.

And yet… for me, that was the moment when *Fairy Films* fell into place.

Focusing solely on films with oblique fairy references fails to do justice to their archetypal power. These essayists focused on how, even in their most sanitized or sensationalized forms, *the core tenets of fairy belief are still preserved in these films* (even if you sometimes have to squint).

The fact that genuine fairy folklore, with qualities faithful to original interpretations, can manage to push through centuries of fantasy baggage from popular culture is, simply put, miraculous. Authentic fairy belief not only overcomes their complete absence; it also overcomes "fairy misinformation," for lack of a better term.

We see this in Dr. Jack Hunter's personal reflections on such staples of the fairy genre as *Labyrinth* and *The Dark Crystal*; Dr. Neil Rushton's thoughtful dissection of *Photographing Fairies*; Susan Demeter's exploration of chilling themes from *The Hole in the Ground*; and Dr. Simon Young's rescue of the ever-contentious Walt Disney fairy tradition. To round things off, Allison Jornlin managed to wrangle several different films, both explicitly fairy-oriented and otherwise, into a thought-provoking meditation on the origins of bogeymen (another term we can attribute to fairy belief).

This collection of essays will not add years to your life. Nor will it solve relationship difficulties or fill your 401K. But it is my sincere hope—my sincere *belief*—that it can reenchant the way you see motion pictures, if not life in general. So many films, whether they realize it or not, owe a debt to the Good Folk.

Read on. Long after you place this book on the shelf, you will still perceive the theme covered herein, wherever they manifest. In doing so, you will recognize that very little about us has changed in the last several millennia. Despite our sophisticated trappings, we remain the same species that left offerings to the spirits, feared the dark, and believed that secret passages beneath our feet led to Fairyland's timelessness. Once you start seeing it, you will never "un-see" it.

Fairy Films will help you see through the glamour.

CONTENTS

Through a Crystal Darkly: Cultural, Experiential and Ontological Reflections on Faerie

Dr. Jack Hunter

In February 2020, when Joshua Cutchin first reached out to me about the possibility of writing a chapter for this book, I was immediately interested in the prospect. I have always wanted to write about *The Dark Crystal*—one of my favourite films growing up—and this seemed like the perfect opportunity to do so.[1] But rather than write a straightforward dissection of the film and its motifs, I wanted instead to do something a little more reflexive and consider its relationship to some of my own personal extraordinary experiences, as well as to broader cultural and folkloric trends. I am especially interested in trying to tease out how my own experiences (and possibly those of others as well) are related to particular images from popular culture—in this case the imagery created by the British faerie artist Brian Froud (1947-), and the films he has designed and influenced. My own experiences, as we will see, seemed, somehow, to be tinted with the essence of Froud's work, while still maintaining an element of spontaneity and unexpectedness. The discussion presented in this chapter, therefore, centres on the interplay of popular culture depictions of faeries and real-life faerie encounters.

In a recent article for the *Folklore Thursday* blog, Simon Young[2] made an interesting distinction between 'folklore' on the one hand—the stories and traditions that are passed down from generation to generation—and 'lived-folklore' on the other—the extraordinary experiences that people continue to report even today, such as my own. He explains the difference between these polarities in relation to two publishing projects he was working on at the same time—*Magical Folk* (2018) and the *Fairy Census* (2018):

> In *Magical Folk* our authors took fragments of folklore and fairy beliefs from a given region, seasoned with the most popular local fairy stories. In *The Fairy Census* respondents talked, instead, about the weirdest, most intimate moments that they had lived: they often confessed that they had told no one or practically no one about what had happened to them. I turned one way, it was a jolly Morris dance with accordions and cymbals: I turned the other way it was a painfully energetic salsa where everyone was nude.[3]

Despite the apparent differences between long established faerie-lore, traditions, beliefs, and practices (which we might call 'popular culture') and the wild nature of real-life extraordinary experiences, Young points out that there are times when elements of traditional folklore pop up in surprising ways right in the middle of the strangeness of contemporary entity encounter narratives. These are instances when:

> …those weird, intimate experiences… contain fragments of 'unknowing tradition'. What I mean by 'unknowing tradition' is that the individuals in question had a fairy experience that echoes experiences in traditional fairylore, but where they had no apparent knowledge of this aspect of fairylore….[4]

My own experiences with faeries, as we will see, were 'weird' and 'intimate', but they also contained elements of tradition. Elements of 'known tradition' included my exposure to the artwork of Brian Froud and the films he designed, while elements of 'unknown tradition' included resonances with traditional faerie lore that I was not aware of at the time. It is important to point out here, at the beginning of our excursion, that I am not presenting my own experiences because I think they provide particularly good evidence for the existence of faeries. Indeed, they provide very little in the way of evidence of this sort, at least at face value. Nevertheless, it is my hope that they will help to elucidate some of the complexities of the relationship between culture and experience, which is not as straightforward as many commentators would have us believe.

Since the 1990s, scholars of religion have paid increasing attention to the relationship between popular culture and various forms of religion and spirituality. Theologian Gordon Lynch, for example, has argued that, far from being a niche concern, studies of the relationship between religion and popular culture have the potential "to make a serious contribution to the academic, cultural and religious life of Western society." He further suggests that by studying this connection we can "develop a clearer understanding of how religion is practiced and perceived today."[5] The same could also be said about the so-called 'faerie faith'[6] as depicted in popular culture—which is indeed the premise of this very volume—that we can learn something about belief in faeries (and maybe even something about the ontological nature of faeries, i.e., what they *are*) by studying popular culture expressions of this belief. With that in mind, I want to turn now turn to consider some of the most potent popular culture expressions of faeries of the last 50 years—the artwork of Brian Froud.

As I started to pull together ideas for this chapter, I remembered that a colleague of mine, the panpsychist philosopher Dr. Peter Sjöstedt-H, had mentioned that he had met with and interviewed Froud in Glastonbury with the aim of writing it up for an article. I instantly got in touch and asked if the interview had been published anywhere, explaining that I was interested in knowing Froud's thoughts on the relationship between his artwork and real-life faerie experiences. To my surprise (and delight), it hadn't yet been transcribed, let alone published. I am immensely grateful, therefore, to have been given the opportunity to listen to and transcribe Sjöstedt-H's interview for use in this chapter, and I have included extracts from the interview throughout. As we will see, Froud's comments shed some interesting light on the relationship between popular culture imagery (which he creates and has contributed to) and real-life extraordinary experiences, such as my own.

Faeries, The Dark Crystal and Labyrinth

Whenever people ask me to describe the faeries that I saw during my own experiences (which are recounted below), I have often resorted to saying something along the lines of: "They looked like creatures from *The Dark Crystal*." Being a child of the 1980s and 1990s, I had essentially grown up watching the movie, which is set in the magical world of *Thra,* and was first released in 1982. The fantastical characters and creatures that inhabit Thra were rendered into puppet form by Jim Henson's (1936-1990) Creature Shop, and were designed by artist Brian Froud, capturing his distinctive faerie aesthetic in three dimensions. The collaboration between Henson and Froud on *The Dark Crystal* gave rise to a very organic image of the faerie-realm—a world of twisting forms, mystical forces, and different kinds of intelligence, good and evil.[7] The tag-line for the movie was, "Another world, another time," and this sense is wonderfully evoked in the film.

The Dark Crystal tells the story of a Gelfling, an elf-like being by the name of Jen, who is tasked with restoring the shattered Dark Crystal and bringing cosmic balance back to Thra. On his quest, beginning from his sanctuary with the uRru—the benevolent Mystics who raised and protected him when his family were slaughtered by the evil Skeksis— Jen meets an array of fantastical characters who help him on his hero's journey. He encounters the enslaved but kindly Podlings, the astromancer Aughra, a whole host of spectacular flora and fauna (some of which seem to blend these categories), and eventually meets another Gelfling called Kira. Together Kira and Jen manage to restore the Dark Crystal, which in turn leads to the re-unification of the uRru and Skeksis (who become the UrSkeks), thus initiating a new golden age of peace and balance in Thra.

Froud added extra detail to this re-imagined Fairyland with his book *The World of the Dark Crystal* (1982), which built upon and embellished the mythology of the film, presenting a sort of natural history of another world. In 2019 the video streaming service Netflix also produced a new ten-part series entitled *The Dark Crystal: Age of Resistance,* which has added new characters, backstory and further depth to the franchise, while suc-cessfully managing to maintain the overall vibe of the original film. This is achieved primarily through its use of practical puppetry, which adds an uncanny element to the world of *The Dark Crystal.*

Froud's unique faerie aesthetic was also faithfully reproduced in the 1986 movie *Labyrinth*—another collaboration with Jim Henson and his workshop—which draws on the classic faerie abduction motif as its cen-tral plot device.[8] The film stars musician-actor David Bowie (1947-2016)[9] in the role of Jareth, the Goblin King, and Jennifer Connelly, who plays the part of a young girl named Sarah. After inadvertently wishing that her little brother Toby be whisked away by the goblins, Sarah is forced to navigate an otherworldly labyrinth in order to rescue the toddler from the Goblin King, all before her parents return home from their night out.

Joshua Cutchin has suggested that of all the cinematic portrayals of the faerie-folk, *Labyrinth* is one of the most faithful to traditional faerie lore.[10] The faerie-folk depicted in *Labyrinth* are dangerous, trickster-like and take on all manner of strange and distorted shapes, sizes and features. In his interview with Sjöstedt-H, Froud explained that:

> … faeries are notorious for… their trickster nature… they will show you forms… I think you have to be very careful around a faerie, and treat them with a great deal of care….

Cutchin also notes parallels with wider features of the alien abduction phenomenon in *Labyrinth*, which echoes many elements of traditional faerie lore.[11] One such similarity is the depiction of the Goblin King as much taller than the smaller goblins swarming around him, doing his bidding. The presence of a taller being who serves as the leader is a common theme in accounts of abductions by the so-called Grey extraterrestrials,[12] for example, and interestingly is a motif that also recurred in one of my own experiences, described below. Like *The Dark Crystal*, *Labyrinth* also very successfully created a 'realistic' faerie-realm consistent with traditional folkloric accounts of visits to the otherworld, even to the extent of twisting the film's time-line, a theme common to many reports of such journeys.[13] Cutchin explains:

> Jareth is shown on numerous occasions manipulating time, and though Sarah's task is supposed to take thirteen hours, she leaves and returns in a single night. Early in the film we see her parents leaving when it is dark outside, telling her they will return by midnight; even if we are generous and declare the hour of their departure 5:00 p.m., that still means Sarah's adventures happen twice as fast as they should.[14]

I was also captivated as a teenager by the images and stories contained in the book *Faeries* (1979), Froud's wonderful collaboration with fantasy artist Alan Lee (who would later work on Peter Jackson's *The Lord of the Rings* trilogy). This book was given to me by a friend of my mother as a gift years after I had first seen *The Dark Crystal*, along with an excellent illustrated encyclopaedia of Tolkien's Middle-Earth, and has evidently had a lasting influence on me.

Froud and Lee's *Faeries* book is something of a field guide to the denizens of the faerie realm. The author-illustrators present themselves as naturalists collecting specimens, much like Victorian butterfly collectors. They beautifully illustrate profiles of mythical and folkloric beings: from Puck, *kobolds*, and *boggles* to *trows*, *selkies*, and Jenny Greenteeth. The work is a phantasmagoria of genuinely enchanting imagery (including some wonderful Cottingley-style photographs at the end of the book) that very effectively conjures the sense of an Otherworld that is close to, if not part of, our own world. Strange and beautiful elfin creatures are realistically rendered alongside grotesque goblins, boggarts, and trolls. An animated film produced in 1981 took its inspiration from the book, though admittedly it failed to completely capture the essence of Froud's imagery in the way that *Labyrinth* and *The Dark Crystal* would. In his interview with Peter Sjöstedt-H, Froud explicitly comments on the effect of his collaboration with Lee on popular perceptions of faeries in the latter half of the 20th century:

> ... the *Faeries* book... did actually change everybody's view of it, because fairies had gone out of favour. I mean they were absolutely considered to be childish and for children... Since that time there has been a revival of fairies, and truly this stuff has come from that book, from that one moment. We did change history with that, only I think because we were being quite truthful and as accurate as possible.[15]

Suffice to say, the imagery projected into popular consciousness by *The Dark Crystal, Labyrinth,* and *Faeries* presented a unique, but accessible, new faerie aesthetic that harked back to traditional folklore, and offered a counterpoint to mainstream imagery. As a consequence of the popularity of his work, Froud's images have left a profound impact on depictions of faerie-folk from other artists and designers over the last forty years. This ultimately shifted the image of faeries away from the Disney conception of the minuscule winged faerie Tinker Bell—grounded in Victorian flower-faerie imagery, inspired by J.M. Barrie's character from *Peter Pan*, and perfected by Disney in the 1953 animated film[16]—towards an altogether darker, earthier, representation.[17] But such shifts in perception are not new to the faeries. Indeed, the faeries have always been *mercurial* in nature—difficult to pin down, and constantly changing in parallel to human culture—and this represents just one of their most recent transformations.

Changelings: The Shifting Forms and Meanings of Faerie

Many of the world's cultures have traditions of belief in beings that would be called 'faeries' in Euro-American societies.[18] There are, for example, extensive 'little people' traditions from indigenous North American cultures,[19] African *tokoloshe* beliefs,[20] the *Yokai* in Japan,[21] and so on. It would prove too monumental a task to follow the connecting and diverging threads within and between different cultural traditions, but it is entirely possible that similar changes in perceptions of such beings have occurred in other cultural contexts.

For our purposes, we will trace changing perceptions of faeries within Western cultures, especially vis-a-vis the context of European and British lore, as these traditions have been the predominant influence on Brian Froud's artwork… as well as on my own experiences. In the context of the *Faeries* book (without which there would be no *Dark Crystal* or *Labyrinth*), Froud explains how he and Lee:

> … just went back to the folklore of England and Ireland, studied that and… tried to accurately portray what people had written about and seen and experienced in the book, and it brought that back to people.

In relation to British faerie lore, then, historian Ronald Hutton has sought to chart how "concepts of faeries developed and mutated from the opening of recorded history to the early modern period."[22] He notes that during the period between the 12th and 17th centuries the terms 'fairy,' or 'fay' gradually made their way across the channel from France to the British Isles. In an examination of the use of the terms 'fairies' and 'elves' in the work of J.R.R. Tolkien, Helios De Rosario Martinez (2010) provides a very useful summary of the original meaning of the term:

> *Fairy* (in Middle English and archaically spelt in various forms, like *fair-ye*, *fayerye*, etc.) is a word adopted from the Old French *faerie*, *faierie*: an abstract noun meaning "magic, enchantment," with connotations of "deceit"; also "enchanting but false speech"… Likewise, its modern synonym *fay* can be traced back to Old French *fae*, *faye*, *fee*, etc., past participle of the verb *faer*, *fayer*: "to enchant, bewitch," and also "to declare by an oracle"… These words denoted some kind of delusive, spoken magic, similar to the concept of *glamour*.[23]

The early association of the term 'fairy,' therefore, is with magic, danger and deceit. In Britain, the term was quickly associated with what the Anglo-Saxons once called 'elves.' Alaric Hall's doctoral research on 'The Meanings of Elf and Elves in Medieval England' (2004) found the extant Anglo-Saxon literature actually gave very little sense of a coherent model or framework for understanding elves, which is either a true reflection of Anglo-Saxon beliefs or the consequence of patchy evidence.[24] Nevertheless, there are a couple of distinctive traits of the elves that have survived the ravages of time, which Hutton summarises:

> It is clear that elves were feared, for maliciously afflicting humans and their animals, but there are also strong hints that they were models of seductive female beauty. There is no unequivocal evidence that elves were

regarded as sources of supernatural power for humans, but some association of them with diviners or prophets.[25]

Furthermore, Hall's research revealed that the assumption that elves
"were incorporeal, small and arrow-shooting proves to be both unfounded and implausible" in light of the literary evidence.[26] By contrast, the
elves were often considered warriors and sources of danger and power,
though they are very rarely explicitly described. Similarly, in the Celtic
traditions of Ireland, Scotland, Wales, Cornwall, and the Isle of Man, the
faeries were more often than not considered to be dangerous—an encounter with a faerie could be portentous of death, for example.[27]

In the Early-Modern period the faeries began changing again, coming to be associated with beings from classical mythology such as *dryads,
nymphs* and *fauns*—nature spirits and minor divinities. This cross-fertilisa-
tion of classical, Anglo-Saxon, Celtic, and other traditions is perhaps best
exemplified in the writings of William Shakespeare (1582-1616), whose
plays crystallised a new faerie archetype for the centuries that followed. In
A Midsummer Night's Dream, for example, the faeries are essentially "counterparts of figures drawn from classical myth," with similar powers to
influence the lives of mortals as the Greek gods.[28] Although they maintain
their mischievous characteristics, the faeries are somewhat domesticated,
losing a sense of their wildness and danger. The trickster character of
Puck, however, manages to resist this domestication process.

By the 19th century, popular culture depictions of faeries began to
change again—most notably perhaps with the faeries diminishing in size.
Laura Forsberg drew a very intriguing parallel between the development
and proliferation of the microscope in Victorian society—and the invisible world this new technology revealed—and the diminishing size of
popular culture conceptions of faerie-folk.[29] In other words, new technological developments gave rise to new modes of conceiving the nature
of faeries. This, in a sense, is the origin of the popular culture idea of the
tiny faerie.

But the late 19th and early 20th centuries also saw a resurgence of Celtic
faerie traditions in British culture, primarily through the influence of Romantic poets such as W.B. Yeats (1865-1939). The Celtic revival brought
with it a return to an earthier, darker perception of the faerie,[30] perhaps
best exemplified in the work of Welsh author, and occasional occultist,
Arthur Machen (1863-1947), and in the artworks of illustrators such as
Arthur Rackham (1867-1939).

Perhaps one of the greatest influences on popular perceptions of faeries in the first half of the 20th century were the infamous Cottingley photographs, taken in the 'beck' at the bottom of a Yorkshire garden by two young girls, first popularised in *Strand Magazine* by Arthur Conan Doyle (1859-1930) a century ago.[31] The faeries here are like miniature ballerinas, dressed in gauzy robes and dancing sweetly around the young girls. Regardless of the veracity of the images,[32] the Cottingley photographs made a major contribution to 20th century perceptions of faeries—crystallising them as childish, small and (above all) fake.

Mythographer Marina Warner, however, takes a slightly more ambiguous perspective, writing that "the young girls themselves…understood [photography's] relation to fantasy and other worlds, and made it the mirror of their dreams."[33] Again, technological innovation—this time in the form of accessible photography—rendered the manifestation of dreams possible for Edwardian schoolgirls, and allowed for the emergence of the new faerie archetype, epitomised by Disney's interpretation of J.M. Barrie's Tinker Bell character from *Peter Pan*. Tinker Bell was literally projected into the popular consciousness on cinema screens across the world—a globalising faerie archetype.

By the end of the 20th century, the good folk would begin to undergo another significant transformation in the cultural imagination. The so-called 'Machine Elves' popularised by psychonaut philosopher Terence McKenna (1946-2000) and experienced by users of psychedelics on a relatively regular basis[34] gave the faeries an overt countercultural edge and a new lease of life.[35] In his epic cultural history of the psychedelic compound DMT, Graham St. John explains:

In the history of DMT contact reports, the decidedly more innocuous elves are as common as rats in your barn. While Leary dropped hints about "merry erotic energy nests" of "elf-like insects" in *The Psychedelic Review* in the mid-1960s, it was McKenna… who later propagated the contact meme throughout underground culture. Also regarded by McKenna as "gnomes" or "tykes," these entities… colored the discourse of psychonaut musicians, authors and sculptors during the 1990s and early 2000s.[36]

Admittedly, however, the term 'Machine Elves,' or often just 'Elves,' is used rather broadly in the psychedelic community to refer to a wide array of entity encounters (perhaps similar to the broad application of its earlier Anglo-Saxon usage)—which may in fact represent a much more diverse spectrum of different entities and beings. This diversity includes the Greys—so familiar in Ufological circles—mantis-beings and other insectoids, beings of light, and creepy interdimensional clowns and jesters, all commonly reported in psychedelic states of consciousness.[37]

Although there is only enough space here for a brief historical sketch, I hope that what I have presented will suffice in demonstrating that cultural perceptions of the faeries are constantly changing, and will likely continue to do so as we move forward into the 21st century. The films and artwork of Brian Froud are, therefore, another node in this long and continuing lineage. My own experiences occurred within, and cannot be extracted from, this wider socio-cultural and historical context.

The Cliff Dwellers and the Psilocybe-Folk

In this section I describe two of my own experiences with what I took to be faeries, one of which occurred at the tail end of the 20th century, the other at the beginning of the 21st. As suggested at the start of this chapter, I do not present these stories as proof of the existence of faeries, but rather as illustrations of the complex ways in which popular culture and extraordinary experience might interact with one another. In the following section I address and explore in-depth the relationship between lore/culture and experience, but it is worthwhile keeping these topics in mind as we consider my own experiential narratives here, and how they might relate to cultural themes and images.

My first encounter with faeries was in a dream. I must have been about 12 or 13 years old at the time. In the dream I climbed up the hill behind my parents' house in Mid-Wales to a place I often visited alongside an old quarry. There was (and still is) a large cliff face there, overgrown with brambles, hanging down over it like a fringe. In the dream I saw through the brambles and rock-face into a small cave or chamber, lined with dry, rust-coloured bracken. In the middle of the warm-looking chamber were two sleeping, troll-like creatures nestled-in as though hibernating. They were smooth-featured, slow-moving, and seemed to reflect the warm glow of the cavern, their home in the rock. They looked up and saw me with wizened faces, noting my intrusion on their slumber. Their eyes radiated a mysterious sense of knowing, and that is about all I can remember of the dream. I have visited the place since, but have not seen the creatures again. The dream has never repeated but remains vivid in my memory.

In spite of their unusual appearance, the cliff-dwelling trolls were oddly familiar. Indeed, the entities I encountered in my dream-state were similar, though not identical, to the Mystics from *The Dark Crystal*—the beneficent urRu who guide Jen on his quest to restore the shattered Dark Crystal. In his interview with Brian Froud, Sjöstedt-H asked about the inspiration for the urRu and their similarity to the appearance of trolls in the work of the Swedish painter and faerie tale illustrator John Bauer (1882-1918). Froud explains that the Mystics, like Bauer's trolls, take their form from the landscape in which they live:

> To me it's just natural that that's the way they look… The forms in general are based on nature, and trolls definitely are based on nature. So you've got the combination of rocks, and trees, and from the shapes of those you get limbs and you get faces. They are the product of the landscape, and they do feel like the spirit of the land. It's very difficult *not* to feel them if you stand in a wood… [W]ith trolls what John Bauer did was to sort of soften it somewhat. I mean, trolls are usually like monsters and they're bad, or evil, or usually grumpy at least, but John Bauer seems to go, "No, they're actually more than that." They really *are* this wood, you know. Woods scare us, and yet woods enchant us. The thing he did was re-enchant the forms of trolls.

The entities that I saw, slumbering in their cozy chamber inside the rock face, appeared (much as Froud suggests here) to be an embodiment of the rock itself; they were part of it. Perhaps they were trolls.

My second experience of the faeries was also in an altered state of consciousness, facilitated via *psilocybin* mushrooms. I first published an account of the experience in an essay in the debut issue of the *Psychedelic Press* (2012), which was later re-published in the book *Out of the Shadows* (2015), an anthology of essays from the journal. I also submitted what I consider to be the definitive account of the experience to Simon Young's *Fairy Census 2014-2017*; I am well aware of the capacity for such experiential narratives to shift and change over numerous retellings, so for the purposes of staying as close to the original narrative as possible I will quote the full version from the *Fairy Census* to set the scene. This time around I was 16-17 years old:

> My experience occurred the very first time I took magic mushrooms. I noticed these small two-dimensional creatures walking in procession in the grain of wood on a chest of drawers. There was one larger member of the procession that appeared to be female and in charge. The enti-

ties had long pointed noses, appeared organic, like beautiful little goblins, and were sort of swirling along in their procession. The largest one
turned to look at me, noticed I was looking, and then continued with its
procession. I shouted out to the other two people in the room 'I can see
fairies,' because I didn't know what else to call them. The fairies just continued to move along the grain of the wood, and I stopped paying attention to them. It was a strange experience – they seemed to be different to
the rest of the psychedelic experience because they were moving along
with deliberate intent, and seemed to possess a consciousness of their
own. They clearly noticed me, but were not concerned that I had spotted them. The memory is still very vivid in my mind...[They were] Like
small, two-dimensional, beautiful goblins. They had long pointed noses.[38]

It was a brief encounter that has stuck with and puzzled me over the
intervening years. It was one of the most extraordinary experiences of
my life—a moment of 'lived-folklore,' to use Simon Young's term. Both
experiences were spontaneous in the sense that they occurred unbidden,
and yet also featured elements of traditional faerie-lore. The larger female leader of the procession in the chest of drawers, for example, was
the only member of the troupe to make eye contact with me, while the
rest remained preoccupied. Folklorist Eddie Bullard explains that in many
alien abduction narratives "[o]ne being serves as a leader or liaison with
the captives and communicates with them by telepathy, giving reassuranc-
es and imparting special messages, while the rest of the crew seem cold
and unfriendly."[39] In addition to such folkloric motifs, the experiences
also seemed to draw from popular culture, especially in the way that the
entities were tinged with elements of Brian Froud's imagery. This naturally raises the question of whence Froud's imagery originates—does he just
'make it up,' or is there something more involved in his artistic process?
When asked whether the images he creates have a deeper underlying reality, Froud gives a particularly interesting response, explaining:

> I did it originally in the abstract. Originally I was intrigued, I guess, by
> fairy art and fairy tales and then gradually got more and more interested
> in the possibility of real fairies. You know, what did that mean? And so I
> was definitely faking it for a long time, although the response I was get-
> ting from certain people was precisely that I was getting it right! People
> saying, "Well, that is how I experience fairies, that's what I see." But it
> does seem to me that sometimes seeing a fairy can be very subjective....

Apparently, I am not alone in noticing similarities between my own experiences and Froud's imagery—it is something other faerie experiencers

have also commented upon. It is equally notable that, although Froud initially believed he was 'faking it,' his process seemed to have stumbled across something that resonated with the real-life experiences of contemporary people. There are echoes here of the mind-bending stories, collected by Jeffrey Kripal,[40] of writers and comic-book illustrators whose artworks seemed to somehow tap into and predict future unknown events, describe real people, or take on a life of their own. There seems to be something deeply weird about the creative process itself and its role in manifesting the 'paranormal.'

Furthermore, what initially started out for Froud as an 'abstract' endeavour eventually became an experiential reality when he began having his own interactions with faeries. Much like my encounters, Froud's first real-life faerie experiences occurred during altered states of consciousness. Interestingly, though, he keenly points out his experiences have never occurred under the influence of psychoactive substances; they did, however, take place under exceptional psycho-physiological circumstances, which is consistent with other research into the expression of extraordinary experiences.[41] Froud explains:

> I think I was at the end of a tour with the second book when I first started seeing them... but I think I must have been discombobulated by travelling across America—you're doing things at funny times, you have to get up early in the morning, going on planes, do a mid-day signing, get on another, have a car journey, then do another signing. So, by the end of it I was really getting exhausted, and not quite getting what the time of day was, and then spontaneously I started to have—it seemed to be— psychic experiences with fairies... they were sort of, like, popping up.

In the next and final section we examine some the ways in which experience and culture interact through feedback loops, before speculating on a possible ontological framework for understanding the nature of faeries in this context.

Cultural and Experiential Feedback Loops in a Participatory Cosmos

The entities I saw in my be-mushroomed state resembled something like Froud's *pixie* depictions in his *Faeries* book, the *goblins* of *Labyrinth*, and the Gelflings from *The Dark Crystal*. The images below are the earliest drawings I have of the entities I saw in the chest of drawers, which I later called '*psilocybe*-folk' (excuse my poor drawing skills).

Fig. 1. Although this experience took place a fair few years ago now, I can still vividly recall it, but describing it with words has proven quite difficult. I drew these pictures as a means to translate, to some extent, the essence of what I saw. As they moved, I got the sense that they were in the process of "doing something," but I don't know what that was—merely a sense of purpose.

Fig. 2. A more detailed picture of the face of the larger being, as best as I can recall. At the time, they definitely seemed two-dimensional—almost like shadow puppets.

Initially, I assumed the likenesses of my *psilocybe*-folk and the uRru-like creatures in the cliff-face—experienced in my altered states of awareness, through tripping and dreaming respectively—were sub-consciously influenced by my adolescent exposure to the images of Brian Froud, through his films and books. My brain—affected as it was by the psychoactive compound *psilocybin* and by the strange state of REM sleep—conjured hallucinations that essentially reconstructed images and ideas I had been exposed to in my youth and adolescence, but nothing more.

This Materialist interpretation is a standard way of explaining away such experiences, including entity encounters in altered states. Even among the spiritually inclined, popular cultural influences in dreams are taken as proof that they are not 'real' experiences. It is a position broadly referred to as the 'cultural-source hypothesis.' Fortean researcher Hillary Evans (1929-2011) summarises this idea, arguing that there is a marked tendency:

> ... for witnesses to encounter the entities they might expect to encounter. Mary appears to Catholics, the devil to fundamentalist Christians, and so on. The witness doesn't necessarily have to subscribe to a belief system to have it affect [their] ideas; awareness of it may well be enough. Both the fact that the experience occurs, and the form it takes, will reflect [their] cultural background.[42]

But the shaping of experience by cultural influence does not necessarily work as a *complete* explanation for such experiences; indeed, the relationship often works the other way around—with experience shaping belief. Furthermore, extraordinary experiences often challenge our expectations, and it is this quality that marks them out as extraordinary in the first place. As noted, my own experiences possessed a spontaneous, unexpected, and unbidden quality, despite their apparent relationship to popular culture imagery. Froud expresses a similar sentiment about his own experiences, explaining:

> ... It doesn't feel in any way a delusion... In many ways, you know, it can have some aspects of illusion, but that really just goes away. Everybody, you know, when they get photographs and they see faces in things—I do that, but I not only see it, I use it in the art, turn something into a face, look at those leaves—but that's not the experience of a fairy encounter... I find it spontaneous, I have no control over it. I can't make it happen....

Contrary to expectations proposed by the 'cultural source' hypothesis—which suggests that we see what our culture has conditioned us to see—there is very often a sense of the unexpected in such encounters, of something *pre-cultural*, perhaps. David Hufford's work demonstrates, in the context of the Newfoundland 'Old Hag' tradition, that many supernatural beliefs actually have an underlying 'experiential source.' These experiences birthed different traditions of belief, each tradition essentially a variation upon the same (or similar) phenomenon. In Hufford's examination, the phenomenon of sleep paralysis provides the underlying experience, occurring independently of culture, yet resulting in the proliferation of different 'supernatural assault' traditions around the world.

Rather than being a direct consequence of my exposure to the artwork of Brian Froud, then, perhaps my extraordinary encounters were evidence of something much more complex. Folklorist Peter Rojcewicz (1986) has referred to this as the 'reflective principle':

> Proponents of the "reflective principle" argue that a percipient's personal and culture-bound values significantly shape their non-ordinary experience. The coloring of experience by a percipient's psychology or cultural beliefs does not invalidate the potential reality of the event; it merely complicates it.[43]

When asked about the issue of objective reality versus cultural expectation, Froud suggested a similarly complex structure. He appeared to adopt a both/and perspective—explaining that entities exist objectively *'out-there,'* but that they, too, are shaped by our cultural expectations:

> I think it genuinely can be a mixture. It does seem to me that if you've got fairies of place, often if they are experienced then they are experienced in a certain way, or similar way. So there seem to be similar shapes or forms that appear to be generated from a particular place. At the same time, you know, if we are expecting to see a gnome with like a red pointy hat on, it's perfectly reasonable that maybe that's what we do see.

Extraordinary encounters with faeries appear, therefore, as contact points between objective, external, phenomena and subjective experiencers. The encounter is moulded and shaped by the expectations of the percipient, but is also influenced by the external phenomenon—it is an interconnected relationship, or feed-back loop that can result in emergent phenomena. It is also interesting to note in this regard that the unusual phenomenon of stigmata—the extraordinary manifestation of signs of the crucifixion on the bodies of (usually) devout believers—did not take on its most dramatic and gory form until a transformation in artistic representations of Christ on the cross took place in the 13th century. Ian Wilson explains:

> There may even be an argument that the whole sudden onset of stigmatisations in the thirteenth century was due to the new, realistic fashion in artistic portrayals of Jesus that came into being shortly before St. Francis of Assisi's time... In previous centuries Christian churches throughout Europe had been decorated according to the stiff and formal Byzantine style.... To show suffering, extreme emotion, or anything more than a token amount of blood, was unthinkable. Around the second half of the twelfth century changes began to creep in. The taking down of Jesus' body from the cross was shown much more realistically... could this have been what prompted the sudden flush of stigmatics within little more than a generation?[44]

The implication is, then, that changes in culture—aesthetic, artistic, technological and imaginative—can also lead to the emergence of new forms of extraordinary experience. Culture and experience exist in a continuous feedback loop. Experience gives rise to new insights that challenge and extend established cultural models, while at the same time cultural models serve to both limit and enable certain kinds of experience. It is because of this two-way (at least) relationship that reduction to either a cultural or experiential source is never quite satisfactory. Brian Froud's artwork and films have provided a new aesthetic framework for perceiving faeries, while at the same time drawing on a combination of folklore (culture) and his own subjective experiences as inspiration. Similarly, my own experiences were spontaneous, extraordinary, and novel, while at the same time containing elements of traditional folklore and hints of Froud's aesthetic.

So where does this leave us in terms of the bigger picture—the ontological nature of faeries? One of the key takeaway points is that faerie encounters are interactive experiences; we project *onto* them as much as they project *into* us. In a sense, such experiences could be seen as collapsing our usual sense of detachment from the world, and drawing us into a participatory relationship with it, e.g. with the faeries or spirits of place.[45]

Interestingly, towards the end of his interview, Sjöstedt-H steers the conversation into explicitly ontological terrain when he asks whether Froud has any sympathy for panpsychism, "the view that mind is inherent in all things." Froud's answer seems a fitting place to end this journey into the worlds between culture and experience:

Yes. I think that's really the secret and the answer to everything. Absolutely, that you're trying to tune in to everything... If you have a nature that's imbued with soul, and then, more particularly, personality, and everything has its own personality, you can have a dialogue with it, and in the dialogue—and even the picturing of it, the seeing of images—there's a possibility of something energetic shifting, or moving...you can have the help of it being shaped in some sort of form that you can understand....

Acknowledgements

My thanks to Joshua Cutchin for inviting this contribution, to Dr. Peter Sjöstedt-H for giving me the opportunity to listen to his interview, and to Brian Froud for his inspiration and permission to publish his comments in this form.

References

Bane, T. (2013). *Encyclopedia of Fairies in World Folklore and Mythology*. Jefferson, NC: McFarland & Company.

Bonafin, M (2009). Relativistic Time and Space in Medieval Journeys to the Other World. *Cognitive Philology*, No. 2.

Bullard, T.E. (1989). UFO Abduction Reports: The Supernatural Kidnap Narrative Returns in Technological Guise. *The Journal of American Folklore 102*(404), pp. 147-170.

Cooper, J. (1997). *The Case of the Cottingley Fairies*. London, UK: Pocket Books.

Cutchin, J. (2015). 'Faerie-fidelity: Cinema's most accurate depiction of the Good Folk' Available Online: https://www.joshuacutchin.com/single-post/2015/06/24/Faeriefidelity-Cinemas-most-accurate-depiction-of-the-Good-Folk [Accessed 05/03/2020].

Cutchin, J. (2018). *Thieves in the Night: A Brief History of Supernatural Child Abductions*. San Antonio, TX: Anomalist Books.

Davis, A.K., Clifton, J.M., Weaver, E.G., Hurwitz, E.S., Johnson, M.W. & Griffiths, R.R. (September 2020). Survey of entity encounter experiences occasioned by inhaled *N,N-dimethyltryptamine*: Phenomenology, interpretation and enduring effects. *Journal of Psychopharmacology 34*(9), pp. 1008-1020.

Day, D. (1979). *A Tolkien Bestiary*. London, UK: Mitchell Beazley Publishers.

De Rosario Martinez, H. (2010). *Fairy* and *Elves* in Tolkien and Traditional Literature. *Mythlore: A Journal of J.R.R. Tolkien, C.S. Lewis, Charles Williams, and Mythopoeic Literature 28*(3), pp. 64-84.

Evans, H. (1987). *Gods, Spirits, Cosmic Guardians: Meetings with Non-Human Beings*. Wellingborough, UK: The Aquarian Press.

Evans Wentz, W.Y. (1911). *The Fairy Faith in Celtic Countries*. London, UK: H. Froude.

Forsberg, L. (2015). 'Nature's Invisibilia: The Victorian Microscope and the Miniature Fairy.' *Victorian Studies 57*(4), pp. 638-666.

Foster, M.D. (2015). *The Book of Yokai: Mysterious Creatures of Japanese Folklore*. Oakland, CA: University of California Press.

Froud, B. & Lee, A. (1979). *Faeries*. London, UK: Pan.

Giuffre, L. (2012). Entering the Labyrinth: How Henson and Bowie Created a Musical Fantasy. in J.K. Halfyard (Ed.), *The Music of Fantasy Cinema* (pp. 95-110). London, UK: Equinox Publishing.

Hall, A.T.P. (2004). *The meanings of elf and elves in medieval England*. PhD Thesis: University of Glasgow. Available Online: http://theses.gla.ac.uk/4924/1/2004Hallphd.pdf [Accessed 29th June 2020].

Hufford, D.J. (1982). *The Terror that Comes in the Night: An Experience-Centered Study of Supernatural Assault Traditions*. Philadelphia, PA: Pennsylvania University Press.

Hunter, J. (2012). 'On the Nature of the Psilocybe Folk.' *Psychedelic Press*, Issue 1, pp. 3-5.

Hunter, J. (2015). On the Nature of the Psilocybe Folk. In R. Dickins & T. Read (Eds.), *Out of the Shadows: A Cornucopia from the Psychedelic Press*. London, UK: Muswell Hill.

Hunter, J. (2019). The Dark Knight Rises: Shamanic Transformations in Gotham City. In D. Caterine & J.W. Morehead (Eds.) *The Paranormal in Popular Culture: A Post-Modern Religious Landscape*. London, UK: Routledge.

Hunter, J. (2020). Mysterium Horrendum: Exploring Otto's Concept of the Numinous in Stoker, Machen and Lovecraft. In B. Grafius & J.W. Morehead (Eds.), *Theology and Horror*. Lanham, MD: Lexington Books.

Hunter, J. (2020). 'Faeries at the Bottom of the Garden: Non-Human Intelligence and Connection to Nature.' *Supernatural Magazine*. Available Online: https://supernaturalmagazine.com/articles/faeries-at-the-bottom-of-the-garden-non-human-intelligence-and-connection-t?fbclid=IwAR0TEKZqMnSeCGdiT7OZwVMSp3GPFwsytQsiy-vqLfQNLwcaW-TMOLBUKLo0

Hutton, R. (2014). 'The Making of the Early Modern British Fairy Tradition.' *The Historical Journal 57*(4), pp. 1135-1156.

Jarrell, R. (2016). UFO Abductions as Mystical Encounter: Faerie Folklore in W.Y. Evans-Wentz, Jacques Vallee, and Whitley Strieber. In J. Hunter (Ed.) *Damned Facts: Fortean Essays on Religion, Folklore and the Paranormal* (pp. 68-80). Paphos, CY: Aporetic Press.

Jones, S. (2015). The Evolution of a Feminine Stereotype: What Tinker Bell Teaches Children about Gender Roles. *Gender Questions 3*(1), pp. 45-61.

Kripal, J.J. (2011). *Mutants and Mystics: Science Fiction, Superhero Comics, and the Paranormal.* Chicago, IL: Chicago University Press.

Lamb, M.E. (2000). Taken by the Fairies: Fairy Practices and the Production of Popular Culture in A Midsummer Night's Dream. *Shakespeare Quarterly 51*(3), pp. 277-312.

Letcher, A. (2001). The Scouring of the Shire: Fairies, Trolls and Pixies in Eco-Protest Culture. *Folklore 112*(2), pp. 147-161.

Luke, D. & Friedman, H. L. (2010). The neurochemistry of psi reports and associated experiences. In S. Krippner & H. L. Friedman (Eds.), *Mysterious minds: The neurobiology of psychics, mediums, and other extraordinary people* (pp. 163–185). Santa Barbara, Ca: ABC-CLIO

Lynch, G. (2005). *Understanding Theology and Popular Culture.* Oxford, UK: Blackwell.

Macnamara, N. & Anderson, W. (1999). *Leprechaun Companion.* London, UK: Pavilion Books Limited.

McAra, C. (2013). A Natural History of "The Dark Crystal": The Conceptual Design of Brian Froud. In J.C. Garlan & A.M. Graham (Eds), *The Wider Worlds of Jim Henson* (pp. 101-116). Jefferson, NC: McFarland.

Mkhize, N. (1996). Mind, gender, and culture: A critical evaluation of the phenomenon of Tokoloshe "sightings" among prepubescent girls in Kwazulu-Natal. Proceedings of the 2nd Annual Qualitative Methods Conference: "The Body Politic" 3 & 4 September 1996. Available Online: https://criticalmethods.org/bodtwo.htm [Accessed 13/07/2020].

Poortvliet, R. & Huygen, W. (1977). *Gnomes.* London, UK: New English Library.

Rojcewicz, P.M. (1986). The extraordinary encounter continuum hypothesis and its implications for the study of belief materials. *Folklore Forum 19*(2), pp. 131-152.

Roth, J.E. (1997). *American Elves: An Encyclopaedia of Little People from the Lore of 380 Ethnic Groups of the Western Hemisphere*. Jefferson, NC: McFarland & Company.

Silver, C. (1986). 'On the Origin of Fairies: Victorians, Romantics, and Folk Belief.' *Browning Institute Studies 14*, pp. 141-156.

St. John, G. (2015). *Mystery School in Hyperspace: A Cultural History of DMT*. Berkeley, CA: Evolver Editions.

Tramacchi, D. (2006). Entheogens, Elves and Other Entities: Encountering the Spirits of Shamanic Plants and Substances. In L. Hume & K. McPhillips (Eds.), *Popular Spiritualities: The Politics of Contemporary Enchantment* (pp. 91-104). London, UK: Routledge.

Warner, M. (2006). *Phantasmagoria: Spirit Visions, Metaphors, and Media into the Twenty-first Century*. Oxford, UK: Oxford University Press.

Wilson, I. (1988). *The Bleeding Mind: An Investigation in the Mysterious Phenomenon of Stigmata*. London, UK: Weidenfeld and Nicolson.

Wood, J. (2006). 'Filming fairies: popular film, audience response and meaning in contemporary fairy lore.' *Folklore 117*(3), pp. 279-296.

Young, S. (2018). *The Fairy Census 2014-2017*. Available Online: http://www.fairyist.com/wp-content/uploads/2014/10/The-Fairy-Census-2014-2017-1.pdf [Accessed 16/02/2020].

Young, S. & Houlbrook, C. (2018). *Magical Folk: British & Irish Fairies from 500 AD to the Present*. London, UK: Gibson Square Books.

Young, S. (2019). 'Lived Folklore in the Fairy Census.' Available Online: https://folklorethursday.com/folklife/lived-folklore-fairy-census/ [Accessed 29/06/2020].

"I Am—We Are": Decoding the Faerie Motifs of Alex van Warmerdam's Borgman

Joshua Cutchin

A house is much more than a building. It is a microcosm, a living being with both a body and a soul. It speaks, even if its language is only creaking and cracking noises for the profane. Its wailings are evidence of a attack by hostile forces. If uncared for, it can grow old and die and, once abandoned, it crumbles away, leaving only its skeleton visible to all.

- Claude Lecouteux, The Tradition of Household Spirits

"All great literature is one of two stories," Leo Tolstoy wrote. "A man goes on a journey or a stranger comes to town." While ostensibly the latter, a cursory viewing of writer-director Alex van Warmerdam's 2013 motion picture *Borgman* leaves viewers questioning whether its eponymous main character is, in fact, *stranger* than a stranger.

The film tells the story of a mysterious vagabond named Camiel Borgman (Jan Bijvoet) who insidiously injects himself into the lives of an upper-class family (Jeroen Perceval & Hadewych Minis), slowly undermining their domestic bliss in a bid to gain control of the household with his confederates. While divisive, the film was mostly lavished with praise, receiving the Palme d'Or nomination at 2013's Cannes Film Festival.[46] While failing to reach final selection, *Borgman* was also chosen as the Dutch entry for Best Foreign Language Film for the 86th Academy Awards.[47]

Critics commonly employed the phrase 'dark fairy tale' in their assessments, but American audiences seemed largely perplexed by the picture, even when delivering favorable reviews. Critic Brian Tallerico, writing for

RogerEbert.com, admitted, "Like a religious parable designed to present more questions than answers, *Borgman* can sometimes frustrate but it is an accomplished piece of work, driven by a uniquely malevolent tonal balance and two fantastic central performances. It sometimes simmers when I wish it would boil over but damn if it isn't fascinating to watch the water bubble."[48]

Other reviewers echoed this sentiment to varying degrees. "What gives the story an edge is that we have no idea why all this is happening," wrote Karin Badt of *The Huffington Post*, who, while appreciating the film, also uncharitably called it "senseless" and lacking in "complete logical sense."[49]

"While conventional narrative rules dictate that answers be supplied, van Warmerdam is content to keep piling on mysteries," said *The Hollywood Reporter*'s David Rooney.[50]

Clayton Dillard of *Slant* decried *Borgman* as "'artsy fartsy,' because it's all hot air with a sleek sheen, yielding no larger point or utility… Perhaps what makes Borgman most disheartening, finally, is its futility as either cinema or critical essay. Is the cult a group of Satanists? Are they affiliated with a particular political regime?"[51]

"After a while, the film's nonstop obfuscation starts to seem irritatingly coy," remarked Mike D'Angelo of *The A.V. Club*. "*Borgman* is both too self-consciously odd and too bluntly punitive to draw real blood. It's a conversation piece of a movie that won't actually start any conversations beyond 'That was freaky.'"[52]

These demands for answers are far too obsessed with the film's literal text, and grossly underinformed regarding folklore.

Critics and audiences alike would have better understood the film had they taken the center word in 'dark fairy tale' to heart. The film begins quite grounded before becoming more unhinged. By the end, what can only be described as magic—full blown, Old World, malicious, enchanting—bursts from the margins of *Borgman* into full view, and that bewitchment seems firmly ensconced in the faerie lore of Western Europe. Viewing Borgman and his troop of lackeys through this lens elucidates many of the movie's more baffling, seemingly random choices.

"COULD I PERHAPS JUST TAKE A BATH HERE?"

A more sophisticated analysis of *Borgman* might jump from point-to-point throughout the film in a non-linear fashion; however, nearly every narrative beat in the motion picture has *some* resonance, no matter how minor, with faerie lore. Ergo, it seems clearer and more prudent (if less elegant) to engage the film methodically, scene-by-scene.

Borgman opens on a quote that has, amongst reviewers and fans, become quasi-infamous: "and they descended upon the earth to strengthen their ranks." This apparent Old Testament quote clearly evokes Biblical accounts of the Nephilim and fallen angels (the latter, worth noting, is one of many Christianized explanations for the origins of faeries).[53] The epigraph is in fact pure fabrication. Though van Warmerdam has referred to this in interviews as "a Bible quote," it has no precedent in any version of the Bible.[54] Warmerdam is fully aware of this contradiction, and claims to have merely desired a subtle, rather than overt, religious context ("I was raised a Catholic, was an altar boy, that is an attractive source to draw from," he said).[55]

From there, the movie presents a striking image: a priest with a shotgun and a dog, rounding up a posse consisting of himself, a forest warden and, notably, a blacksmith, themselves armed with an axe and a lance. They then set about searching for, and driving away, several individuals living in underground chambers. They stab at the ground, revealing Borgman and his confederates, who flee the forest.

"I was longing for something nasty, but also enigmatic," said van Warmerdam. "And I wanted, like Borgman says in the film, to play. There's a man in a hole in the woods, there's a priest with a gun (an old dream), and then I start writing. Writing brings the ideas."[56]

Even at this early juncture, the parallels are abundantly apparent. The antagonism of the priest and the blacksmith have clear antecedents in faerie lore; the former often labeled faeries as demons and sought to exorcise them from pagan lands,[57] while the latter were equally "called upon to resolve, in one way or another, cases of witchcraft or fairy aggression."[58] Faeries had strong connections with the underground in practically every European culture, with Fairyland itself often depicted as subterranean.[59] More tenuously, the lance might evoke an Irish legend in which Finn of the Fianna thwarted faerie musician Aillen Mac Midhna with a magical spear.[60]

When piercing the ground, the blacksmith's lance breaks several eggs Borgman is storing. Eggs are a common tool in folk magic, and appear regularly in stories of faerie changelings. Why eggs are imbued with magical power is up for debate, however. (Keble College professor Diane Purkiss speculated, "Chickens very rarely get bewitched… so I wonder if the egg has some kind of power derived from being an enclosed but living thing?")[61]

Outed, our faerie stand-ins scatter, their leader escaping to gather himself in a gas station restroom. Notably, the bathroom is clearly marked unisex; such a designation is not uncommon in Europe, but may hint at Borgman's embodiment of The Trickster archetype. Folkloric Tricksters (Loki, Coyote, Anansi, etc.) were commonly gender fluid, and share many attributes with the character, including heightened sexuality, a penchant for deception and manipulation, and a dark sense of humor.[62]

We then see Borgman wandering a neighborhood, stopping at a house in the traditional 'Amsterdamse Stijl' before being rejected and continuing on.[63] If he can indeed be interpreted as a faerie or troll, it is possible the homeowner—perhaps more old-fashioned, as suggested by the traditional architecture—was able to recognize Borgman's true nature. Instead, he settles upon a much more austere, contemporary home (built especially for the film), all concrete and glass.[64]

The cinematic language of the building's prominent floor-to-ceiling windows is apparent, reflecting the family's vulnerability. The folkloric significance is less recognizable, yet equally important: we see a woman, later identified as Marina van Schendel, opening a second-floor window, an act recognized in countless cultures as exposing one's home to supernatural forces.

From former Sorbonne professor of medieval literature and civilizations Claude Lecouteux: "The window is… a magical location… This aperture is closely linked to misfortunate and death, either because it allows such forces to enter or to escape, or because it is an alternate opening used when there is a desire to avoid contaminating the threshold."[65] Marina van Schendel essentially invites a spirit into her home (she is later revealed as an artist, a vocation closely associated with European fae folk).[66]

The late Professor John O. Buffinga of Memorial University in St. John's, Newfoundland, elaborated:

A window and a door are opened at the beginning of the film, thereby letting in the intruder and his conspirators. As Borgman approaches the villa, he stops to survey the property, and as his eyes glance upwards a point of view shot shows a woman opening an upstairs window. It is a classic motif in horror tales such as F. W. Murnau's *Nosferatu* (1924), based on Bram Stoker's *Dracula* (1897), in which Lucy stands in front of an open window thereby luring in the vampire Count. Spying the woman at the upstairs window provides Borgman with the boldness to ring the doorbell.[67]

Approaching the door, Borgman introduces himself to Marina's husband, Richard, as 'Anton Breskens.' This alias holds little symbolic significance; 'Anton' means one worthy of praise or value, while 'Breskens' is merely a Dutch harbor town.[68] However, his actual name, 'Camiel Borgman' (revealed to Marina later in the film) is replete with symbolism. In Abrahamic religion, 'Camiel' (or Camael, Khamuel, Camiel, Cameel, Camniel) is an Archangel, calling to mind the opening epigraph.

The surname "Borgman" rewards multiple interpretations. In Old Norse, 'borg' means 'fort'—we are reminded of the close association throughout Europe of ringforts with spirits of the land, ergo 'Borgman' = 'Man of the Fort,' i.e. a faerie.[69] Equally compelling, Dutch folklore describes a race of trolls known as the *Berg* people, a cognate close enough to warrant contemplation.[70]

"Could I perhaps just take a bath here?" Borgman asks. This simple request—a small, simple favor, a basic staple of existence—is reflected throughout folklore in the propitiation of household spirits with various food offerings and simple demonstrations of respect.[71] The request for a bath carries extra significance, since faeries detested filth of any kind.[72]

Richard thrice denies this small kindness.

"You're turning it into a problem," Borgman warns; one wonders, had he been shown the slightest hospitality, if the remaining plot would have unfolded at all. Faeries were renowned throughout Europe for enacting fearsome retribution, should they be scorned; in his seminal *The Fairy Faith in Celtic Countries*, Walter Evans Wentz describes individuals blinded, abducted, crippled, and even killed for disrespecting customs and traditions surrounding the fae folk, denying offerings, harming faerie property, and violating their privacy.[73]

Anatole le Braz, University of Rennes Professor of French Literature, wrote of Brittany's house spirit, the *lutin*:

It was, in a word, the good genius of the house, but conditionally on every one paying to it the respect to which it had the right. If neglected, ever so little, its kindness changed into spite, and there was no unkind trick of which it was not capable towards people who had offended it, such as upsetting the contents of the pots on the hearth, entangling wool round distaffs, making tobacco unsmokeable, mixing a horse's mane in inextricable confusion, drying up the udders of cows, or stripping the backs of sheep. Therefore care was taken not to annoy it.[74]

In desperation, Borgman claims to know Marina, asserting she cared for him as a nurse in hospital. This falsehood is patently obvious, as she is neither a nurse, nor does she recognize him. Simultaneously, the mysterious stranger still possesses a vague knowledge of her, calling her 'Maria,' a name startlingly close to her own. Borgman's insistence is rewarded with a severely violent beating from Richard. That evening, Marina hears a voice calling out from what is either a pantry or a laundry room. It is the bloodied Borgman, cowering in the corner. Choosing to shelter in this utilitarian room echoes how a variety of household spirits sought refuge in similar spaces, dwelling in chimneys, sheds, barns, etc.

"The Dutch *Kaboutermannekin* worked in mills, as well as in houses," wrote essayist Louise Imogen Guiney. "He was gentle and kind, but 'touchy,' as Brownie-people are."[75]

Marina tends to her visitor's wounds, finally allowing him to bathe. (Various faeries were attributed powers of divination… perhaps, while introducing himself, Borgman mistook Marina's future compassion for an event in the past.)[76] She then escorts him to a tiny, traditional guest cottage (the 'summer house') on the edge of their landscaped backyard.

A faerie taking up residence in "the bottom of the garden" needs no explanation.

It is at this point that, viewed through a faerie interpretation, the film's narrative coalesces: *Borgman* is the story of a land spirit transitioning into a household spirit. Lecouteux cites "the difficulty we have in making a clear distinction between the *genius loci* from the domestic deity, inasmuch as this latter can be a former place spirit that has been tamed or satisfied by the offerings or worship it has been given."[77]

Lecouteux later adds, "… it is not uncommon to see that the *genius domesticus* does not live directly inside the house but rather in the garden, vineyard, or yard… the farm or residence, or even in a tree or stone that stands in the yard. Perhaps what we have here is the intermediary stage preceding the spirit's move into the heart of the house."[78]

"ISOLDE'S NOT FEELING WELL."

The following morning Stine, the van Schendel au pair, informs Richard and Marina that their youngest daughter, Isolde, has taken ill. She presents no fever, however, only claiming she saw 'a magician.' Isolde's affliction may represent a variation of the faerie stroke or kiss. From Carole Silver's *Strange & Secret Peoples*:

> To be fairy-kist could mean… that one was shell-shocked or traumatized; the fairy's kiss could strike one dumb… Epilepsy was, to many, clearly a result of the fairy stroke. The trows or drows of Shetland had a touch that paralyzed… Possessing "great power and malignity," they were responsible for paralysis (they were thought to steal the affected limb and to substitute a log in its place) and for consumption (in which they took away the heart). They punished mortals with disease for touching their property, stepping into their rings, or venturing too near their fairy forts; they even punished human beings with illness for merely seeing them.[79]

Perhaps making this connection, Marina demands Borgman leave. He begs to stay and she acquiesces, provided he remains hidden. Borgman later approaches Marina while she paints, asking for another bath, and, while met with similar protests, his request is granted again. Isolde, having earlier seen Borgman, shares a brief exchange while he washes.

The film cuts to that evening, when all three of the van Schendel children are regaled by a fairy tale from their new friend (the story Borgman tells, which we will address later, stretches over several scenes, and allegorically reflects his own actions). Storytime is interrupted by the unheralded appearance of two large, dark haired dogs.

"You're early," Borgman hisses to the hounds. "Off with you." For viewers, this is undoubtedly one of the more perplexing moments in *Borgman*; the animals' significance is never elaborated upon.

However, we are granted a degree of clarity when applying the folklore of faeries, who often possessed shape shifting abilities. For example, the *farfollet*, a household spirit and faerie native to the French Alps, "appears in the form of a calf, a dog, or a cat,"[80] while the Irish *púca* was known to take many forms, including that of a black hound.[81] Anomalous black dogs in the British Isles—the *cù-sìth*, Black Shuck, *barghest*, the *Moddey*

Doo[82]—were either directly associated with the Little People or were in fact themselves fae folk in disguise.[83] Indeed, Marina encounters a white specimen of the same breed later in the film, and briefly wonders for a moment if she isn't actually looking at Borgman in disguise.

Walter Evans Wentz chronicled the testimony of a Galway piper: "In the course of another conversation, Steven pointed to a rocky knoll in a field not far from his home, and said:—'I saw a dog with a white ring around his neck by that hill there, and the oldest men round Galway have seen him, too, for he has been here for one hundred years or more. He is a dog of the good people, and only appears at certain hours of the night.'"[84]

Ergo, it is reasonable to interpret these mysterious canines as members of Borgman's crew in disguise. This interpretation is further supported by a text message received from one of Borgman's confederates in a scene immediately prior: "Has the time come yet?"

"IT'S POSSIBLE... BUT IT WILL HAVE CONSEQUENCES."

Easily the film's most arresting image is that of Borgman nude, atop Marina. The scene is often compared to Henry Fuseli's *The Nightmare*, an inspiration made obvious by the fact Marina indeed suffers terrible dreams each time her guest sits upon her chest. Nightmares have long been attributed to fae folk; the German term *Albtraum* literally translates as "elf dream,"[85] and elsewhere in Eurasia disruptive dreams were blamed upon household spirits including *dracs*, *sotrés*, and *domoviye*. Of the last, Lecouteux writes, it "hurls himself at night on the woman he loves and braids her hair."[86]

"In Germany, while outright possession is not explicitly described, the Elben [Elves] are clearly connected to both madness and nightmares, two things that are closely tied to the ideas of fairy possession," wrote author and researcher Morgan Daimler. "Grimm, for example, relates that in German there were two closely related expressions for nightmares: '*dich hat geriten der mar*' [the night-mare has ridden you] and '*ein alp zoumet dich*' [an elf bridles you i.e. has a horse's bridle on you]."[87]

Following her first nightmare, Marina coldly watches Richard depart on a business trip before finding the guest cottage empty. Borgman is traipsing back into the forest, proclaiming he is "bored," "wants to play," and "doesn't feel like hiding." In a surprising change of heart—likely influenced by her dream—Marina pleads, "Can't you come back in another capacity?"

"It's possible," he answers, "But it will have consequences."

This exchange serves as the catalyst for an elaborate plan to usurp the van Schendel gardener. Borgman immediately contacts his crew, last seen in the opening: Brenda, Ilonka, Pascal, and Ludwig (played by van Warmerdam himself).

The game is afoot.

Borgman uses a tiny, poisoned blow dart, fired from the bushes, to incapacitate the family gardener. This is one of the most overt faerie parallels in *Borgman*, directly analogous to *elf-shot*. In older times, it was believed faeries literally shot tiny arrows at their victims, afflicting them with symptoms of the faerie stroke or any other numerous incapacitating maladies.[88]

An excerpt from Daimler's *A New Dictionary of Fairies: A 21st Century Exploration of Celtic and Related Western European Fairies* practically describes the gardener's ensuing reaction.

> 'Elfshot' or 'elf-arrows' appear in both Irish and Scottish fairylore as a type of small weapon used against people and livestock by the fairies… One of the most common weapons of the fairies, elfshot had various negative effects on those struck by them. The arrows do tangibly exist and can be found as small, Neolithic flint arrowheads… when they are used by the fairies they are invisible and so are the wounds they cause, requiring a special practitioner to be brought in to identify the site of the impact.

> … The most distinctive type of elshot injury was a sudden, internal shooting pain, without any clear explanation…

> The fairies might use elfshot for a variety of purposes, including punishing humans for slight offenses, tormenting them over greater violations, and stealing humans and livestock into Fairy. If the purposes was a minor punishment the effect might be minor and only last for a short time while if they were truly angry it might involve great pain and suffering indefinitely or even result in the person's death.[89]

The gardener, gravely doubled over in pain, is taken by Borgman to his home and wife. A series of ruses ensues wherein Brenda arrives, masquerading as a doctor (a 'toxicologist,' specifically, calling to mind Daimler's 'special practitioner'). However, Brenda and Ilonka kill both the gardener and his wife. Their heads entombed in concrete, the couple is unceremoniously disposed of in a lake.

It is perhaps appropriate at this juncture to address a recurring image seen throughout the film: a spinal scar shared between Borgman and his cohort. Predictably, it is implied within the film that this is a literal, physical procedure, and while we obtain glimpses into that process, it is never elaborated upon in any significant way, save to imply that some type of surgery enrolls the patient into Borgman's company.

From a folkloric perspective, these curious scars may well suggest a common fae folk trope, that of the hollow back; this motif appears throughout Europe, from Italy[90] to Scandinavia,[91] and commonly describes faeries as possessed of a hole or void in their back through which food is consumed. This belief is particularly engrained in Dutch culture, which describes their native *ellefolk* as hollow-backed.[92]

Returning to the narrative, the bodies of the gardener and his wife end up drifting, feet up, like some type of seaweed or perverse 'submarine sculpture.'[93] This image is alluded to throughout the film, most overtly via the fairy tale Borgman tells the van Schendel children.

In his story, a young boy has been consumed by a hideous monster at the bottom of a lake. The bereft boy's mother pleads for his body to be returned, to no avail until the crippled Antonius—sharing a name with the storyteller—steps forth and volunteers to dive to the bottom of the lake, earning the mother's gratitude. While the story is never properly concluded, it obviously parallels Marina's inexplicable affinity for Borgman, as well as his crew's preferred method of disposing of corpses.

From a broader, folkloric perspective, lakes were commonly sites of faerie interaction: "We most often meet fairies by the shores of lakes, fountains, or springs," wrote Lecouteux. "… fairies could very often be considered as aquatic spirits: an anthropomorphic expression of the *Numen* reputed to dwell in such places. Fairies rarely wander far from what clearly seems to be their natural element…."[94]

"THERE IS SOMETHING THAT SURROUNDS US."

At last fully comprehending the reason behind the gardener's disappearance, Marina makes a final plea to her Richard, one that summarizes the insidious nature of their faerie infestation: "There is something that surrounds us. Something that is outside us, but slips in now and then. A warmth… a pleasant warmth that intoxicates, but also confuses. The shell of something that means harm. At least that's what I think. I'm not sure."

To further secure his role of gardener, Borgman and his accomplices stage a sham job interview process, paying a handful of inexperienced candidates to apply. These are presumably immigrants who functionally serve to showcase Richard's racism and character deficits: "A black!" he remarks after turning away an applicant of African descent.

Simultaneously, Borgman's confederates incapacitate another candidate applying for the job in earnest; Isolde later murders this wounded man in cold blood using a small boulder. This likely signifies how these strangers have begun to assert their influence over the van Schendels, but can also be interpreted as typical faerie possession.

"That fairies or elves are capable of possessing humans may seem like a strange concept to some people reading this, but it is a power that they were always understood to have until recently," wrote Daimler. "Just as they can influence a person's perceptions through the use of illusion—glamour—they can also directly influence a person's mind by bringing madness or even by displacing the spirit and taking over control of the person's actions."[95]

It seems important that, immediately prior to Isolde's bloodthirsty act, all three children see and recognize Borgman for who he actually is: their former house guest, not some random gardener. Their recognition is accompanied by a minor hand gesture and meaningful look from Borgman (the possessing act itself?) as well as a subtle aural cue: the buzzing of insects.

This sound effect is first heard after Borgman's initial rejection by the owner of the first home he visits, then later after abandoning the van Schendel property. The buzzing is only associated with Borgman, Brenda, Ilonka, Pascal, and Ludwig, and always accompanies a significant plot pivot, typically an act of deception.

The number of times witnesses to the supernatural—those experiencing altered states of consciousness, having out-of-body experiences, claiming alien abductions, etc.—have described this exact same noise is innumerable. While those with a strictly Judeo-Christian outlook may cite anecdotal reports of 'buzzing fly' sounds in reports of demonic possession, it is equally present in stories of faerie abduction and bewitchment.

After taking ill in 1645, famed faerie abductee Anne Jeffries claimed to have heard "a thousand flies... buzzing around her," after which her soul was whisked away to Fairyland.[96]

Having the path to success paved for him, Borgman appears once more at the van Schendel doorstep, shaven and clean.

Richard's reaction is much warmer than after Borgman's initial appearance. He easily secures the position of gardener and bypasses the summer house completely, securing an invitation to sleep under the van Schendels' own roof.

From Leiden University assistant professor of film Peter Verstraten:

> The fact that [Richard] does not recognize the shorn and scrubbed applicant as the bedraggled tramp he had previously mistreated is a token of his self-absorption. By contrast, Marina immediately sees through his appearance. Having Borgman around the house gives her the idea that she might become close with the gardener, but he discourages any advance as "too early." He insists that he plays the gardener, and that as such Richard is his superior, and one is not supposed to mess with the boss' wife.[97]

Borgman's transformation also echoes faerie shape shifting, a feature addressed earlier.

"I WANT TO KNOW WHAT I'VE GOT UNDER MY ROOF"

Not only has our titular *genius loci* graduated to *genius domesticus* status, he has also secured space on the property for his confederates, who begin changing the backyard to suit their needs—specifically, enlarging the backyard pond, an act closely resonant with Lecouteux's descriptions of faeries as aquatic spirits. In the process, they inadvertently create large mounds of earth; while likely circumstantial, this may obliquely reference the close international association of fae folk with earthworks.

Borgman sets about looking as busy as possible, driving stakes into the ground. Marina approaches him with a simple lunch of bread rolls and water, which Borgman declines. She leaves it in the garden instead. This simple exchange is important for a variety of reasons, all related to the tradition of making offerings to faeries.

"Food-sacrifice plays a very important role in the modern Fairy-Faith, being still practised, as our evidence shows, in each one of the Celtic countries," wrote Evans Wentz. "Without any doubt it is a survival from pagan times, when, as we shall observe later, propitiatory offerings were regularly made to the Tuatha De Danann as gods of the earth, and, apparently, to other orders of spiritual beings. The anthropological significance of such food-sacrifice is unmistakable."[98]

With Borgman now fully ensconced as a 'household spirit,' it seems only natural for Marina to make him an offering. What she brings is equally significant, as faeries were not only commonly offered bread[99] but also, in some instances, fresh water.[100]

Borgman's refusal is thematically resonant, and can be viewed in several ways. Perhaps he harbors a grudge for his earlier mistreatment, when he was initially denied a bath. It is just as possible that, as with most faerie offerings, Marina's lunch should not be given directly to the spirits, but rather left in a pre-designated place for them to find of their own accord.

Marina's dialogue supports this interpretation: "Shall I leave the water bottle behind?... I'll put in in the shade... I'm putting it down here. You've got to look or you can't find it," she says, leaving the offering under a bush at the garden's border.

"Are you done?" her surly gardener replies. "Don't you have any feelers? I am the new gardener. I have an assignment."

"You wanted to play, you said," Marina whimpers.

"I am playing. I play at being a gardener."

Despite his outward irritation, Borgman still keeps Marina under his spell, as highlighted in the following scene. Stine politely asks her employer if she might invite her boyfriend over to spend the night, to which Marina ironically says, "My answer is very simple: no. Ask him for dinner one day, then I can look at him, listen to him, see if I can trust him... I want to know what I've got under my roof." This reply comes from a woman who only discovered the actual name of her enigmatic gardener one scene earlier and who, in the following scene, meets Ludwig and Pascal for the first time and allows them into her summer house.

The *only* explanation for this character inconsistency is faerie enchantment. This erratic behavior seems to be a specific choice by van Warmerdam; in an interview, Hadewych Minis (Marina) said, "It is difficult to play. [Marina is] so intrigued by Borgman. He bewitched me in a way. The mother transforms to being an almost robot, and that's very millimeter acting."[101]

Marina's blindness leaves her open to Borgman's slow, insidious home invasion. He continues inducing nightmares, and she becomes infatuated with him. Most egregiously, she allows Ludwig and Pascal to take her children from the house and into an underground bunker. They are offered a mysterious orange liquid to drink, and we see Borgman's associates unpacking a surgeon's kit.

The literal, textual implication of this scene is that the children are about to undergo the same spinal surgery shared by this crew of transient 'gardeners'—but we again find strong parallels in faerie folklore. The food taboo when entering Fairy Land is well documented. In *Ancient Legends, Mystic Charms, and Superstitions of Ireland*, Lady Wilde writes about a faerie prince who entices a young girl underground.

> At the end of the stairs they came upon a large hall, all bright and beautiful with gold and silver and lights; and the table was covered with everything good to eat, and wine was poured out in golden cups for them to drink. When she sat down they all pressed her to eat the food and to drink the wine; and as she was weary after the dancing, she took the golden cup the prince handed to her, and raised it to her lips to drink. Just then, a man passed close to her, and whispered—
>
> "Eat no food, and drink no wine, or you will never reach your home again."
>
> So she laid down the cup, and refused to drink. On this they were angry, and a great noise arose, and a fierce, dark man stood up, and said—
>
> "Whoever comes to us must drink with us."[102]

Depending upon the culture, the unwitting victim who eats or drinks in Fairyland may be held captive by the faeries or absorbed into their ranks. In *Borgman*, the latter is implied, as the children are allowed to return home, but arrive mysteriously changed: Isolde is asleep, her siblings near-catatonic. Anyone with even a cursory knowledge of faerie lore can see this is a transparent variation on the tradition of changelings, faerie imposters left in the place of abducted human children.

As with most faerie folklore, the precise definition of what changelings were is culture-dependent. In some stories, they are 'stocks' or 'fetches,' literally logs cloaked in faerie glamour to appear like human children;[103] in other traditions they are elderly faeries who look like wizened human children;[104] still other mythologies describe them as malformed faerie babies.[105] The motivations behind faerie abductions of human children are equally debatable, suffice to say that adolescent kidnappings are a hallmark of faerie belief worldwide.[106]

In any instance, changelings invariably appear listless and sickly, with an insatiable appetite. Among those practicing some form of the Fairy Faith, any change in a child's behavior was blamed upon faeries. It is clear that the van Schendel children exemplify the changeling trope (the argument for this interpretation strengthens in the final frames of the film).

"PAST THE SUMMER HOUSE"

As per Marina's request, Stine invites her boyfriend over for dinner. Leaving him to watch television with the zombified van Schendel children, she is dispatched to the garden to collect a bouquet for the event. While doing so, Stine encounters Pascal, who insistently invites her to sit with him in the summer house while he explains where to find the flowers. When she finally relents, he hastily shuts the door.

Because her errand is taking far too long, Stine's boyfriend goes looking for her, but only finds Pascal, who claims she has already returned to the kitchen. It is immediately apparent that Stine has changed. She angrily refuses her boyfriend's affection and is abruptly petulant with Marina: "There are no flowers in the garden at the moment, as you know perhaps," she snaps. "I had to go way past the summer house to find any."

Here we have yet another example of a scene where small details reward greater thematic resonance. While children were most at risk for faerie abduction and substitution, the next most common changeling demographic was younger women; we later see Stine drinking the same orange liquid shared with the children, solidifying this connection.

The fact that Stine was forced to venture "way past the summer house" (i.e. into the woods) is also important. Across a variety of cultures, foraging in the forest—particularly alone—placed one at especial risk for encountering the fae folk. While not flower-picking, berry-gathering was often marked with danger.

"Encounters were sometimes characterized by mortal perceptions of the actual physical presence of fairies, but more often by an awareness of a dreamlike, psychic presence which caused pickers to lose their sense of time and get lost by being 'taken astray' or 'led astray,' or 'fairy-led,' or being 'in the fairies,'" wrote Peter Narváez, folklore professor at Memorial University of Newfoundland.[107]

In *Borgman*, Stine is sent to forage in the woods alone, only to take far too long with such a simple task, during which she encounters a supernatural being with the powers of persuasion. She then returns changed. "Once they had you in their powers they could keep you in a trance for days," a Newfoundland informant told Narváez.[108]

It becomes apparent there is a sexual component to Stine's sudden connection to Pascal. She later offers herself to him, but he appears disinterested in sleeping with her. Narváez's research provides additional insight, and closely aligns with Stine's encounter:

> In keeping with the traditional gender alignment of berry pickers, over two-thirds of the protagonists in these stories are women... When age is mentioned or alluded to, it is clear that most of these women are young and subject to parental authority and community norms regarding sexual morality. Thus, there are interdictions about the dangers of going out alone without taking the proper precautionary measures. But temptations to deviate from these norms are strong and sometimes take the form of seductive voices... calling the woman's name or imploring "come here!" Admonitions not heeded, the temptations of solitude prove irresistible and the interdiction is violated... Without the assistance of women friends the young woman is led "astray," a term which commonly signifies either wandering off or committing moral error.[109]

Richard returns from work in time for supper, to which everyone is invited: the van Schendels, their children, Borgman, Pascal, Ludwig, Stine, and her boyfriend.. After asserting his control of Marina one final time (demanding no alcohol be served at the meal), an extremely awkward dinner party begins. It emerges that not only has Richard been fired, but that his boss is in fact the father of Stine's boyfriend. A literal fistfight ensures, ended by a swift right hook from Ludwig, who perfunctorily dumps Stine's unconscious boyfriend at a bus stop without any objections.

The children continue eating. Richard pulls Marina into another room—perhaps the very room in which she first discovered a beaten Borgman—and shows her a mysterious "X" that has been tattooed upon his shoulder.

"I've been marked," he says, claiming it is the source of his recent misfortune.

"Marked?" she asks, either oblivious or playing the part. "By who?"

Several loose candidates exist in faerie folklore. Individuals taken by faeries sometimes displayed physical marks. While not a cross, the *breac shìth*, 'elfin pox,' or 'fairy spots,' were blemishes upon the skin.[110] The 'fairy blast'—'blast,' sharing the same Germanic root as 'blustery' and 'blister'—was a mark upon the skin obtained by offending faeries, who by means of a magic gust of wind caused a blister filled with all manner of detritus: bones, rocks, feathers, teeth, etc.[111]

We also find an interesting, if by no means exact, congruency in the following excerpt from Evans Wentz:

> A conception like that among the Chinese, of how an evil spirit may dispossess the soul inhabiting a child's or adult's body, seems to be the basis and original conception behind the fairy-changeling belief in all Celtic and other countries. When a child has been changed by fairies, and an old fairy left in its place, the child has been, according to this theory, dispossessed of its body by an evil fairy, which a Chinaman calls a demon, while the leaving behind of the old fairy accounts for the changed personality and changed facial expression of the demon-possessed infant. The Chinese demon enters into and takes complete possession of the child's body while the child's soul is out of it during sleep—and all fairies make changelings when a babe is asleep in its cradle at night, or during the day when it is left alone for a short time. The Chinese child-soul is then unable to return into its body until some kind of magical ceremony or exorcism expels the possessing demon; and through precisely similar methods, often aided by Christian priests, Celts cure changelings made by fairies, pixies, and *corrigans*. In the following account, therefore, apparently lies the root explanation of the puzzling beliefs concerning fairy changelings so commonly met with in the Celtic Fairy-Faith:—'To avert the calamity of nursing a demon, dried banana-skin is burnt to ashes, which are then mixed with water. Into this the mother dips her finger and paints a cross upon the sleeping babe's forehead. In a short time the demon soul returns—for the soul wanders from the body during sleep and is free—but, failing to recognize the body thus disguised, flies off. The true soul, which has been waiting for an opportunity, now approaches the dormant body, and, if the mark has been washed off in time, takes possession of it; but if not, it, like the demon, failing to recognize the body, departs, and the child dies in its sleep.'[112]

None of the above are truly suitable points of comparison for the 'X' on Richard's shoulder—for example, the Chinese cross dispels, rather than encourages, misfortune—but the fingerprints of faerie folklore remain nonetheless.

"I AM—WE ARE"

Perhaps blinded by the household drama, Marina and Richard fail to notice—or perhaps fail to care—that Borgman, Ludwig, and Pascal seem to be doing very *un*garden-y things in their backyard. The trio are seen welding giant scaffolding and driving stakes into the ground; at this juncture, their purpose remains unclear.

Marina awakens when Stine informs her all three children have taken ill. They appear absolutely exhausted. Faeries were commonly ascribed control over human sleep; our modern *Sandman* possibly began as a menacing Scandinavian nursery *Bogle* who employed sleep-inducing magic, a role filled in France by *La Dormette* and in Germany by the *Pechamnderlin*.[113] It is equally important to note that some folklore holds Dreamland and *Tír na nÓg*—Fairyland—occupy the same reality.[114]

Stine reports to Pascal that Marina has phoned the doctor, hinting the children's illness may be part of some unspoken plan (Stine appears more thoroughly bewitched than Marina in many respects). Borgman phones Brenda and Ilonka, who assassinate the doctor and make the house call in his stead.

The moment they appear onscreen with the children, we are once more greeted by the curious buzzing sound—its first use heard indoors, explicitly indicating this audio cue is not merely an ambient noise employed during outdoor scenes.

Brenda diagnoses the children as "overtired from the modern world." While the root of their malady likely lies in their journey to Pascal and Ludwig's 'Fairyland,' it is important to examine Brenda's aversion to modernity. Chaucer was among the first to describe faeries departing the mortal world in droves; the 'passing of the faeries' has been attributed many motives, from Christianity to industrialization to, indeed, the modern world.[115] Some even go so far as to speculate the reason faeries are rarely observed is because science and technology have supplanted magic and wonder, disenchanting our world to the extent that fae or faerie folk can simply no longer be perceived because of societal conditioning. Ergo, if we read Borgman & Co. as a troupe of faeries, a rejection of modernity makes perfect sense.

Borgman continues to influence Marina's dreams, generating night-mares where Richard abuses and tries to kill her. This naturally widens the rift between the couple, and Marina asks Borgman to murder Richard. Like any spirit or devil, it was once thought possible to bind faeries and enlist them to enact one's bidding; these pacts sometimes involved sexual intercourse, a desire Marina shares with Borgman at several points during the film.[116]

After spending the night elsewhere, Richard returns in good spirits, ea-ger for reconciliation. He has somehow removed the tattoo on his shoul-der, and the instant he arrives Borgman invites the family to the back lawn. Here, Borgman, Brenda, Ilonka, Pascal, and Ludwig reveal the fruits of their labor: a stage show produced for the film's core cast. The details of the performance are, by-and-large, inconsequential and played for ab-surdism.

(At the risk of branching into a discipline beyond this essay's purview, the paranormal or supernatural, however one defines it, seems obsessed with theatricality. This is especially true in the UFO phenomenon, where experiences commonly display nonsensical details, or seem highly incon-gruent with the concept of extraterrestrial visitation.[117] Jacques Vallee was among the first to address the similarities between faerie lore and the modern 'extraterrestrial' contact experience, therefore providing a ten-uous link between the nonsensicality of UFO reports and the theatrical absurdity at hand in *Borgman*.)

That being said, there is one moment in this performative act worth mentioning: Ilonka trails sandwich boards behind her, worn by Pascal and Ludwig, reading "ICH BIN" and "WIR SIND": "I am—we are."

From Buffinga's insightful interpretation of this 'playlet':

> One could be tempted to interpret the cryptic words on the storyboards as an introductory lesson in the conjugation system of German irregular verbs, specifically the verb 'to be'. However, as they also happen to be the first person singular and the first person plural of this verb, along with the multiplication effect that is implied, one is reminded of the pseudo-biblical motto that briefly appears on the screen at the beginning of the movie: "And they descended on earth in order to increase their ranks." The words on the storyboard therefore seem to be a veiled refer-ence to the conspirators' recruitment policy that the viewer might almost have forgotten. The fact that the text is in German may well be another directorial trick...

In the final analysis, the stage and the performance are a 'play within the film', a kind of synopsis of the movie's plot. It is also a *mise en abyme*, a kind of self-reflection or introspection that the movie's leads may or may not have understood as a veiled reference perhaps to their own fate. The surreal dramatic piece, finally, is another kind of window, one that gives us, the viewer, some insight into Van Warmerdam as a directorial trickster. His ludic approach to filmmaking makes him toy with us as much as he toys with his characters. Through the economy of its style, the paring down to the essentials, the symmetry, choreography, and framing in terms of the positioning of his characters, the playlet re-enacts on a symbolic level what the characters have gone through in the film, and, by extension, what the viewer has gone through while watching it. Finally, the staging of the performance itself on the lawn that separates the man-made world—with its straight lines and right angles—from the elemental or natural world beyond reinforces the notion that the primordial can erupt at any time.

This theme closely corresponds with traditional notions that the fae folk actively abducted individuals to strengthen their ranks, either through progenation or via straightforward assimilation. At this point in *Borgman*, all three van Schendel children and Stine have been successfully recruited into the faerie ranks.

I am—we are.

"THE GARDEN IS FINISHED"

Though Richard appears a changed man—gracious, affectionate, amicable toward his new gardeners—the plot to end his life remains in play. Following the performance, Stine tucks the children into bed, and the parents enjoy a glass of reconciliatory wine. Tragically (despite his deplorable character), Richard succumbs to his poisoned drink, dying on the floor.

Borgman finally introduces Marina to his female cohort. All have been invited into the house, where an impromptu (albeit awkward and silent) house party ensues, the invaders casually listening to Thelonious Monk's *Let's Call This*. Marina pulls Borgman aside and expresses her concerns not only for Richard's corpse—still collapsed underneath the piano—but also for his friends.

"Why all these people?" she asks. "I want to be with you."

"You are with me, aren't you?" he retorts. I am—we are.

Borgman produces a pill to help Marina calm her nerves.

"The garden is finished," she whispers breathlessly. "You are no longer a gardener."

She makes romantic advances towards her (now former) gardener, but is once again spurned, igniting a jealousy which intensifies after Borgman chooses to dance with Brenda. She flees to her car with the remainder of the wine bottle to sit and drink, and a violent thunderstorm erupts. Ludwig and Pascal use this opportunity to dispose of Richard's body in the freshly-dug pond.

"Fairies are namely in medieval, and subsequent, popular and literary tradition notorious for their ability to influence weather, not least to unleash storms," wrote McGill University Lecturer in Old and Medieval English Literature Martin Puhvel.[118] Faeries of Aranmore caused squalls over the Irish Sea.[119] Along the Rance River in France, *fées* could be seen during storms.[120]

"In the darkness of the black midnight, a powerful great storm shook the place," wrote Bampton Hunt in his *Folk Tales of Breffny*. "It was like as if the four winds of Heaven were striving together, and they horrid vexed with one another. There were strange noises in it too, music and shouting, the way it was easy knowing the Good People were out playing themselves, or maybe disputing in a war."[121]

The storm in the film provides additional thematic significance beyond its strong faerie connotations. Not only have we reached the climax of the film— *Sturm und Drang*—but, as Puhvel notes, storms in medieval literature often portend a transition to the Otherworld, from our reality to the beyond.

Though Marina is unaware, her return home will result in such a journey—the ultimate transition, in fact. Once inside, Borgman takes her to the bedroom, where they share another glass of wine. Marina obviously expects long-overdue intimacy; unfortunately, she dies as they kiss, poisoned in the same manner as her late husband. Marina is dumped in the pond, which is filled in with dirt and sewn with grass.

The final shot of *Borgman* shows our mysterious strangers—Borgman, Brenda, Ilonka, Pascal, and Ludwig—leading Stine and the three van Schendel children into the forest from whence they came, accompanied by the ominous buzzing sound effect. Faeries, abducting the vulnerable to Fairyland.

I am—we are.

"And they descended upon the earth to strengthen their ranks."

"FRIENDLY, RUTHLESS, BUT NOT SADISTIC"

Are the fae folk a suitable lens through which to view *Borgman*? It would be easy to paint Borgman and his confederates as evil. Hadewych Minis herself described him as "a dark kind of demon." [122] Famed critic Leonard Maltin said of the film, "What starts as a darkly surreal satire of the bourgeoisie turns into a strange, disturbing meditation on the nature of evil, open to a myriad of interpretations."[123]

Van Warmerdam is more charitable in his characterization, casting doubt on Borgman's malignancy while hinting that a definitive, if unspoken, interpretation of the film may indeed exist.

"I see the film as a poem, a song, it is crystal clear, there are no false leads, I give the [necessary] information," he cryptically told one interviewer. "It is important to know that Borgman and his cronies are players, they are indeed stoic, but they enjoy their work... They are friendly, ruthless, but not sadistic."[124]

We might infer from this statement that the neutrality of the central antagonists (antiheroes?) is key ("important") to understanding these "leads" and arriving at a "crystal clear" interpretation of the film. Notably, faeries and their ilk commonly occupied a morally grey area in folklore: neither positive nor negative, mere forces of nature akin to the weather.

Yet this insinuation that *Borgman* possesses an internal logic is directly at odds with other interviews from van Warmerdam. "I can't explain," the director told reporters about the film's more abstruse elements. "I know nothing more than you."[125] On another occasion, he told interviewers, "I want it all to mean nothing, but in such a way that it could mean something."[126]

(This dream logic permeates not only Fairy Tales, but other modern day supernatural encounters as well. J. Allen Hynek, progenitor of modern Ufology, coined the term "High Strangeness" in the 1970s to describe for the nonsensical, ineffable, and peculiar absurdities found in so many UFO reports.)

Might the director be embodying The Trickster archetype himself? Van Warmerdam's contradictory statements may be a deliberate method to avoid robbing his art of its power. When asked whether or not over-explanation is harmful to cinema, he replied, "Harmful, I don't know, but it makes boring movies. People want to understand everything, they even get angry if there's not a clear plot."[127]

"From the beginning I didn't want to explain too much," van Warmerdam declared in another interview. "Explaining brings you to forced [shots], and worse, to stupid dialogue. Although, in the first rough cut there was still a lot of…explanation. We cut a lot of it because we found out that [cutting the explanation] makes the film stronger."[128] (Oh, to see those deleted scenes!)

This appears to be direct confirmation that *Borgman* possesses its own internal logic, and strengthens the validity of a faerie lore reading. Van Warmerdam also wrote and directed 2003's *Grimm*, a film drawing upon both urban legends and the work of The Brothers Grimm—ergo, it is safe to assume he is the sort of personality familiar with faerie lore.

Should we adopt a 'Death of the Author' stance, van Warmerdam's inspiration is unimportant; archetypes, including those of the fae folk and household spirit variety, are so strong they emerge independently of intent, bubbling to the surface with a will all their own. If a reading of *Borgman*-as-faerie-lore is justified, and it seems to be, then how does van Warmerdam implement that tradition? How are the fae folk used to provide additional insight into the two primary themes of the motion picture: nature and class?

"WE ARE FORTUNATE—AND THE FORTUNATE MUST BE PUNISHED"

Upon release, many critics theorized Borgman might be a personification of Nature itself. "Is Borgman the Devil?" asked Sasha Stone of *The Wrap*. "Is he the underclass? Is he nature?"[129]

James Teitelbaum speculated Borgman might be "the anthropomorphic incarnation of a force of nature beyond human comprehension. Perhaps Borgman and his crew represent nature itself. Don't look too hard though: there are no answers to be found on screen."[130]

"Clearly, one of *Borgman*'s big themes is the simmering resentment between the haves and the have-nots, but van Warmerdam also flirts with the idea that in the process of making our lives so comfortable, we've lost sight of our essential animal nature," wrote *The Village Voice*'s Stephanie Zacharek.[131]

From his first introduction—filthy, subterranean, and dwelling in the wilderness—*Borgman*'s titular character could not be more strongly tied to the Earth. As a spirit of the land, his very identity is inseparable from the environment itself, and it is in this capacity that Nature reinserts itself into the modern, austere lives of the van Schendel family.

"Van Warmerdam's film shows not only a world estranged and a lack of harmony in the world as it is presented to us, but also in the viewer's response to this world, as it is no longer recognizable," Buffinga wrote.[132]

Short of living in an urban center, Richard and Marina's property could not be further removed from the primordial forest that spawned Borgman. In truth, their home is *worse* than any metropolitan area; instead of outright destroying the natural world, properties like the van Schendels' make the hubristic mistake of trying to *tame* nature. This is no better exemplified than in their garden, a location whose maintenance is a central plot point of the film. The garden clearly illustrates a perverted urge to subjugate and enslave the wild for mankind's own satisfaction.

This subtext may have become muddied had van Warmerdam set the film in a denser, more developed neighborhood. Instead, it is highlighted by the juxtaposition of the van Schendel garden directly abutting the woods. In fact, *Borgman*'s filming site was a protected nature zone.[133]

"Next to water, the forest is the great lair or refuge of land spirits," wrote Lecouteux. "It is a haunted place, an outlying place full of violence; a site of excursion; a refuge of outcasts and exiles as well as pagan beliefs; a place of marvels and perils; a savage, marginal, dreadful space; as well as a focal point of peasant memory... A headquarters for strange phenomena that represent all sorts of theophanies...."[134]

Once hired, Borgman and his crew immediately set about re-shaping the van Schendel garden, an effort to reclaim the artificiality of the residence's landscape for Nature. This endeavor is only fully realized once the pond is filled in once more, the area sewn with grass. In some traditions, Camael the Archangel was the force in charge of Adam and Eve's expulsion from the Garden of Eden; Borgman fulfills a similar role, casting humans out of the wilderness.

Before returning to his forest, Borgman takes one, final, sentimental look at the home—and it could not appear more lifeless, more in contrast, with its vibrant, initial introduction full of human life. For years, presumably, the van Schendel garden has served as the frontline of a war between Nature and man, until one day the faeries came and waged the final battle.

Among cinephiles, it is significantly less popular to interpret *Borgman* as a commentary on Nature versus Modernity than it is to approach it as a critique of class warfare. While the temptation to interpret every film as a commentary on class has become fatiguing as of late, this reading has a great deal of merit, and is explicitly (and bluntly) present in the film's text.

Wrote blogger David Perretta:

> Why does Marina let this stranger into her home? If you take away all the supernatural elements of the film you're left with bourgeois etiquette and standard conventions of what it means to be a "good citizen." Marina doesn't really want to let him into [her] home, but since her husband beat him up pretty badly she feels guilty. She also can't kick him out of the house once he's getting better, because not only could he sue them, but again that's not very polite.[135]

"We are fortunate," Marina cries at one point in the film. "And the fortunate much be punished." The van Schendel family's privilege is exemplified in the small bourgeoisie flourishes van Warmerdam includes in their lives. Their home is spacious and immaculate. They have an au pair who not only supervises the children at home, but also takes them to school. They have a quaint guest cottage in their garden, which itself has a dedicated landscaper. Richard exhibits a distaste for 'lower' classes, buys his wife jewelry in lieu of offering apologies, and holds a white collar occupation.

Borgman, on the other hand, is filthy, homeless, and unemployed.

Around the same time in the film that Isolde murders the gardener candidate, she also dismembers her favorite stuffed animal. Marina discovers the gutted teddy bear filled with sand from the sandbox and confronts her daughter:

> That bear was lovingly put together by human hands. Maybe even by children's hands. Children who haven't a life as good as yours. Children who can't go to school, or to a doctor when they are ill. That bear was brought into this country in a plane or on a boat. And then it went in a van to the city, to the toy shop. That bear has travelled an enormous distance. One day I was looking for a present for you and I saw this bear in the shop window. And Mummy had never seen such a sweet bear before.

She bought it to make you happy. But Mummy shouldn't have done that. Nothing gets deliberately broken in this house! Understand?

Marina's concern for the working class that constructed the teddy bear is immediately undermined by her husband who, serving as an avatar for the upper class—privileged, grossly capitalist, wasteful—suggests she is being too hard on Isolde.

Of this destroyed toy, one critic wrote, "the pinnacle of the imagery related to the kids is when the little killer girl [Isolde] is in the sandbox, where she's gutting her teddy bear of its straw stuffing and filling it with sand. Symbolically, this is the emptying of the human soul—the child, as evidenced by the teddy bear as an image—and its being refilled with dirt (i.e. consumerism, commodities, et cetera)."[136] While it seems equally likely that the refilled stuffed animal represents how Borgman's confederates have opened the children and replaced something inside of them (their souls?), both readings are entirely valid and not necessarily at odds with one another.

What does class have to do with faerie lore? Class-based language has been involved since the earliest days to codify faeries; their euphemism 'The Gentry' clearly exemplifies this trend. Moreover, faeries have been used to represent the plight of the working class for centuries. Wrote Professor of English at Roosevelt University in Chicago Regina Buccola:

> The increased involvement of the "yeoman class" in literature generated greater attention to issues of concern among the laboring classes and impoverished. In many plays, these concerns are depicted (and, at times, deflected) through fairy plots. Many of the household chores that fairies are imagined to do align them with one of the lowest social classes—female domestic servants. However, fairies are not controlled through mortal masters but, rather, have the power to career through human lives wreaking havoc or granting favors at will. They are subject to no reprisals (such as corporal punishment or withheld wages) if they do not perform household duties well. Thus, they adhere to neither gender nor class codes, although they perform tasks and posses role-based identities that are accounted for in such structures. They are creatures liberated from the strictures of class and gender; theatrical depictions or tales of their antics could, therefore, have been liberatory for the members of the working classes and women long confined to particular social positions and the conduct considered appropriate to them. The theatrical and popular discourses about fairies presented creatures that both were and were not like the domestic workers whose daily work they mimicked.

It is in the gap between their similarities to their human counterparts and their differences from them that fairy characters suggest alternatives to sociocultural norms.[137]

When one considers how regularly artists utilized faeries through-out history to dramatize *Borgman*'s two most-cited themes—nature and class—it becomes highly likely that van Warmerdam drew upon this rich vein of folklore to craft the film. That its internal logic should largely be lost on modern audiences is unsurprising; western culture is shockingly illiterate regarding faerie traditions today, despite how inextricably em-bedded they are in our art and language. The persistence of these themes and motifs is a testament to faerie lore's resilient nature; it endures, like Fairyland, beneath the surface of cultural consciousness, influencing our imaginations long after we foolishly deem it irrelevant.

"More wind please!": The Magic, Myth, and Mystery of Twin Peaks

Mark Anthony Wyatt

During the filming of *Twin Peaks*, the talented cast of actors soon came to understand, via David Lynch's direction, that if he asked for 'more wind' he was asking them to express more mystery. The wind blowing through the treetops of the forests in Twin Peaks was a consistent image, not limited to the opening credits—it blew throughout the series, a metaphor for the mystery of the forest.

I'm making an assumption you are reasonably familiar with the television series *Twin Peaks* and its film prequel, *Fire Walk with Me*. I won't explain who the characters were, their motivations, or sub-plots, but will occasionally mention characters, places, scenes, and locations for reference purposes. However, I'll give you a quick refresher of the basic initial *Twin Peaks* storyline. If you have not seen the series or film, I highly recommend that you do; if you have, I am hoping that my essay will encourage you to watch it again.

Twin Peaks was created by David Lynch and Mark Frost, two talents that rightly stand shoulder-to-shoulder in the highest echelons of American television drama writers, alongside greats such as Steven Bochco and David Milch.

(As this essay progresses, I may give credit to Lynch when it may well have been Frost's intellectual property. It's difficult to know exactly who posited every idea to the series, so I apologise to Mark Frost in advance if I have gotten anything wrong.)

Twin Peaks is, on the surface at least, a story about the investigation into high school student Laura Palmer's murder; her dead body is discovered by Pete Martell, a local fisherman, washed up on a stony riverside beach, wrapped in plastic, in the first episode's attention-grabbing, iconic opening scene. The tale is set in Twin Peaks, a fictional, seemingly idyllic American town in the Pacific Northwest, situated close to the Canadian border. In real life, as in the series, the region has a distinctive feel: a sense of damp menace seems to hang expectantly in the air, along with the fresh, pungent aroma of a multitude of coniferous trees thriving in the temperate climate.

Special Agent Dale Cooper, a charismatic young investigator, is swiftly dispatched by the Federal Bureau of Investigation to the town to lead the investigation into Laura's mysterious, horrific death, where he is ably assisted by the straight-up Sheriff of Twin Peaks, Harry S. Truman, and his local police department. Cooper later receives additional help from a bright FBI colleague, Albert Rosenfield, both agents having been assigned to the case by the regional FBI Chief, Gordon Cole. Cole is a deep-thinking, partially deaf man in his sixties, who is—as you may recall—memorably played by David Lynch himself.

When we first 'meet' FBI Special Agent Dale Cooper, we see him pick up his voice recorder and address his co-worker, Diane, for the first time as he drives toward town. He tells her, "I'm entering the town of Twin Peaks. Five miles south of the Canadian border, and 12 miles west of the state line. I have never seen so many trees in my life!" Shortly afterwards, having met Sheriff Truman for the first time—immediately making his superior rank clear in a firm but polite way—he lightens up and asks Harry, with wide-eyed boyish enthusiasm, "Sheriff, what kind of fantastic trees have you got growing around here?"

Cooper investigates the crime using tried, tested, conventional scientific means, but also listens to his gut instincts as he unravels and interprets his dreams with deep philosophical insights. Some of these insights are passed to him by other characters in the story, for example the sagacious Margaret (a.k.a. 'the Log Lady') or the enigmatic Major Garland Briggs. Cooper's investigation shines a light not only on Laura's double-life (despite the salacious circumstances surrounding her death, most Twin Peaks town folk had previously seen her as a wholesome, 'Home-Coming Queen' kind of a girl), but also on the hidden, chthonic darkness and murky secrets of the town itself and its surrounding mysterious forest. Cooper, forever skirting the liminal edges, is on a personal shaman-like journey of discovery as he tries to unify dualities, to find balance between two different worlds. Cooper unifies the rational and the supernatural in an Arthurian quest—backed up by his own trusty Knights of the Round Table, Albert, Andy, Harry, and Hawk—to track down Laura's killer, navigating a sea of seediness surrounding the awful crime. Cooper's noble quest would eventually lead to him facing his own demons, and a 'Dark Night of the Soul.'

I recall viewing the 90-minute pilot episode of *Twin Peaks*, which aired in England on BBC Two on October 23, 1990, and subsequent episodes in the weeks that followed. I remember excitedly looking forward to each new episode, and sometimes having to set my VCR to record it if I was going to be out, in those far-off days of anxiously waiting an entire week for the next installment of your favourite TV shows! Right from the start, I loved *Twin Peaks*, but mostly (in retrospect I think) for the bizarre humour, the references to the presence of the other, and the cast of pretty ladies. I know my youthful, more day-dreamy self would have enjoyed hanging out at the Double R Diner, being served damn fine coffee by sultry Norma, trying to prise classified government UFO information out of that wise old owl Major Briggs, and watching Audrey's sensual dancing to strange jazz music by the jukebox. Back in those days I was not quite ready for that odd music and not too aware of the deeper content: the folklore of course, as well as the metaphysical, the esoteric, religion, theosophy, philosophy, alchemy, surrealism, psychology and so, so much more.

A common trope in many of Lynch's films, as it was in *Blue Velvet* for example, is to present a scene where everything appears just perfect before we soon discover that when we look deeper, there is always a darkness, an evil lurking, a seething underbelly of sleaze and decay, hidden from our gaze but ready to reveal itself at a moment's notice. The town of Twin Peaks has that in common with *Blue Velvet*'s Lumberton, as both logging towns seem idyllic at first. They share an iceberg-like feeling of pending doom. To casual viewers of *Twin Peaks* and *Blue Velvet* there probably didn't appear to be that much going on at first glance, but a deep, dark abyss lies hidden away just beneath the surface.

One of *Twin Peaks'* major themes is the unification of dualities, the *yin* and the *yang*, and the pursuit of balance—both within ourselves and in the wider world—with an overarching message that we should strive to find a healthier balance with nature. The series does this through many different visual and audio cues, for example via dual pairings such as mountains, golf balls, waterfalls, accounts, books, diaries, and, of course, doppel-gängers.

Margaret, the Log Lady, who seems to spend most of her waking hours drinking coffee at the Double R Diner or delivering Taoist parables to unsuspecting recipients—who had only popped by to eat a delicious slice of cherry pie—says directly to the camera at one point, "Balance is the key. Balance is the key to many things. Do we understand balance?" Lynch, via the Log Lady, cuts the 'middleman' (the story) out to address us, the viewers, directly.

THE OLD GODS

The Green Man (a.k.a. 'Jack of the Green,' also connected to John Barleycorn) has long been associated in English folklore with the balance between man and the natural world, particularly with the dark woods. Half man, half tree, a spiritual guardian of the forests, he is a symbol of nature's changing seasons, fertility and annual rebirth. His image can still be seen on old Roman artifacts, his face sprouting foliage instead of hair, his body strong, lean and tree trunk-like.

The Green Man's earliest roots are uncertain. Some historians compare his likeness to the Roman god Bacchus, but if you look closely at some of his surviving imagery he has dolphins, seashells, and other sea-related paraphernalia around his head, so I suggest that he was more likely derived from an ancient sea deity. Wherever he came from, we do know that the Celts held him in high regard: for example, there is a small sculpture of the Green Man in Scotland's medieval Rosslyn Chapel. More recently, green eco-groups in England have adopted him as a mascot, and there is a highly-rated annual Green Man cultural/music summer festival in the Brecon Beacons of Wales. The Green Man shares some characteristics with the Greek god Pan. Agent Cooper's long time secretary and confidant, Diane, shares an onomastic link to the Greek/Roman mythological figure of Artemis/Diana, goddess of the hunt, who was a kind of early female version of the Green Man, given her association with spirit animals such as deer, bears and hunting dogs.

Do you recall the sweet little bird sitting balanced on a tree limb in *Twin Peaks'* opening credits? A beautiful songbird, the Bewick's wren was historically associated with the Yuletide in Anglo-Celtic, Saxon, and Druidic folklore. Lynch uses that scene as a metaphor for balance, just as he used a delightful little bird in *Blue Velvet* (this time a robin) as a symbol for equilibrium. There is an old Anglo-Saxon saying: "The robin and the wren are God's almighty cock and hen."

Interestingly, in old English and Cornish folklore, robins were harbingers of death if they should fly into your home or workplace. I recall my mother getting very agitated when a bird flew into our home sometime in the late 1960s. I remember running around trying to help it leave by a window or door. I'm confident that mum would have known of the superstition, and she always had a fear of birds 'fluttering' around near her; I can't recall if the event did foreshadow a death, but it may well have.

A few years later, some elderly local country people (including our sweet lady neighbour, 'Mrs. G,' who had been born in the late 1890s or early 1900s) would have still considered an appearance of a tame robin or wren *around* your home (but not *in* it) as a visit by the spirit of a recently departed loved one. I recall a little robin sat on a tiny conifer shrub at the top of her garden in about 1975. Mrs. G, my younger brother, sister, and I stood by the shrub taking it in turns to stroke the little bird, and we held her gently in the palms of our hands. I still have a treasured photo of my little brother petting that beautiful little robin (robins are tiny in the UK). That experience, so long ago now, made me wonder if Lynch intended the little wren we all saw at the beginning of every episode, balanced on the bough, to be Laura's spirit.

As I have found out by studying Lynch's work, he does hide big clues in plain sight that only seem obvious with hindsight. Another example of this is the appearance of an owl—another harbinger of death. It flies through the forest immediately after Leland dies in the Twin Peaks police cell, after 'Bob' withdraws from Leland's body. A coincidence? I think not.

Coincidences frequently crop up in *Twin Peaks*. Cooper says, in slightly different ways on more than one occasion throughout the series: "Coincidence and fate figure largely in our lives." As a further example, he later says, "Gentlemen, when two separate events occur simultaneously, pertaining to the same object in enquiry, we must always pay strict attention!" Lynch also uses the tool of repetition frequently and loudly. He obviously wants us to take notice, to absorb the information he presents.

The gradual (some might say cancerous) invasion of humans and our housing developments, businesses, and infrastructure into our ancient forests is a process that began in North America after the first European settlers arrived. Bear in mind, Europeans had already cleared Europe's forests centuries before, as their numbers had grown. Nature, Lynch tells us, needs to be respected; it will fight back and has time on its side. We see this both in Twin Peaks' failed country club development and the fire destroying the sawmill in the forest. If we exploit nature by failing to control our human greed, we will suffer the consequences. You could argue that Lynch's message was many years ahead of the modern 'green' curve.

Back in the 1600s, those new arrivals in North America were rapidly clearing ancient forests to create farmland and space for their homes. It was the practical thing to do. By clearing the trees, they provided themselves not just with land to grow crops, but also materials with which to build their homes—but there was more to it than just providing food and shelter. By their clearance, the early settlers were also giving themselves greater security. With a clear view, they could see any dangerous predators, animal, human, or any undefined 'other,' that may have been intent on attacking their communities. The removal of the woods meant that, theoretically, there was nowhere for their enemies to hide. A cleared forest of shallow tree stumps held no secrets, no hidden monsters. Simon Schama, in his book *Landscape and Memory*, wrote, "Beauty laid in clearance, danger and horror lurked in the pagan woods."

THE ANGRY FOREST

In his book *Don't Look Behind You*, Timothy Renner discusses how First Nations people in the American northeast warned the newly arrived European settlers about what they called 'The Hide-Behinds.' These creatures—known by various names in different parts of North America and elsewhere—are most commonly referred to nowadays as 'bigfoot,' and followed along behind travellers in Pennsylvania's deep, dark woods, just out of sight. They were known to occasionally abduct the last person in line, never to be seen again. Only the bravest people, or perhaps the most foolish, would volunteer to be last in line. These creatures, whether physical or interdimensional, and the bizarre disappearances of people in dense woodlands and forests, are still with us today.

Fear and darkness have always attached to the dark forests like parasites. In *Twin Peaks*, Lynch bridged the generations, tapping into a modern version of an ancient fear. Legends of forest spirits abound all over the world. In rural parts of Russia, for example, local fathers tell their children that if they go into the woods alone, they should never veer off the beaten path. If they do, the *leshy*, a huge wild man with blue skin, green eyes and hair, would surely lure them deeper into the forest until they are exhausted, lost, or both. On first reading that, I was reminded of the Cornish piskies who were said to have done much the same thing in old legends of Cornwall; the Cornish called this being 'pisky-led.'

In 1972 a story emerged from Romania about a beautiful female spirit (*Fata Padourri*) who had tempted a male forestry worker deeper into the woods than he would ordinarily have walked. Thinking that he was on to a good thing, and not yet realising that she was not a 'normal' girl, he followed her, whereupon she suddenly turned into a tree. He had great difficulty finding his way back to his work crew. Another forestry worker in the area came forward and said that he had experienced something similar in the same area. He had been followed by an attractive young lady who had teased and beckoned him, deeper and deeper into the woods, only to find that she had suddenly disappeared into a wisp of smoke. He had trouble finding his way back out of the woods too.

Whilst researching *Twin Peaks* and the literature that may have influenced Lynch, I found several major literary possibilities. The best known of these influences are perhaps the works of J.R.R. Tolkien, most notably his *Lord of the Rings* trilogy. You may recall how the Ents, tree-like forest custodians of Middle Earth, alongside the Huorns, inspired by Treebeard, attacked the enemy fortress at Isengard, where the war-like Orcs and men had exploited their forest home. Lynch was also possibly inspired by the ancient Saxon *Beowulf* saga, as well as ubiquitous medieval Teutonic folktales of monsters and werewolves roaming the gothic woods of Northern Europe.

Lynch may also have been influenced by some slightly more recent literature from 1916. Arthur Machen, a Welsh writer of supernatural and fantasy novels, wrote *The Coming of the Terror*, a short story in which the trees came to life to aid the animals in an uprising against humans (specifically British civilians) during World War I.

Machen's creepy story has a similar style to that of the great H.G. Wells (who lived a stone's throw from my Nan in Woking). I believe Machen also inspired James Herbert's *The Rats* and George Orwell's *Animal Farm*, both of which feature rebellions from the animal world. (I will leave what could well have been Lynch's major literary influence, a short story from

1926, for my final paragraphs, as it ties several writers' ideas of living, animated forests fighting back against man's greed directly to *Twin Peaks*.)

Twin Peaks has many references to folklore from Northern Europe (Odin, Thor, Yggdrasil, etc.), but at first I found little in the way of truly authentic Native American folklore in the series, which may surprise some readers. Having said that, during my research I did later re-discover the works of Algernon Blackwood, a supreme storyteller I had read voraciously in my youth. On re-reading Blackwood's wonderful, atmospheric masterpiece *The Wendigo* (1910), I soon realised that it may have been a big influence on Lynch's *Twin Peaks*. The Wendigo is either mythological or an unclassified creature—either way it's said to be a terrifying, flesh-eating, bigfoot-like monster, and the Algonquian peoples of North America do believe it exists, naturally or supernaturally, in the dense forests surrounding the Great Lakes and St. Lawrence River. As with the vampire legends of Northern Europe, where a vampire's victim later becomes a vampire, Wendigos are said to turn their victims into Wendigos. Others believe that the Wendigo is merely symbolic, a symbol for winter and greed. The idea of 'Bob,' the possessing evil spirit that moves parasitically from host to host, is a similar concept, and Lynch also explored the notion of mankind's greed. You may well have thought that the major source of possible Native American folklore in the series would have come via Hawk, the honourable indigenous law enforcement officer, but the lore he generally quoted was largely imported by European settlers. That said, Native American folklore in *Twin Peaks* is definitely represented visually, by way of set-dressing and those awesome Pacific North West locations.

As an example, Washington's stunning Snoqualmie Waterfalls have long been revered as a place of power by the indigenous people of that region. The Snoqualmie people say that their ancestors sometimes show themselves in those misty waterfalls, and similar falls in the region. Laura's image in *Twin Peaks*, you may recall, is seen floating through the canopy of the trees, amongst the mists caused by the water crashing on to the rocks far below. The indigenous tribes say the Giant Redwoods (Sequoias) are 'Standing People ' which contain 'the Great Spirit.' Redwoods are thought of as symbols of time and strength, the wind that blows through them their life-breath, a kind of spiritual highway on which their ancestors travel.

FOLKLORE WALK WITH ME

I will now present a swift overview of some of the folklore tropes I found in *Twin Peaks*. I will also stress it is nowhere near an exhaustive study, as my main focus in this essay is upon the folklore of the forests.

One of the very first things I noticed whilst re-watching the show recently was the proliferation of the colour red; red, international colour of danger, literally all over *Twin Peaks*, inescapable, even down to red filters on the cameras at times. Doubles are prevalent too, so many that I stopped jotting them down in the end! The two mountain peaks are, of course, one of the first examples of doubles to crop up in the series, alongside the twin waterfall of Snoqualmie, seen at the beginning of every episode. (I have since noticed that the number of waterfalls over the edge of the cliff varies according to recent rainfall.) There are plenty of abductions too... after all, the show's basic premise is built upon the abduction of two local schoolgirls, Laura and Ronette, and we are also led to believe that Major Garland Briggs has been abducted by aliens/faeries/ultra-terrestrials (take your pick). You could argue too that there are changelings in *Twin Peaks*, in the guise of thought-forms or *tulpas* from 'the other place' replacing characters (Dougie and Diane spring immediately to mind).

I believe that there are symbolic faerie food offerings as well (and I emphasise the word *symbolic*), for example in the form of damn fine cherry pie and great coffee from Norma's Double R Diner; this repast beguiles visitors to linger and stay in the town. On the flipside, at the nearby Deer Meadow Café, the cherry pie is apparently awful, the coffee abysmal. The small, fictional Pacific Northwest town of 'Deer Meadow' serves as Twin Peaks' Jungian shadow-self, its dark side.

This 'shadow-self' leads neatly into the motif of split-personalities. Laura and her father Leland both have good and bad sides to their personalities, brought about by possession in Leland's case, and an abusive upbringing in Laura's. They are unable to find that elusive balance that Lynch teaches, their human behaviour and characteristics swinging erratically from good to bad, like out-of-control pendulums.

Cyclops, the one-eyed Greek mythological monster, is represented in *Twin Peaks* by Nadine Hurley and her eyepatch, and of course we also have the One Eyed Jacks Bar. Phillip Jeffries (quirkily played by David Bowie) and Major Briggs travel back and forth in time, as does Agent Cooper as he tries to rescue Laura before she is murdered; but, as with Orpheus in

Greek mythology, Cooper makes the critical mistake of looking behind himself, losing Laura just as Orpheus lost Eurydice. The Icelandic *Eddas*, the Saxon *Beowulf*, and other classic writings all influenced Tolkien's *Lord of the Rings* saga, which, in turn, may have also inspired Lynch. We see their symbology in the passage of the rings through various owners, and the circles, mounds, and dwarves, for example.

The symbolism of crossing the River Styx makes a very early appearance in *Twin Peaks* during the opening scene at the river's edge; it is how Laura is delivered to us, the viewers, as she arrives in the story, having floated across the water. This made me think of the way that many Christian 'saints' arrived in Cornwall (a region of Britain I know well) in the 4th and 5th centuries from Wales, Brittany, Scotland and Ireland. Legend tells us that these saints, like St. Ia for example, mostly arrived still breathing, and obviously, back in those long-gone times, not wrapped in plastic! Speaking of saints and Christianity, we could perhaps push that analogy a little further, suggesting that Laura's death at the outset of the *Twin Peaks* saga signals her re-birth, in that she too rises again—not literally, of course—but that her character is 'reborn' as the major focus of the storyline, especially during the film prequel *Fire Walk With Me*.

There are giants in *Twin Peaks* too, like the 'Fireman' who works as an elderly waiter at the Great Northern Hotel and as a stage compere at The Roadhouse introducing musical acts. This brings me to the constant repetition of trinities throughout the series, including, of course, in series three (!) the Trinity nuclear tests, and the three pretty, but very odd, casino girls, Sandy, Mandy, and Candy. Are they perhaps a visual representation of the *Moirai*, the Greek Fates? Is that why they are present at the big showdown towards the end of series three, in the Twin Peaks Police Station?

There are several women in the series and film primarily, if not all, placed in distress at the hands of men, a common trope in folklore. Laura is the obvious one that comes to mind, as well as her school friend and fellow trauma and abuse victim Ronette Pulaski. Shelly Johnson is beaten and mentally belittled by the thug Leo, and Laura's mother, Sarah Palmer, suffers something no mother should ever have to endure, the death of her daughter.

There are, of course, other distressed women in *Twin Peaks*. Audrey Horne comes to mind, although her peril is at a lesser and almost (but not quite, given the abusive implications) comical level. I'm thinking back to the scene where Audrey is trapped in the One Eyed Jacks brothel prior to her rescue, at great risk of being discovered by her own father, Benjamin—who, to Audrey's horror, is unaware she works there and has entered her boudoir intent on being her next customer. In the scene, Audrey looks suspiciously like 'Snow White,' and the entrapment of a young beauty by a monstrous captor reminded me of other classic faerie tales of my youth, such as *Beauty and the Beast*.

Stags and their antlers feature heavily in the various hotels, clubs, and homes of *Twin Peaks*. These are, in Norse folklore, symbols of masculinity, war, and conquest, and mainly appear in centres of male power within the saga, such as in Sheriff Truman's and Benjamin Horne's offices. We also see iron in the opening credits, in the form of timber cutting tooling, on mechanised machinery at the Packard Sawmills. 'Cold iron' has traditionally been thought of as a material to ward off both the fae and various other evils; that's why, for example, you see it used as perimeter fencing surrounding old graveyards, and in the form of a horseshoe (in the shape of a U) for good luck above entrance doors into people's homes.

When I began my recent *Twin Peaks* research, I began right at the opening sequences of the pilot and the earlier episodes of the television series. I had watched those opening visuals many times over the last few decades, but until then I had never peeled back that metaphorical carpet in the Red Room of my mind to look at the show from a snake's eye view, similar to the way that Lynch's cameras showed us what lay beneath the pretty white picket fence at the outset of *Blue Velvet*. When I finally did that, I soon became aware of something far deeper, surprising, and genuinely magical about those introductory scenes. I was now, 30 years later, watching *Twin Peaks* with far more enlightened eyes than I had in my younger years. What I noticed was something so blatant and 'in-your-face' that once I had seen it, I could not unsee it. Whether there was any real intent behind what I noticed is for you to consider, but I believe it wasn't happenstance.

THE WIZARD

Please cast your mind back to the opening sequences, the images that follow the pretty songbird, with 'cast' being the operative word. Consider those swaying Douglas firs with the wind (*air*) blowing through their tops, and do you recall the smoke rising up from the chimneys (smoke from *fire*), and, to reinforce it, the iron grinding wheels throwing off fiery sparks (*fire*) as they sharpened the cutting blades? Then Lynch shows us the literal down to *earth* image of the road leading into the town of Twin Peaks, and the majestic Snoqualmie twin waterfalls (*water*) cascading down into the river far below.

Lynch effectively invokes The Four Elements: Air, Fire, Earth, and Water, at the very outset of each episode. He then shows us a cast circle, a known source of power and protection in magic rituals. The visual presents 12 lit candles, quickly followed by those same 12 candles, but all snuffed out. Blink and you would have missed it. I believe this represents the light and the dark, the nature of duality. These opening sequences are Lynch-as-wizard, performing spell-work onscreen. This was something that, to my knowledge, wasn't attempted again until the advent of 2019's hit reality web-series *Hellier*, but whether the creators and players of *Hellier* were actually cognizant that they were doing so—with occultist Allen Greenfield possibly playing the wizard role—is perhaps a deep discussion for another day.

Lynch may well have been calling in the 'directions' in the opening sequences too, north, south, east and west, but I can't be sure, as I wasn't with him and his camera crews to check their compass bearings! What I do know is that Lynch grabs our attention, and Angelo Badalamenti's haunting theme music works in unison with Lynch's wand wizardry as it goes out across the airwaves, lulling us all into a relaxed state of mind, all the better to receive his deeper messages within the show. Magic is all about the power of suggestion, and most importantly, our intent, and it is closely tied into the so called mythological faerie realms, which I discuss elsewhere in this essay.

Lynch loves numerology. You will see it all over his films if you pay attention. Using numerology, the population of Twin Peaks of 51,201 (shown on the road sign in the 'earth' image), reduces to the number nine, which is a very powerful numeral in Norse/Germanic mythology. Did Lynch use the number nine to 'power-up' his spell by the maximum single digit available? You could argue that the population number was randomly chosen, and therefore I am just clutching at straws, but if you do the math, and look at the probability of outcomes, you may ponder Cooper's words on coincidences again. The number nine also signifies Odin hanging for nine days and nights in the 'Tree of Life' (Yggdrasil, the Lord of Ghosts/Lord of the Hanged) in order to gain power over the runes, to learn their hidden secrets. Norse legend also tell us that there are nine worlds in creation.

"THE TREES, THEY WORSHIP THEM!"

Whilst the Ghostwood Estate's business negotiations were ongoing with the Norwegian delegation, Jerry Horne—brother to Benjamin, owner of the Great Northern Hotel—excitedly exclaims, "You should have seen them Ben, the trees, *they worship them!*" This description of the Norwegian party is a nod, if ever there was one, to the abundant Norse heritage on display in *Twin Peaks*.

It's also worth pointing out here that some of the Redwood trees in the forests around the 'Twin Peaks' area are ancient. Amazing lifeforms, their heights can easily exceed 200 feet. Giant Douglas Firs, Redwoods, and Spruces are very hardy and resilient, designed by nature to withstand several months every year of immersion in deep snowfall, and they are much the stronger for it. Despite that heavy snow, the trees continue to grow well in the winter months and into their old age. The trees convert their energy into extra growth around their circumference, not unlike a middle aged/elderly person who may put weight on around their waist during the winter!

Trees, science now tells us, communicate with each other, linked together by their roots and symbiotic fungi. It is not uncommon for these trees to live between 2,000-3,000 years. If 'old' equals 'wise,' some of these monolithic Pacific Northwestern trees—which have seen so many human generations coming and going in the trails beneath them—must be extremely wise! Oh, the stories they could tell us. Speaking of wise trees, I will be discussing wise owls a little later too, but a little spoiler first: *The owls may not be what they seem!*

If you were to take a survey asking *Twin Peaks* fans who their favourite characters are, you would probably get as many different responses as there were people asked, and there would be no wrong answers. (Well, except perhaps for Mike Nelson, ha, ha! Poor Mike, he didn't have the best storylines or character development, did he?) Some people may of course say 'Agent Cooper,' others 'Audrey Horne,' or perhaps even 'Bobby Briggs.' There are just so many great characters from which to choose. In my recent re-watch, I absolutely loved Albert Rosenfield, a character for which my more youthful personality of the 1990s may not have been quite ready.

But for me now the real stars of *Twin Peaks* are the trees. They give the story; as my personal writing mentor, the late Cornish supernatural researcher and author Michael Williams, always instilled into me, *a sense of place*. It's what the Romans once referred to as the *genius loci*. When I say 'trees,' I'm not merely talking about the actual trees *per se*, I am alluding to the unseen realms that the forests encompass. Our eyes can only see less than one percent of what is out there in the world that we inhabit, and that, naturally, includes our woods and forests. Indeed, many people down through the centuries have claimed to have seen diverse creatures of the faerie realms in our many varied landscapes throughout the world, for example in our lakes and rivers, in the seas, and on our hills, moors and mountains.

When I say *faerie* I'm referring to the likes of creatures of all shapes and sizes that nevertheless do have two things in common: they remain unclassified to modern science, and mainstream science and its dogmatic followers don't believe in them! Of course, naturally, some of my more materialist readers may scoff at the notion, believing that creatures such as bigfoot, knockers, piskies, leprechauns, trolls, and even mermaids are merely mythological creatures, and we are somehow backwards to believe in such things… but I beg to differ.

Perhaps there's no smoke without fire. There have been sightings of all manner of unclassified, perhaps inter-dimensional, faerie creatures since man was first able to record such events. Every culture has these faerie legends, some of which are unique to a particular area, whereas others may be similar, but have been given different names by cultures that until recent times never communicated. The point being that they have always been with us, but we are only now beginning to realise it—well, some of us are, anyway.

As the researcher Timothy Renner once said, "We have forgotten the faeries, giants, and monsters who have always lurked in the dark woods beside us, and we have made the tragic mistake of confusing folklore with fiction." Timothy should know, as he hosts the excellent *Strange Familiars* podcast where he regularly interviews honest, intelligent people about their experiences of strange, unclassified creatures, and—most notably for this essay—their sightings of bigfoot! He himself, alongside witnesses, has seen unexplainable (by our current level of science) faerie lights/orbs, and has experienced that weird feeling of otherworldliness that permeates our dense woodlands.

The woods are the setting for some of the most important scenes in *Twin Peaks*. It's where Cooper finds the entrance to the Black Lodge, where Laura first goes missing, where the nasty Jacques Renault resides in his log cabin, where One Eyed Jacks, the sleazy club, is located, where Bobby and Mike make a sleazy drug deal with crazy Leo, where Benjamin Horne does some even shadier business with Leo, and where in season three, we see the macabre 'Woodsmen' hanging around the old gas station. The woods are where Margaret, the Log Lady, a kind of good witch, resides. She always keeps her curtains closed so the owls can't see her, and communes, animist-style, with her talking log. It is also where James and Donna hide Laura's half of the love-heart locket under a dirt mound; shades of the *Eddas* and Tolkien again.

David Lynch was partly raised in Spokane, Washington, so he was already familiar with the Snoqualmie Valley area when a film location scout suggested it to him and his writing partner, Mark Frost, as a location for the budding series. Lynch's youth was spent amongst the dark forests where Native American tribes once hunted. He called the area his 'Inland Empire' and I'm sure he soon came to accept that there is an unknown, unseen presence lurking in those forests; we could perhaps refer to it as 'The Other.' Lynch's father was a scientist for the United States Department of Agriculture, his research focusing on the local trees. Lynch, in his typical under-stated verbal manner, once said of his childhood home: "I was in the woods a lot, and the woods for a child are magical." I too spent a lot of time in the woods, a topic I will discuss soon.

The great Chief Sealth would have known what to call that strange presence in the forests of the Pacific Northwest in his native tongue. Sealth was the leader of the Suquamish and Duwamish tribes, best remembered for being a spiritual, peaceful man with a love of language. Born in 1786, Sealth was revered in his time as a negotiator between the indigenous people and the growing European immigrant population. His name was the inspiration for the city of Seattle, as the European settler leaders couldn't pronounce his name correctly!

Chief Sealth delivered a fine speech to European emigrants in 1854, which I've taken the liberty of editing down to the most relevant part for this essay, and I have subtly (but honestly) altered it to aid in the translation. In this short piece, Sealth is warning the settlers that his people will always be present long after their generation has passed from this material world:

> These shores will swarm with the spirits of my people, when your children's children think they are alone in the woods, they won't be. My people loved this land and they will always return, they may not see them, but they will feel their presence.

The oak tree—a tree I spent so much of my youth in southeastern England climbing—was venerated by many ancient cultures and societies. The Celts and Druids of Britain and Gaul (France), for example, revered the oak and all had sacred groves. The Greeks and Romans associated the oak with Zeus and Jupiter, respectively. Interestingly, Jupiter was also the god of thunder, the word 'thunder' deriving from the Norse '*thunar*,' as in Thunar's day: Thursday. The Norse tribes called their thunder god Thor, which comes from the same source. It is believed by some that the Celts and Druids made human and animal sacrifices to their oak tree gods in times of drought, to bring rain, or for sundry other purposes.

Lynch uses thunder in *Twin Peaks* as a device to increase tension, to foreshadow dramatic life-and-death moments. You may recall the scene in the second season where judge Clinton Sternwood (there's that wood reference again!), arrives at the Great Northern bar in Twin Peaks with Cooper and Truman in order to preside over a legal hearing regarding Leland Palmer's incarceration and guilt. If you do, then you will also remember the dramatic thunderstorm accompanying Sternwood's arrival. (Lynch uses the same thunder device in his excellent 1999 film *The Straight Story*). A little later, Sternwood says to Cooper, "Coop, I advise you to keep your eyes on the woods. The woods are wondrous here, but strange."

THE BLACK FOREST

The woods are omnipresent throughout the *Twin Peaks* tale, the 'elephant in the room'; not always mentioned, but everyone knows they are there, and none of the characters would wish to be lost in them alone. Those woods are majestic to look at as we speed past them in our modern, comfortable vehicles, but those vast, ancient forests can also be relied upon to send a shiver of unexpected discomfort, if not outright fear, up our spines. There is a memorable scene where Jerry Horne is hopelessly lost in the woods, not a little high, and we see him recoil in absolute terror as a primal fear envelops him. Jerry has just realised, in that moment, that he may not survive his latest wanderings in the woods, may never see his beloved brother Ben again.

When the first Sheriff Truman informally inducts Cooper into the Bookhouse Boys' Club at the Double R Diner prior to their raid to rescue Audrey Horne from the brothel, he warns Cooper that, "There's an evil that lurks in the woods, a darkness. It has been around longer than any of us can remember." That line brought back half-forgotten memories of my own youth in rural Surrey. I was raised alongside the Tillingbourne, a small river that meanders its way through the Surrey Hills alongside many old woods. Some of these would have once been a part of King Henry VIII's hunting estate, but the known history of the area goes back much further.

My home village, Shalford, would have been somewhere in the middle of a huge forest that stretched from the south coast of England up to where London stands today. That forest was approximately 60 miles from south to north, and maybe as much as 80 miles from east to west. It was said that at one time a squirrel could have leapt across the forest's length or width from tree to tree without once touching the forest floor. The ancient Britons called the area *Coed Andred*, which means 'Great Woodland,' the Romans called it *Anderida*, and the Saxons knew it as *Andred's Weald* (wood). It was also known by some as the Black Forest, aptly named as it was so dense.

I spent my boyhood years playing in the local woodlands with my friends or sometimes alone, just wandering around, occasionally climbing the ancient oaks. You may see how, being born and raised there, I still feel a real connection with southern English woods, or what remains of them.

I can recall regularly reading books from my dad's bookcase at an early age, one of which was a collection of horror stories by legendary English supernatural writer Algernon Blackwood; his surname so apt. On the cover of that short story collection was a sinister illustration that has never left me: a dark, hairy wild man of the woods, a 'bogeyman' as my dad liked to call it—as opposed to a boogieman, which I picture more as a late 1970s disco dancer wearing a white suit (it is all in the pronunciation!). Dad would tease me that there was a bogeyman living in the woods just across the river and field behind our home, and, for a few years at least, I believed it. I never saw the bogeyman—despite often staring from my dad's bedroom window, hoping to catch a quick glimpse—but there was something odd about those woods, a strange unworldly presence that I couldn't quite put my finger on.

I was in there alone once, around 12 years old, just ambling through the decaying woodland floor, hearing the usual natural woodland chatter of birds and the occasional swift movement of startled deer, when suddenly, and for no knowable reason, everything went deathly quiet. The birds stopped singing their songs, and for what felt like five minutes (but was more than likely only a minute) I felt transported elsewhere, to another place. I knew there were eyes on me, I had instinctively felt their gaze… but human or otherwise? I didn't know. A chill went through me and then—just as suddenly as it had all begun—normal service, woodland-style, returned with a flourish as the birds took up their songs again.

Had I momentarily been taken out of this reality, and then returned? That experience echoes the way that those who claim to have encountered mermaids and faeries say they have felt. Today, modern UFO and bigfoot witnesses describe similar occurrences, and this unearthly silence features in many of the strange encounters reported by disappearance researcher David Paulides; that feeling of being out-of-time and the sudden lack of sound.

Lynch's forests in the Pacific Northwest are undoubtedly broader and taller than ours in the southeast of England, but in their own smaller way, ours are just as dark and mysterious. Perhaps they are some strange remnants of an earlier time, and the faerie folk may still linger there.

Algernon Blackwood's stories frequently had creepy, faerie/monster-inhabited woods as their major theme/setting, most famously of course in his tale *The Wendigo* (which I discussed earlier), but there were several other great yarns, too. Among them was "Ancient Lights" (1914), a story about a middle-aged surveyor's clerk from my home county, Surrey, lured ever deeper into 'The Faerie Wood,' a local copse of oak and hornbeam, by mischievous faerie folk. His task was to survey and appraise a client's wish to cut down some trees in order to improve the view from his home. As the clerk enters the ancient copse he immediately notes the peculiar stillness, the entire woods having turned dark and silently watching him enter. Was my odd experience a result of reading that story at a younger age? Or was Blackwood's art just imitating life?

It seems clear that I am not alone in having experienced that sense of 'The Other' in a woodland setting. The trees in Blackwood's "Ancient

Lights" appeared to come to life, along with unseen, but heard, faerie presences—perhaps even the Green Man, too—all of them intent on stopping the clerk from giving permission to to have the trees chopped down. I will revisit similar stories of trees, and their associated faeries, coming to life and fighting back against humans a little later.

I have often wondered if my English ancestors took their bogeymen and faerie legends with them when they emigrated to the New World, or if those legends were already there but with different names; I am confident that it's a bit of both. The same thinking, of course, applies to 'knockers,' short, subterranean faerie inhabitants of Cornwall's tin mines who 'travelled' with immigrant miners to North America. Here they eventually evolved into 'Tommy-Knockers,' as the novelist Stephen King is aware.

An elderly friend of mine, Will, raised in the Appalachian backwoods, is of Scots/Irish ancestry. He grew up in the wooded hills having to hunt fish and game to survive, as there was little money coming into his family's household. Will is still a tough man, not someone who would ever have been easily frightened, but has told me of a couple of occasions where he too had felt that same otherworldly presence and how it scared him. Will learned that if he chose to ignore that fear, rather than running away from it, the terrifying presence would slowly fade, suggesting that the presence feeds off our fear. Paranormal researchers have found, in poltergeist cases for example, that observation and reaction do ensure continuity. Perhaps the town of Twin Peaks thrives on fear?

"THE OWLS ARE NOT WHAT THEY SEEM!"

Especially when discussing the woodlands aspect, no look at the embedded folklore of *Twin Peaks* would be complete without talking about the strange otherworldly nature of owls, both in the *Twin Peaks* story and in the wider world. We often read about owls in ancient folklore, where they were purveyors of wisdom and magic, harbingers of death, guardians of secrets and the underworld. They are the birds of Athena and Minerva, goddesses of wisdom, and they give us the impression of living between two worlds, travelling in those liminal spaces that we in the paranormal world love to discuss on our podcasts!

Owls are frequently seen in *Twin Peaks*. Lynch uses them to foreshadow important events, like the death of a character, or sometimes in another one of their traditional roles: as messengers. Owls are, to me, a direct link between the old and new folklore, and I believe that owls are not always—as Agent Cooper was advised several times during his investigations into Laura's murder—what they seem to be.

Let me take you back to a dramatic scene in *Twin Peaks*. Agent Cooper has just been shot after answering a knock at his door at the Great Northern Hotel. He lays helpless on the floor, his consciousness perhaps hovering between the two worlds, when he is visited by a giant. The giant says to Cooper: "The Owls are not what they seem."

Shortly after the giant delivers that intriguing line (and this happens so quickly many of you may have missed it), we see a very brief visual clue. That clue is in the form of what looks very much like a Steven Spielberg-style UFO, and the image has accompanying emanations of throbbing and electrical humming sounds. We then see a look of wonder come into Cooper's eyes and hear him quietly say: "They're here."

This scene quickly morphs, the UFO image revealed as a medical device in a clinical hospital setting, keeping it unclear as to what we really witnessed. Shortly afterwards the log lady prompts Major Garland Briggs—whom we discover has been working on the top secret, real-life UFO government project 'Blue Book'—to share important classified information with Cooper. This is delivered in the form of an old computer printout (this was the '90s after all) of endless binary code showing Cooper's name and that intriguing line again, "The owls are not what they seem," randomly appearing alongside all the digits. Importantly, we also learn that these weird coded messages, previously assumed to be from so called 'extraterrestrials' from far flung galaxies, have actually been emanating from within nearby forests in the Twin Peaks area.

My present thoughts, which may well change in time as I consider fresh information, are that yesterday's faeries may be today's aliens, only the language that we use to describe these strange beings and our encounters with them has changed (and perhaps the environments that we live in, too). Even a small amount of research makes us aware that faerie lore and alien lore have so much in common, including abductions, missing time, and strange food offerings. I am confident that whoever 'they' are, they are already here, and they've probably been here at least as long as we have, and perhaps even longer. (Having said that, I don't completely write off the Extraterrestrial Hypothesis either.)

So, you may be wondering, how do I see the owls fitting into this folk-lore, into our modern Ufology? The weirdness of owls features heavily in the works of Whitley Strieber and Mike Clelland. In Streiber's 1987 book *Communion*, he talks about his own personal encounters with odd owls whilst staying in a log cabin in the remote woods of Upstate New York. A famous alien abductee, Strieber was convinced that these were not mundane, corporeal owls, but rather some form of 'alien' intelligence monitoring him and his family. The book was published a few years before *Twin Peaks* was written/filmed, so it is likely that Lynch was aware of Strieber's book and 'the owl connection.'

Clelland is also an experiencer with numerous, very odd, very personal experiences with owls, as detailed in his book *The Messengers: Owls, Synchronicity and the UFO Abductee*. His first encounter featured several owls who flew over him and a friend for an unnaturally long time whilst they were resting on a hilltop during a hike in the wilds; like the denizens of Twin Peaks, Clelland felt sure that they were more than just owls, too. In true Lynchian style, I will now repeat what I wrote earlier, and like Gordon Cole, the FBI character Lynch plays in *Twin Peaks*, I'll shout it out:

"THE OWLS ARE NOT WHAT THEY SEEM!"

The UFO literature suggests that some 'other' intelligence (I don't feel comfortable using the word 'alien,' as it comes with all that extraterrestrial baggage attached) may be—and I'll stress *may be*—projecting images of owls, or perhaps deer in some cases, as a kind of 'screen memory' when wishing to interact with us humans. They may feel we are less scared of them, and perhaps less likely to be violent, if the image they project is of something with which we are more comfortable.

I do wonder whether they sometimes get their calculations wrong, which might explain the sightings of so many unfeasibly large owls! I admit that I too have seen an oversized owl, back in 2015. The owl stood taller than my old Suzuki Vitara's front bonnet—just over four feet high (1.2 metres). As my son Dexter said to me when I told him about it, "Owls aren't that big, Dad." He was right of course.

Meeting huge 'owls' on quiet country roads, sometimes in conjunction with 'missing time,' is a lot more common than you might think. Ask your family and friends if they have seen any huge owls and be prepared to be surprised. To sum up my thoughts on the connection between ancient faeries, modern aliens, and owls, I would say that they are *'complimentary verses of the same song.'*

THE WOMAN OF THE WOOD

Whilst conducting my research on this essay, I was fortunate enough to stumble across some excellent sources of information on *Twin Peaks* (all listed in my bibliography), but none more so than from the podcast *Counter Esperanto: Winds of the Weird Podcast/Tangents about Twin Peaks*, hosted by Karl Eckler and Jubel Brosseau. On one episode while discussing the Twin Peaks area (they both grew up in the Pacific Northwest), their conversation turned toward the modern concept of psychogeography, the idea that an area itself is thought to influence the behaviours of those living within it. (I am familiar with this concept, as I have written about a similar thing happening in the far west of Cornwall.)

Karl and Jubel talked about how the Pacific Northwest has always attracted High Strangeness and they provided a few examples. The 'Satanic Panic' was particularly rife in the region, and to this day there are still plenty of rumours of witchcraft and rituals taking place deep in the forests. The FBI continue to have a heavy presence in the area too, though they are likely tackling the terrible problems of human trafficking and prostitution across the US/Canadian border. Strange, unmarked black helicopters are regularly seen, and there are reports of Men-in-Black, Black-Eyed Kids, and plenty of UFO activity too. It remains to be seen whether *Twin Peaks* will return to our screens for a fourth series, but, in real life, the weirdness does appear to be on-going.

I stumbled upon an interesting article from May 19, 2017 in the U.S. edition of the *Guardian* online newspaper about the hidden darkness of the Snoqualmie (Twin Peaks) area. The writer, Maria L. La Ganger, told her readers how the area, 30 miles east of Seattle, is a popular suicide spot, and how misadventure regularly claims the lives of many hikers and skiers as well. A local police chief had this to say: "Some are hikers that have died, some have killed themselves, and others are either undetermined or victims of homicide. If you think about it, Seattle is a very populated area, and the Snoqualmie Valley is the first really empty place outside the city."

As Maria remarked: "The body of Twin Peaks homecoming queen Laura Palmer wasn't the first discovered in the region, and it certainly will not be the last." During the 1980s the 'Green River Killer' went on a killing spree throughout the Pacific Northwest. Gary L. Ridgway, who was once described as America's most prolific serial killer, buried many of his victims around the Snoqualmie area. It's certainly worth remembering too that not all of our monsters come from some strange, undefined alternate universe; many of them have lived amongst us and, no doubt, they continue to live amongst us. Like the fictional *Twin Peaks* character Leland Palmer (and probably Ridgway, too) they may have looked as harmless as the rest of us.

In recent years I have followed the work of David Paulides, an ex-police detective from the San Jose Police Department. In his *Missing 411* book series, Paulides investigates extremely odd, modern, on-going disappearances of people in forests across North America and elsewhere. These are not people who have been murdered, savaged by wild animals, or wandered off the trails; their disappearances are far more bizarre, and currently unexplainable by our established mainstream science. Paulides knows only too well that there is an unseen, often malevolent presence in the woods and forests that we do not yet understand.

As I was digging deeply into the literature that may have partly inspired Lynch's *Twin Peaks*, I stumbled across a fantastic book called: *Tales Before Tolkien: The Roots of Modern Fantasy*. Inside I discovered a short story by Abraham Merritt (1884-1943), an American writer. His 1926 "The Woman of the Wood" is a strange, animism-inspired story about trees defending themselves against men intent on their total destruction (shades of Blackwood's "Ancient Lights"). In the preface to the tale, editor Douglas A. Anderson writes, "Tolkien is unlikely to have known of the story but would have sympathised with the impulse behind the story, which tells of how trees might defend themselves."

Anderson said this because Tolkien himself remarked in 1972, "In all my works I take the part of trees as against all their enemies." It is my contention that this equally applies to Lynch, in that he too would likely have been unaware of this book, but has also been a stalwart supporter of the trees in *Twin Peaks*.

The main protagonist of "The Woman of the Wood" is a man named McKay, a slightly shell-shocked, war-weary, ex-pilot of an undisclosed military airforce in World War I. McKay is recuperating, post-war, in a quiet country area of France, resting and feeling loved by the surrounding trees in a small coppice by a lake. As he rests, he feels that the trees are communicating their fear to him, their fear of being wiped out by men.

To cut a longer story short, there is a small dwelling on the other side of the lake where a brutish man, Polleau, and his two equally tough sons live, spending their days busily cutting down trees. While out on a boat on the lake one day, McKay is disturbed by the sounds of an axe being swung in anger at a slim birch tree by one of the two sons. McKay hears the anguished wails of the dying tree, and the terrified sighs from all the other trees in the area. He tries to save the trees by confronting the ax-eman directly, man-to-man.

I won't spoil the story by saying any more, but will just point out that in *Twin Peaks*, which has the same background theme of a territorial 'war' between man and the forest, there is a similar, updated, macro-version of that scene. Think about the sawmills in the opening images of *Twin Peaks*, where we see the double-mechanised movement of the machinery sharpening the sawmill's cutting blades. If we were to look at the series in purely animist terms, we would note that the living, conscious trees are being mass-murdered by the human tool of the sawmill's cutting blades, savagely slaughtered on an industrial scale, as opposed to Polleau and his son's random killings by axe many decades earlier.

These huge advances in efficient wood cutting (tree-slaughtering?) technology, from axes to sawmills, is a metaphor. In the last 100 plus years, mankind's inter-human wars have become more industrialized with our death camps and nuclear weapons. We have stupidly mass-hewed ourselves with our short-sighted and callous disdain for our fellow man, the same way that we have treated our invaluable, life-giving forests. The sword has given way to the rifle, the axe has ceded to the buzz-saw. Perhaps we may someday realize that we not only hurt the trees as we clear-cut the land... we also hurt ourselves, and those numinous, mostly unseen denizens of the forest, the faeries. The beings that, in our modern lives, we had arrogantly begun to disbelieve, because we, with our Darwinian materialist science, thought we were now far too sophisticated and grown up to believe in them.

Well, I have news for the disbelievers; *they* believe in *us*! They (the faeries, aliens, inter-dimensionals, or whatever else you want to label them) have been quietly watching us for time immemorial, and I will bet they're fearful of a race of beings who think nothing of hurting each other, let alone them. It's no wonder that bigfoot and the rest of the faerie gang have always been so elusive.

Still, I live in hope that our intelligence will one day outweigh our evil ways and ignorance, and our science will eventually catch up with what our folklore has been telling us for hundreds of years. I'll say this in true Gordon Cole style:

"FAERIES DO EXIST!"

"All the world is made of faith, and trust, and pixie dust," wrote J.M. Barrie. I believe I know what scientific rationalists would think of that light-hearted quote by the creator of Peter Pan, but I resonate with the first two-thirds of it—we are all still learning about the final third.

We have a long way to go yet, and we have so much more to discover. I quite like it that way. I am enjoying the journey. While we have intelligent minds on our side working on it, we need mainstream scientists to wake up and smell Cooper's coffee too, so they can join us in our faerie quest. Lynch taught us about balance in *Twin Peaks*, a balance we need between our left and right brains.

A balance between us and nature, needed now more than ever.

Acknowledgements

Special thanks go to the following people who have helped me, in one way and another, to put this essay together: Janice L. Maier, Will Collins, Robert E. Wyatt, and Joshua Cutchin.

Bibliography

Anderson, D. (Ed.). (2003). Tales *Before Tolkien: The Roots of Modern Fantasy*. New York, NY: Ballantine

Baker, F. (1976). *The Call of Cornwall*. London, UK: Robert Hale.

Barrie, J.M. (1911). *Peter Pan*. London, UK: Hodder & Stoughton.

Biron, E. L. (May 22, 2017). The Trees of Twin Peaks. Retrieved May 22, 2020 from https://papierhuis.com/2017/05/22/the-trees-of-twin-peaks/

Blackwood, A. (1910). *The Wendigo*. London, UK: Eveleigh Nash.

Blackwood, A. (1914). *Ancient Lights*. Retrieved May 20, 2020 from http://algernonblackwood.org/Z-files/ancient%20lights.pdf

Blackwood, A. (1950). *Tales of the Uncanny and Supernatural*. London, UK: Peter Nevill.

Burden, Z. (2015). Another Place: The Esoteric Symbolism of Twin Peaks. Agent on the Threshold: The Taoism and Alchemy of Twin Peaks. Retrieved May 21, 2020 from https://zoraburden.weebly.com/the-esoteric-symbolism-of-twin-peaks.html

Clelland, M. (2015). *The Messengers: Owls, Synchronicity and the UFO Abductee.* New York: Richard Dolan Press.

Cutchin, J. (2015). *A Trojan Feast: The Food and Drink Offerings of Aliens, Faeries and Sasquatch.* San Antonio, TX: Anomalist Books.

Cutchin, J. and Renner, T. (2020). *Where the Footprints End: High Strangeness and the Bigfoot Phenomenon. -Volume 1: Folklore.* Red Lion, PA: Dark Holler Arts.

Eckler, K. & Brosseau, J. (2016). *Counter Esperanto: Winds of the Weird Podcast/Tangents about Twin Peaks.* Retreived May 23, 2020 from https://american-podcasts.com/podcast/counter-esperanto-podcast-tangents-about-twin-peak

Fraser, J. G. (1890). *The Golden Bough* (abridged version: 1922). New York, NY: Touchstone/Simon and Schuster.

La Ganga, M. (May 19, 2017). The town where Twin Peaks was filmed has its own share of mysterious deaths. Retrieved May 20, 2020 from https://www.theguardian.com/us-news/2017/may/19/twin-peaks-snoqualmie-washington-mysterious-deaths

Lynch, D. (2007). *Catching the Big Fish: Meditation, Consciousness, and Creativity.* New York, NY: TarcherPerigee.

Machen, A. (1916). *The Coming of the Terror.* New York, NY: Ballantine.

Merritt, A. 1926. *The Woman of the Woods.* New York, NY: Ballantine.

Paulides, D. (2012). *Missing 411: Western United States and Canada/Unexplained disappearances of North Americans that have never been solved.* Charleston, SC: CreateSpace Independent Publishing Platform.

Quammen, D. (2012). Where the Giants Grow. *National Geographic 222*(6), pp. 34-41.

Renner, T. (2018). *Don't Look Behind You.* Charleston, SC: CreateSpace Independent Publishing Platform.

Schama, S. (1995). *Landscape and Memory.* New York, NY: Alfred A. Knopf.

Simpson, J. (1987). *European Mythology: Library of the World's Myths and Legends Series.* New York, NY: Peter Bedrick/Hamlyn.

Strieber, W. (1987). *Communion.* New York, NY: Avon Books.

Tolkien, J.R.R. (1954-1955). *The Lord of the Rings Trilogy*. London, UK: Allen and Unwin.

Williams, M. 1982. *Superstition and Folklore*. Bodmin, UK: Bossiney Books.

Wyatt, M.A. (2019). *The Spirit of Cornwall: A Haunted Legacy (Volumes 1 and 2)*. Leviathan Productions.

Handmaidens of the Eternal: Consciousness and Death in Photographing Fairies

Dr. Neil Rushton

'We humans are not alone. We share our planet with a quite
different order of life. Fairies. They are spoken of in every
culture of the world from New Zealand to the New Hebrides.
Handmaidens of nature according to some, assisting in
propagation and growth. Another theory: Exiles from heaven,
God's orphans straddling this world and the next; messengers
between the two worlds.'

Photographing Fairies is a 1997 British film based on the 1992 novel by Steve Szilagyi.[138] It was directed by Nick Willing, who also co-wrote the screenplay with Chris Harrald, and was Willing's first outing as a film director, after previously directing music videos through the 1980s and 1990s. This background is apparent in the aura and mood of the film, which relies much on the musical backdrop to create its metaphysical atmosphere, from Simon Boswell's original score to the frequent interjections of the *Allegretto* from Beethoven's 7th Symphony.

The film also benefits from the acting acumen of Toby Stephens, Ben Kingsley, Emily Woof, Frances Barber, and Philip Davis, as well as the two child actors Hannah Bould and Miriam Grant, who seem preternaturally disposed to their roles. The exquisite cinematography of John de Borman adds much impressionistic ambience, and while the visual effects may seem somewhat primitive from the perspective of 2020, they retain an authenticity in line with the tenor of the film. The production company was PolyGram Filmed Entertainment (mooted as a European equivalent to Hollywood, but which folded in 1999), which joined forces with BBC Films and The Arts Council of England to fund, produce, and distribute the film. Its budget was *c.* $1.1 million and it made *c.* $4.7 million at the box office, despite receiving only limited release in cinemas.[139]

It is a film operating on many levels, rooted in the effects of World War I yet managing to incorporate a myriad of cultural and supernatural tropes: the British class system, Theosophy, regional identity, religious faith, familial affiliations, the relatively new profession of photography, altered states of consciousness, and, of course, the fairies. While its love story is also a central theme, the main emphasis of the film is death. Death has long been an important province of fairy folklore, and a study of *Photographing Fairies* gives an opportunity to bring this into relief; to understand the relationship between the fairies, consciousness, and death.

Photographing Fairies

The standard spoiler alerts apply, but the film goes something like this (although such a brief summary cannot convey the existential magic that only watching it can transmit): Charles Castle (Stephens) marries Anna-Marie (Rachel Shelley) in the Alps just prior to WWI. While taking an ill-advised walk along a high peak, the couple is trapped in a storm, sucking Anna-Marie into a crevice in the ice. She dies, leaving Castle with nothing more than a pocket-watch containing her image, and which plays a Strauss-like musical tune. This segues into Castle in the trenches of the war, evidently not valuing his life as a bomb falls close to him while he carries out his photography of dead soldiers, heedless of the ticking explosive. Within a few minutes we have been introduced to death, both at a very personal level and also at the industrial level of WWI casualties.

In London after the war, Castle runs a photography business with his partner Roy (Davis). One moving scene shows the parents of a dead soldier coming to the studio to have their photo taken with Roy, whose face is afterwards photomontaged with that of the son. As he carries out the procedure, Castle recites John 11:25: 'I am the resurrection and the life.' This portrays him as a somewhat hard and cynical character, magnified when he visits the headquarters of the Theosophical Society. There, Castle turns his nose up at glimpsed séances taking place in side rooms before castigating the gullibility of Gardner (Clive Merrison) as he delivers a lecture showing one of the infamous (and fake) Cottingley Fairy photos, which he proclaimed as evidence of inter-dimensional beings.

Things are about to change for Castle, however. An attendee at the lecture, Beatrice Templeton (Barber), turns up at his studio with a photograph of her daughter, which seems to show an entity balancing on the palm of her hand. Castle dismisses it, but concedes to magnify the image for closer examination. When he does, he sees the image of the entity in the girl's hand reflected laterally in her eye. It is the turning point in the film; the dissolving of his scepticism. Off he goes to the village of Birkenwell, where Beatrice lives, to find out some truths.

He meets Beatrice's daughters (Bould and Grant) who evade his questioning, but then he agrees to meet Beatrice at what they have dubbed 'The Great Tree' in the local woods. She is there already, and we get our first glimpse of the unnamed white flower, which Beatrice eats to alter her state of consciousness. In her altered state, she climbs the tree and falls to her death—Castle arrives to find her body beneath the tree. This brings Anglican minister and Beatrice's husband Reverend Templeton (Kingsley) into the story, immediately rendered with Kingsley's characteristic style: sinister, overlain with an air of compassion.

There follows an amazing five-minute scene, starting at the inn where Castle is staying. He procured one of the flowers from Beatrice's dead hand and, after reading her description of its effects in her notebook, pops it into his mouth. The next few minutes are a portrayal of a psychedelic experience: tracers, time dilation, changes in colour, a skewed musical backdrop, and, after Castle runs to The Great Tree, a numinous episode where the fairies appear as luminous, small humanoids flying around the tree, able to penetrate matter. They are evidently only partly within physical reality.

Castle climbs the tree to get closer to them and falls, transporting him to a white-out bedroom with his deceased wife. The non-linear frames end with them making love before she rolls over in the bed and whispers (albeit rendered with enhanced volume): "This is not a dream." The power of this scene is difficult to convey (as is a real psychedelic experience), but changes the tenor of the film from 'period drama' to 'supernatural magical realism' in an instant.

From this moment forward, Castle knows the fairies are real. After regaining consciousness from his fall and attending Beatrice's funeral (with a bloodied head and not all his wits), he directs Roy to bring a load of photographic equipment to Birkenwell in an attempt to capture them on film. The girls' governess/nanny, Linda (Woof) enters the story and is soon falling in love with Castle. Both she and Roy provide the grounded rational counterpoint to Castle's new evangelical belief in the existence of the fairies… but, then again, they haven't taken the flower.

The film quickens its pace from here: Linda falls deeper in love with Castle (unrequited, as he is still in love with his dead wife); the girls perform a very risqué pseudo-mass beneath the tree; the Reverend Templeton shows his true colours by threatening to kill Castle, whom he believes had designs on his wife; and Castle ends up taking another flower beneath the tree as Roy and Linda operate cameras to capture an image of the fairies—the results are ambiguous. Amidst this, the youngest girl, Clara, takes the flower, climbs the tree and enters 'slow time' (as announced by her sister Ana). She falls, but survives.

This finally leads to Templeton appearing at the tree in a disordered state, destroying the photographic equipment Castle had set up on timers to capture the fairies and cutting down and burning the tree itself. Castle arrives and once more enters an altered state of consciousness by swallowing another flower. He sees some of the fairies on fire, attacks Templeton, and accidentally pushes him onto a sharpened spike from the equipment. Templeton dies. Yet more death; but there is, of course, even more to come.

The film's denouement comes with Castle's trial for Templeton's murder. He pleads guilty and delivers a speech in which he suggests that death is not what it seems: "There is another world, as close to this one as I am to you. I have seen it and I have felt its force… death is a small thing. Death is merely a change of state. The soul is a fresh expression of the self."

Castle is convicted, and the final scene shows him being led to the prison gallows and hanged (where the minister repeats the line Castle uttered from John 11:25: "I am the resurrection and the life"). It is a brutal end to the film (set to Beethoven's *Allegretto*), but as he drops through the trapdoor to his death there is one last hallucinogenic treat: a luminous fairy appears again and his consciousness is ushered back to the mountaintop with his wife. This time, he manages to save her from the fall into the crevice and they are together again in the last frame. Death is, after all, an illusion, and the fairies are arbiters between this world and the Otherworld.

Tropes, Themes and Sources

There is much to unpack from this film. The fairies themselves appear only fleetingly, and the main emphasis is on the concept of death and how it came to be perceived in the aftermath of the First World War. The counterpoints are primarily between secular rationalism, a traditional religious view (represented by Reverend Templeton), and a more animistic idea of consciousness, reliant on supernatural entities to ease the passage from life to death and back to a new transcendence. This is achieved in a number of ways. Perhaps the best starting point is to assess how the secular reductionism prevalent in the years after the war conflicted with the revived Theosophical movement, which sought to give hope of a supernatural reality to the millions of people who had lost loved ones in the carnage of the Great War.

The Theosophical Society was founded in 1875 in the United States by Russian immigrant Helena Petrovna Blavatsky along with Americans Henry Olcott and William Quan Judge.[140] They described the Theosophy movement as an occult esoteric philosophy, which taught that a secretive order of adepts, or masters, existed throughout the world, with access to supernatural wisdom which they were able to disseminate via Blavatsky. In the decades following its founding the society underwent numerous schisms as differing belief systems diluted the original vision into factions, and as Theosophy spread to other countries, it became sometimes unrecognizable from its initial incarnation. Rudolf Steiner was one prominent adherent to Theosophy in the early 20th century who became disillusioned with the constant maneuvering of precepts, and so founded his own (Theosophy-based) Anthroposophical Society in 1913.[141] His ideas about how to interact with the fairies ('elementals' or 'nature spirits' as he termed them, following the 16th-century alchemist Paracelsus) were an important influence on later occult groups.[142]

But in Britain, after the First World War, the Theosophical Society had quickly integrated many aspects of Spiritualism, most especially mediumship (relying on psychics able to directly contact the dead) and the concept of supernatural entities existing alongside physical reality, who were sometimes able to interact with it. With so many grieving in the aftermath of the war, the movement gained popular traction as people sought to reassure themselves of a transcendent supernatural reality in the face of the mass death brought about by the conflict. For over a decade after the end of the war, Theosophically-tinged Spiritualism threatened to overtake traditional religion as the default belief system.

And so we find Charles Castle making his visit to the Theosophical Society headquarters in 1920 London. As with so much in the film, there is a subtlety of approach: the inscribed brass plaque outside the society's HQ is only glimpsed in a few frames as he enters, and to the uninitiated, it would be missed or mean nothing. He passes a couple of rooms where séances are in progress, with the distinct insinuation they are fraudulent. He curls his lip and proceeds to the main event: a lecture where the audience is being assured that a final proof of the existence of fairies has been discovered.

Here is another subtlety. While the film is not about the Cottingley Fairies—although it does hold many similarities to the story, and the two young girls, Ana and Clara, are evidently based in part on the Cottingley children Elsie Wright and Frances Griffiths—the lecture shows Gardner presenting one of the Cottingley photographs as proof of inter-dimensional beings in our midst: "We humans are not alone. We share our planet with a quite different order of life. Fairies… the handmaidens of nature… messengers between the worlds." (Incidentally, Gardner is based on Edward Gardner, a member of the executive committee of the Theosophical Society.)

Castle interrupts proceedings and demonstrates the fallacy of the image from a photographic perspective. His intervention breaks up the meeting and we are introduced to Sir Arthur Conan Doyle (Edward Hardwicke), a member of the society, who extends some words of solace to Gardner and his audience: "We're travelling in the dark. We must expect to bark our shins now and again. We are pioneers exploring the borderland between this world and a better one."

The trope of Theosophy/Spiritualism seems to have been discredited as a deluded belief system on par with Castle's customers, the parents who were happy to have a photomontaged fake photo of their son from the earlier scene. But there is evidently an undercurrent to the phenomenon; the balance of rational scepticism against supernatural belief is about to be tipped. It's easy to mock gullible people believing in ghosts and fairies, but one of the most important elements of the film is how it draws us into that reductionist mindset before pulling it apart to reveal something more dynamic.

This is achieved, in part, through the trope of distillation through the photographic record. The theme of photography is core to the film's narrative. The first scene shows Castle setting up a camera to capture his own wedding, he is evidently employed in WWI's trenches to photograph the dead, he runs a photography studio after the war, and the Cottingley incident itself was based on the photos of Elsie Wright and Frances Griffiths with their fairies.[143]

These scenes all suggest that photography—still a relatively new technology in the first decades of the 20th century—provides an absolute, impartial record of reality, and that when events are faked (as per the Cottingley fairies) photographs offer confirmation, provided photographic expertise is deployed. The photographic record is unimpeachable. Therefore, when Castle blows up the image of Templeton's daughter holding the blurred fairy on her palm and notices its presence in a reflection on her eye, we immediately realise that, due to its physicality captured on film, there may be something supernatural which is nonetheless *real*.

This is brought to fruition when Castle brings a full kit of photographic equipment to The Great Tree in order to photograph the fairies, which he has already seen. The technical details for the job are described by Castle to a suspicious and sceptical Roy. Something fast-moving needs to be captured: "Hence the special emulsions and lenses. We'll be using fast shutter speeds and flashes throughout." The scientific method is employed to record something beyond physical reality. Photography, already demonstrated as a means of capturing the mundane, is to be used as the ultimate method of proving the supernatural's existence.

By the time Castle gets Roy and Linda to take photographs of him communing with the fairies at The Great Tree (after taking the consciousness-altering flower), we are in no doubt that the absolutism of photography is the means through which the truth will be told. If a photographic image shows something, it must be true.

But, of course, the resulting images, while intriguing, are indecisive. Even Sir Arthur Conan Doyle, when shown the photographs of Castle surrounded by light-emitting fairies, is unconvinced. It turns out that photographs are not definitive arbiters of truth after all. By the time Reverend Templeton destroys Castle's photographic equipment beside the tree, we are confronted by a complex dichotomy. Photography is scientific; it is a means to capture an absolute record. But here it is used to give testimony to something outside physical reality. This highlights another important trope in the film: faith.

In some ways Castle has put his faith in the photographic testimony. Throughout the film he uses photography to arbitrate reality. It is the means with which he understands the world and records it. By the time he comes up against Reverend Templeton, he has already shifted his faith, so that instead of using his photographic knowledge to debunk fraudulence—as in the Cottingley images—he utilises it in an attempt to prove the existence of supernatural entities.

This brings him into direct conflict with Templeton's absolute Christian faith. The friction between the two can be seen as that between a pagan animism and a faith-based Christianity. Templeton makes several pronouncements on the need for faith and has no time for any investigation of anything outside of doctrine.

A pivotal example of his attitude appears during an exchange between the two while sacking up flour, milled from the recent harvest in the village. Templeton throws down sacks of flour from the upper loading door of the storage barn to Castle, and they exchange a terse dialogue, ending with Castle being floored by a full flour sack:

TEMPLETON: Are you going to turn our woods into a laboratory? You can't capture God with a camera.

CASTLE: It's not God I'm looking for.

TEMPLETON: It's not proof you need, it's faith.

CASTLE: Tell me about your faith reverend.

TEMPLETON: Faith? It's what a man must live by.

CASTLE: Sometimes a man can hide behind it.

When Templeton destroys the photographic equipment, chops down the tree, and is accidentally impaled after his fight with Castle, he still refuses to accept any belief-system not built on faith in God, even as he takes his last breath. Castle implores him to swallow the flower, but he does not want any type of gnosis. Templeton represents an ingrained Christian worldview built on faith, which cannot allow any intrusion from a metaphysics outside its system, even when offered the opportunity to embrace it directly. This theme of faith in the film finds a counterpoint in the gnosticism of explicit experience—experience presenting the fairies as its primary element.

The fairies (despite only making fleeting appearances in the film, to-taling less than four minutes) are the primary movers in the plot-line. A bona-fide folklorist might criticise their representation as winged beings, and point out that folkloric fairies, while often able to fly, were never de-scribed as having wings in the traditional record. While there are instances of winged fairies from as early as the 17th century, their portrayal as aile-ron creatures dates mostly to 19th century artists such as John Atkinson Grimshaw and Richard Doyle (uncle of Sir Arthur Conan Doyle), further popularised by J.M. Barrie's Tinker Bell in the early 20th century.[144] This type of fairy has, of course, been mainstreamed by the Disney version of *Peter Pan* and the subsequent morphing of folkloric fairies into the winged entities of popular culture.

While the film's depiction of the fairies does show them buzzing through the air in the manner of dragonflies (the buzz itself is a clever and sensual auditory addition), they are evidently sourced from more le-gitimate folkloric roots. On the few occasions they are seen in close-up, the fairies appear more like Brian Froud-designed entities than Tinker Bell.[145] They are mostly amorphous, naked females (although there is also a portly, bald male) with a sinister edge. They have no compunction about dealing Castle some blows as they penetrate his material body and even climb out of his mouth. Although they never speak, they seem suspicious of his motives and don't mind harm coming to him. They predicate Be-atrice's death, and even allow her young daughter, Clara, to fall from the tree during her communion with them.

These are the fairies of folklore; interested in humanity but *mad, bad, and dangerous to know*. They are rendered as winged fairies, recognisable to a modern audience, but they are based upon the supernatural charac-ters found in thousands of folkloric stories and testimonies of people who have interacted with the fairies over centuries. Most of these people were terrified of the fairies and did what they could to propitiate them. They were alluring, but best avoided. And as in many of those stories and testimonies, the fairies make their appearance when the protagonists, by whatever means, alter their states of consciousness.

Altered States of Consciousness and the Fairies

There are three episodes in the film where an altered state of conscious-ness is portrayed. All are seen from Castle's perspective after he has consumed the white flower, which seems to grow in and around The Great Tree. We also see the youngest Templeton daughter, Clara, enter 'slow time' after taking the flower, but her experience is implicit and viewed only by her sister and Linda as she climbs the tree, carries out a communion with the unseen fairies, then falls from a high bough.

This is quite a bold move by the filmmakers, particularly in 1997—showing a young girl taking a psychedelic compound and experiencing the results, for better and worse. And the flower is certainly a psychedelic. Its provenance and attributes are never explained, but it might be seen as a discursive way to render a known psychedelic such as *psilocybin* or *Amanita muscaria* mushrooms.

The first time Castle ingests the flower we are dipped into an altered state of consciousness with him, which, in many ways, mimics a psychedelic experience. Apart from the well-constructed visual and audio gymnastics, the main design of this episode is to introduce viewers to the fairies. It is made explicit that they can only be interacted with via altered states of consciousness. Castle sees them, is knocked around by them, and then climbs The Great Tree before falling to the ground and experiencing a numinous interlude with his dead wife. When she whispers in his ear, "This is not a dream," Castle (and we) are convinced there is a supernatural reality, which appears accessible by altering consciousness with a prescribed compound. This taps into a deep vein of both folkloric and modern testimonies of people who have encountered fairylike entities while under the influence of either a mind-altering aggregate or through more spontaneous means.[146]

This can be taken back a very long way. Graham Hancock has called Palaeolithic cave art "the earliest folklore," and recent anthropological studies convincingly suggest that many of these ancient depictions of entoptic geometric patterns and humanoid entities were created by people under the influence of mind-altering substances.[147] As a greater anthropological understanding of indigenous shamanism developed, most especially through the work of Mircea Eliade and his 1951 publication *Shamanism: Archaic Techniques of Ecstasy*,[148] a new awareness evolved that the rock art produced by Palaeolithic cultures might be the artistic result of shamanic processes, preeminently those brought about by inducing altered states of consciousness.

This was mainstreamed in the 1980s by anthropologists David Lewis-Williams and Thomas Dowson, when they advanced a neuropsychological model for analysing the motifs of parietal art of this period, proposing that the geometric images are in fact artistic representations of universal optical patterns, intrinsic to the human visual system, once perceived by our shamanic ancestors during altered states of consciousness.[149] An important element of this model is the entoptic imagery displayed in the rock art and how it matches closely the geometric patterns seen by people in modern clinical conditions who have altered their state of consciousness. But the cave art also includes copious examples of *therianthropes*, humanoid/animal creatures often bearing a striking resemblance to the fairies of historic folklore, as well as entities encountered in the modern era by people who have undergone a transformation of consciousness.[150]

There is a growing body of evidence that suggests much historic folklore can be related intimately to the type of stories told in cave art by Palaeolithic shamans, with which the descriptions are often remarkably similar. Writers such as Carlo Ginzburg and Emma Wilby have argued a direct link exists between prehistoric shamanism and the folklore embodied in classical, medieval and later periods, often incorporating entities such as nymphs and fairies: supernatural beings who interact with humanity when the conditions are right.[151]

Those conditions may well be reliant on the human participants undergoing an altered state of consciousness as a result of the ingestion of psychedelic compounds. There is certainly a preponderance of mushroom imagery present in historic depictions of fairies, most especially the highly psychedelic red and white *Amanita muscaria* (fly agaric) mushroom and the *psilocybin* mushroom, both prevalent throughout Europe and Asia. If these historic folkloric manifestations of interactions with supernatural entities can be linked to the cave art of prehistory and preliterate societies, then we see a continuous relationship with an alternative reality over a very long period of time. Katherine Briggs pointed out in *The Fairies in Tradition and Literature* that many British fairy motifs repeated in stories and anecdotes through the centuries through the present day were already in place during the medieval period.[152] When folklorists began collecting these stories in earnest from the 19th century onwards, they found a belief in fairies amongst the rural population that was probably very close to the medieval belief and understanding of what fairies were, and how they interacted with humanity.

Many of the stories include situations where the protagonist interacts with the fairies in what seems an altered state of consciousness: Fairyland doesn't comply with Newtonian physics, it is consistently inhabited by strange humanoids and therianthropes (the fairies), and there are mountains of recurring story motifs that are highly suggestive of an autonomous reality being described. But this is not consensus reality; this is folklore recording stories from people operating *outside* consensus reality. They may have arrived there through a variety of means apart from the ingestion of psychotropic plants or mushrooms, many of which are part of the plot device in these stories: dancing in circles, sitting out on cold hillsides, crying emotional tears, becoming panicked whilst lost... there are many ways these stories drop clues as to what is really taking place. The folktales about fairies have been overlain with much allegorical storytelling, but at their root the realities they describe are of people entering altered states of consciousness, perhaps not too far from the realities experienced by the Palaeolithic cave painters.

One folkloric story, in particular, describes an interaction with diminutive fairies following an episode that sounds like Temporal Lobe Epilepsy. This is the 17th century story of Anne Jefferies, who apparently suffered from this neurological condition and ended up consorting with the fairies during her altered state.[153] It is an unusually well-documented story perhaps lending weight to the hypothesis that altered states of consciousness were responsible for many of the testimonies and stories collected from more nebulous folklore.

However, alongside the folkloric record there is the archive of European witch trials, which exist from the 16th to 18th century.[154] With caveats as to the genuine nature of confessions obtained during intimidation and torture, many of the accused witches described meeting with *familiars*, sometimes animals but just as often fairies, who assumed humanoid shape. This was often achieved through the use of salves, unctions, and potions. Although rarely described in detail during the trials, Early-Modern authors were able to define the ingredients consumed by witches in order to alter their state of consciousness: belladonna, henbane bell, jimson weed, black henbane, mandrake, hemlock, and wolfsbane, all of which contain atropine, hyoscyamine, and scopolamine, which can cause psychotropic effects when absorbed orally or transdermally. The accused witches seem to have taken these psychotropic substances and were then able to commune with supernatural entities, some of which were recognised as fairies. While historic records of these communions can be subjected to the usual critical analyses, modern testimonies—although always anecdotal—are more immediate. People continue to witness the fairies.

This can happen spontaneously, as demonstrated by approximately 500 testimonies from the 2017 'census' conducted by *The Fairy Investigation Society*.[155] But there is an ever-burgeoning amount of evidence indicating people who have altered their states of consciousness with a wide-range of psychedelic compounds are likely to encounter fairy-like entities during their trips.[156] There appears to be a clear correlation between the fairy-like creatures turning up during psychedelic episodes (most especially those instigated by the compound *N,N-dimethyltryptamine* [DMT]) and the beings reported in folkloric and modern fairy encounters.

Some of the best clinical evidence for these correlations is the research study conducted between 1990 and 1995 in the General Clinical Research Center of the University of New Mexico Hospital by Dr. Rick Strassman, which found that volunteers injected with varying amounts of DMT underwent profound alterations of consciousness.[157] This involved immediate cessation of normal consciousness and perceived transportation to a different realm of reality with divergent physical properties, inhabited by a range of creatures described as elves, fairies, lizards, reptiles, insects, aliens, clowns (yes, clowns) and various therianthropic entities. One woman even described a pulsating entity she called 'Tinker Bell-like.' The experiences, especially at higher doses, represented to the participants a parallel reality that was 'super real', i.e. not a hallucination, not a dream, but a substantially-built reality with full sensory interaction and telepathy.

The experiences reported from the study are irrational, absurd, frightening, illogical, and surreal. There is no question of any of the volunteers physically leaving the hospital bed during their experiences, but for all of them (without exception) the DMT world was every bit as real as the one their minds left behind. After the injections, participants frequently talked about 'blasting through' or 'breaking through a barrier,' after which they found themselves in a realm with its own laws of physical space, movement, and its own inhabitants. There are dozens of recorded experiences from the study, and the participants all engaged in a non-physical reality directly via their consciousness, seemingly separated from their physical selves. Some of the experiences agree in type to certain aspects of the fairy phenomenon, but what the research demonstrates is that—under the right conditions—human consciousness can operate within a distinct and separate universe inhabited by a range of apparently autonomous entities. These entities may be one-and-the-same: the metaphysical beings recorded in folklore and modern fairy encounters, and the beings met during various types of altered states of consciousness, brought on either actively or passively.

Since around 2010 there has been a quickly-growing literature[158] devoted to the fairy-types appearing in the DMT world, and however uncomfortable it may be for people who have not taken psychedelics to accept any authenticity in these accounts, the consistency of the experiences should make us take notice and accept them as a dataset worthy of analysis. While it may seem a stretch to equate "real world" fairy encounters with the entities turning up in a chemically-induced reality, the data insinuates very strongly that there is a parallel equivalence demanding to be taken seriously.

The producers of *Photographing Fairies* would have likely been unaware of Strassman's study, but they evidently tapped into the folklore that suggests the fairies can be encountered during altered states of consciousness. The unidentified white flower is clearly a surrogate for a psychedelic substance, and the scenes where Castle consumes it (and even when Clara takes it — snaking her fingers and staring at invisible entities) demonstrate his altered state is a psychedelic episode. The scenes in which he witnesses the fairies beneath The Great Tree are replete with motifs recognisable as psychedelic: tracers, slowed-time, enhanced colours, and, of course, the appearance of supernatural entities.

Director Nick Willing and his compatriots knew what they were doing. They understood the psychedelic state and they appreciated and appropriated the folklore, which included it. The fairies exist, but consciousness needs to be tweaked to see them and interact with them. The genius of the film is to incorporate all of this into a narrative that allows anyone (whether they have experienced psychedelics or not) to be subsumed into the intimacy of the numinosity. This is brought to denouement during the final scenes, where the theme of death—ever present in the film—is incorporated into the altered state of consciousness trope. Death is, after all, the ultimate altered state, and here we understand that the fairies are the arbiters between physical reality and what lays beyond.

The Fairies and Death

When Castle clicks open his pocket watch with its Straussian tune to attract Ana and Clara, they notice the portrait of his dead wife inside. "She's alright, you know," says Ana. The girls have taken the flower (implicitly many times) and seem aware that their communions with the fairies overlap with the world of the dead. They even set up an altar beneath The Great Tree and hold their own mass for their dead mother—the flower is centrepiece to the altar.

Apart from the death of Castle's wife in the opening scenes, the fairies have a role in all other fatalities in the film. This is made most explicit in Castle's own death at the end. It is unequivocal: he is executed by hanging, he enters a tunnel of light (filmed from his perspective), and a fairy appears with an expression suggesting he should have known what to expect. The fairy disintegrates, and Castle returns to the Alpine mountain—evidently now a post-mortem Otherworld—to be reunited with his wife. The film sets up the fairies as psychopomps, facilitators between this world and the next, perhaps suggesting they are in league with the dead, or even the dead themselves, manifesting as luminous entities in physical reality when certain conditions are met, or when someone's life ends. Just as with the altered state of consciousness motif, the fairies have a deep connection with the dead in folklore, which is repurposed by the film, creating another layer of authenticity.

The relationship in folklore between the fairies and death, and/or the land of the dead, is illustrated in a variety of ways. In fact, many of the folktales and anecdotes involving fairies invoke some kind of transcendence from consensual reality. One of the most typical motifs is the dilation or expansion of time in Fairyland, rendered in the film as 'slow time'—even if death is not an explicit part of the story. It would seem as if the fairies are with us but not with us at the same time... much like the dead.

One rooted tradition is that the fairies are the Pagan dead (or perhaps post-Purgatory Christians not good enough for heaven but too good for hell, a concept explained by Conan Doyle to Castle in the film). They live in a world of limbo occasionally coinciding with our own.

A story capturing this idea well was collected by the folklorist William Bottrell in Cornwall in the early 1870s.[159] In *The Fairy Dwelling on Selena Moor*, we find Mr. Noy, a farmer in the district of Buryan, lost and bewildered on the moors at night, a common motif in fairy folklore and perhaps an embedded code or metaphor in the story for the protagonist entering an altered state of consciousness. Noy is missing for three days before a search-party on Selena Moor finds him with his horse and dogs tied up nearby.

Incredulous at the passage of time—he was convinced he had spent no more than a few hours sleeping—Noy tells the story of what happened to him after becoming disorientated on the moor. This involved meeting an old-flame, Grace, who had died three years previously. Noy recounts what she told him about her existence with the fairies:

> Their mode of life seemed somewhat unnatural to her, for all among them is mere illusion or acting and sham. They have no hearts, she believed, and but little sense or feeling; what serves them, in a way, as such, is merely the remembrance of whatever pleased them when they lived as mortals—maybe thousands of years ago... "For you must remember they are not of our religion, but star-worshippers. They don't always live together like Christians; considering their long existence such constancy would be tiresome for them."

When Noy returns to consensus reality he explains that many of the fairies he saw:

> ... bore a sort of family-likeness to people he knew, and he had no doubt but some of them were changelings of recent date, and others their forefathers who died in days of yore, when they were not good enough to be admitted into heaven, nor so wicked as to be doomed to the worst of all places. Over a while, it is supposed they cease to exist as living beings, for which reason fewer of them are now beheld than were seen in old times.

This idea was encountered many times by W.Y. Evans Wentz as he travelled throughout Britain, Ireland, and Brittany between 1907-1911, collecting the fairy traditions that he would ultimately publish as *The Fairy-Faith in Celtic Countries*.[160] The belief that the fairies were intimately connected to the dead seemed to be especially prevalent in Ireland and Brittany, where Evans Wentz repeatedly encountered the view that they were one-and-the-same, summed up by an unnamed Dublin engineer talking about the folk traditions in his home county: "The old people in County Armagh seriously believe that the fairies are the spirits of the dead; and they say that if you have many friends deceased you have many friendly fairies, or if you have many enemies deceased you have many fairies looking out to do you harm."

In Brittany, the fairies were known as *fées* or *corrigans*, and were usually understood as ancestral spirits, often appearing to warn of, or predict, death. Evans Wentz found many folktales about the fées and the dead in and around the village of Carnac, where there are extensive remains of prehistoric megalithic stone rows and burial chambers. One M. Goulven Le Scour was a source of many traditions:

> My grandmother, Marie Le Bras, had related to me that one evening an old fée arrived in my village, Kerouledic (Finistère), and asked for hospitality. It was about the year 1830. The fée was received; and before going to bed she predicted that the little daughter whom the mother was dressing in night-clothes would be found dead in the cradle the next day. This prediction was only laughed at; but in the morning the little one was dead in her cradle, her eyes raised toward Heaven. The fée, who had slept in the stable, was gone.[161]

There are many more testimonies along these lines in all the regions visited by Evans Wentz. They are often confused and ambiguous, and some of his interviewees deny any connection between the fairies and the dead. But there is an underlying consistency in the belief, allowing Evans Wentz to summarize: "The animistic character of the Celtic Legend of the Dead is apparent; and the striking likenesses constantly appearing in our evidence between the ordinary apparitional fairies and the ghosts of the dead show that there is often no essential and sometimes no distinguishable difference between these two orders of beings, nor between the world of the dead and fairyland."[162]

This links the folklore to the psychogenesis that created it; the stories, anecdotes and testimonies are embedded with meaning. This meaning is our culture's attempt to understand what death is and who might be around to help us, be with us, or warn us, when death is close or upon us. Folklore sends us messages which seem to infer that there are metaphysical entities more familiar with the land of the dead than we are, and that death is simply an alternative form of consciousness, available to everyone given the right circumstances, and perhaps not something to fear. Folklore portraying the fairies as inhabiting the land of the dead, and occasionally showing up in our living reality, shows them as representatives of the past and what is gone. In the same way as a memory of someone dead can be conjured up in consciousness before disappearing into the subconscious, so the fairies are able to make appearances in our collective stories that attempt to understand death and its connection with life. Their somewhat wacky behaviour perhaps exemplifies our fear of the unknown—they live in an undiscovered country, and have their own customs and rules. But it's a place that can be accessed and brought into our comprehension of reality—physically and metaphysically—so as to come to terms with death, both our own and of others.

The folkloric relationship between the fairies and the dead are filtered throughout *Photographing Fairies*. Its filmic artistic licence transforms all this into a watchable piece of cinema, where the fairies become representatives of not only the supernatural but also purveyors of death. They become 'the in-betweeners,' partly based on the folklore but transformed into something new, which can be understood by a modern audience who may have no knowledge of fairy folklore.

But in many ways, the fairies are peripheral characters in the film. The main emphases in the story are upon death and grief, dealt with at a level that does not require supernatural entities. Castle's attempt to come to terms with the death of his wife is the primary running theme, but the movie presents many other takes on death and grief: Castle's ambivalence to the dead soldiers in the trenches, the parents' stoic attempt at understanding their son's death in the photographic studio, Templeton's confused and wavering reaction to his wife's death, the young girls' apparent nonchalance to both their parents' deaths, and Linda's and Roy's uncomprehending distress at Castle's unnecessary death at the hands of the state executioner. It is only when we see the fairy usher Castle into an after life that we finally understand the necessity for supernatural arbiters between the physical and the metaphysical.

This is one of the accomplishments of *Photographing Fairies*—the presence of the fairies is fundamental and yet the emotional resonance of the storyline is achieved not through their appearances, but rather through a study on how various characters deal with death. The insinuation is that consciousness survives physical death and that the fairies are messengers of this fact.

"We stand on the boundary," Castle tells Doyle. "Touch them and that's what you feel. The physical reality of the next world. A taste of heaven; a place where all wounds are healed and fractures mended. Where people are made complete." He proposes that "the next world is as real as Clacton-on-Sea."

This is always grounded in the everyday throughout the film, which, of course, makes the idea more persuasive. Linda sums it up as she visits Castle in his cell prior to his trial: "Out there's the real world. With trams, and tea dances, and bills to pay, and children to raise. Where real live people fall in love with other real live people. It's my world and I want you in it." Linda is, indeed, the lightning rod in the film, giving a materialistic, yet sympathetic view on proceedings. She witnesses all the death (albeit second hand) and is always a conduit through which the viewer can associate, whether or not they want to believe in the fairies.

Castle's comeback to her speech in the cell is the parting of the ways between the everyday reality of Linda and the metaphysics of death: "But it isn't the only world."

Pulling Together the Threads — Can We Photograph Fairies?

But can the fairies be photographed? Castle's attempts to do so are inconclusive, yet his early 20th century equipment is able to record something. This brings us to the most important question: what are these entities that have been a part of humanity for thousands of years, and where do they come from? They may be adapting to cultural codes, even evolving into new forms, but at what level of reality do they exist?

An answer may be to utilize the three-part interpretation for metaphysical entity contact proposed by David Luke, Senior Lecturer for Psychology at the University of Greenwich (based on Peter Meyer's 2006 study).[163] Luke used this rubric to assess a study into the Otherworldly beings (many of which had fairy attributes) encountered by people who entered altered states of consciousness with DMT. However, it is also a valid tool to evaluate what may be happening to anyone reporting a numinous experience that includes interaction with non-ordinary entities such as the fairies:

1. They are subjective hallucinations without any objective reality. Such a position is favoured by those taking a purely materialist (i.e. physicalist), reductionist, neuropsychological approach to the phenomena.

2. They are psychological/transpersonal manifestations. The communicating entities appear alien but are actually unfamiliar aspects of ourselves, be they our 'reptilian brain' or our cells, molecules, or sub-atomic particles.

3. The entities objectively exist in Otherworlds and can interact with our physical reality. A numinous experience provides access to a true alternate dimension inhabited by independently existing intelligent entities in a stand-alone reality, which exists co-laterally with ours, perhaps interacting with our world when certain conditions are met. The identity of these entities remains speculative.

Of course, all three interpretations may be true at different times and under various circumstances. From a materialist-reductionist standpoint, all fairy experiences could be reduced to hallucinatory events. There is no physical residue as an after-effect of the interactions, and the reports are all limited to visual and aural experiences. While the specific adjuncts allowing for these hallucinations to take place cannot be properly analysed, seeing them all as sensory aberrations remains one legitimate interpretation. The film allows this interpretative model to any viewer unable to make the conceptual leap into accepting the existence of fairies.

This explanatory model is reliant on the theory that consciousness is an epiphenomenon of the brain. The implication is that the brain, for whatever reason, is simply misconstruing sensory input from a physical world where things like fairies simply do not exist. This is the hard and fast materialist-reductionist standpoint, which is deeply embedded in Western culture.

It is also a standpoint that is now challenged at a fundamental level not only by religious and mystical traditions, but also by the recently reinvented philosophy of Kantian Idealism, panpsychism, and by a growing number of quantum physicists, who—using a wide range of methodologies—suggest that the brain is a *reducer* of consciousness, not a *creator* of it.[164] This model sees consciousness, not matter, as primary; it is everywhere and it is everything, and individual human (and animal) brains are merely conveying it within the remit of what then becomes physical reality. For the most part, this physical reality has a closely defined rule-set, but under certain conditions the usual laws break down and metaphysical events can occur. These supernatural occurrences are thus as legitimate as any natural occurrence. The philosopher Jeffrey Kripal describes this in relation to traumatic episodes that cause apparently non-ordinary experiences, which include entity contact:

> The body-brain crafts consciousness into a human form through a vast network of highly evolved biology, neurology, culture, language, family, and social interactions until a more or less stable ego or 'I' emerges,

rather like the way the software and hardware of your laptop can pick up a Wi-Fi signal and translate the Internet into the specificities of your screen and social media. The analogy is a rough and imperfect one, but it gets the basic point across. Sometimes, however, the reducer is compromised or temporarily suppressed. The filtering or reduction of consciousness does not quite work, and other forms of mind or dimensions of consciousness, perhaps even other species or forms of life, that are normally shut out now 'pop in.' In extreme cases, it may seem that the cosmos itself has suddenly come alive and is all there. Perhaps it is.[165]

While most fairy encounters are not the result of trauma, this perspective helps us perhaps understand preternatural fairy experiences as something metaphysical being allowed to 'pop in' from either a greater, transcendent form of consciousness, or from an alternative reality to which humans do not typically have access. This would fit with either of David Luke's second and third interpretations for supernatural entity contact. Simply put, a numinous zone has been entered and the participant is able to make contact with what usually resides external to their ordinary consciousness.

One of the achievements of *Photographing Fairies* is to tie much of this together and present us with a layered and nuanced view of what role metaphysical creatures like the fairies might play in our world. By using folkloric and Theosophical tropes as manifested in the immediate post-WWI period, we are opened up to the possibility of the fairies existing at some level. Photography is the means with which they may be brought into view in physical reality, but it is only through an altered state of consciousness that this actually occurs, thus plugging into the plausible concept that this is how non-physical entities have been experienced from prehistory through to the present day.

This is accomplished with much artistic licence, relying on a skilful screenplay and outstanding acting, but is always rooted in an understanding of the cultural role of the fairies. Perhaps most importantly, *Photographing Fairies* integrates the idea that the fairies are handmaidens of the eternal; they are arbiters between physical existence and what is usually thought of as death, with the ultimate cosmic message that there is no death... only a continuance of consciousness.

You Are Not My Son! Revealing the Changeling in The Hole in the Ground

Susan Demeter

Come away, O, human child!
To the woods and waters wild
With a fairy hand in hand,
For the world's more full of weeping than
you can understand.
- W.B. Yeats, The Stolen Child

S omewhere between myth and our collective imagination, deep in a rural Celtic landscape, there is a hole in the ground. Not just an ordinary hole, but a giant, ominous crater that serves as a doorway between this world and another one. And that other world is filled with impossible, monstrous humanoid beings, whose intentions towards us are unknown, and seemingly unfriendly. This setting is the backdrop to the film *The Hole in the Ground.*

The Hole in the Ground is an independent Irish horror film which debuted at the Sundance Film Festival in January 2019. I am a huge fan of folk horror and the supernatural, so I had been eagerly anticipating its release, and I was not disappointed. There is nothing in its promotional materials nor story which overtly mentions fairy lore, nor is it the type of movie one might immediately associate with fairies, especially if the viewer is primarily acquainted with the Little People through Disney—and yet, this movie is definitely marked by the fay.

This chapter takes a deep dive into *The Hole in the Ground*, exposing its fairy motifs, symbolism, and the sinister, trickster qualities of the Fair Folk who lurk throughout this film, and are so often found in unexpected ways in modern cinema. The story follows Sarah O'Neill, a young mother, and her son Christopher as they transition to a new life in the countryside. After the discovery of a large, mysterious hole near their rented house, the boy's behaviour becomes progressively disturbing and bizarre.

The choice for the lead characters' surname intrigued me because it has a very strong tie to bad dealings with the fairies. I have no idea if the writers knew of the fairy folklore attached to the O'Neill name or not, but it represents a noteworthy synchronicity with the film's plot.

Shane's Castle, located in County Antrim, Northern Ireland is an ancestral home of the Royal House of O'Neill. Built sometime during the 12th century, it served as the O'Neills' home for hundreds of years until a mysterious fire gutted it in 1816. Today the castle lies in ruin, and has become a popular tourist destination because of its regular appearances in HBO's *Game of Thrones* series. The O'Neill family is among the oldest in Ireland, and they have a strong tradition of a banshee appearing to them at times of misfortune and death. One room in Shane's castle was traditionally kept for the use of *Maeveen, the White Lady of Sorrow*. Historians have suggested that because the O'Neill banshee is named, and had a specific room within their home, she was likely a family member in life. The origin of the O'Neill banshee is said to have come from an offense committed by the family against the local fairies.

> One of the early O'Neills was returning from a raid when he found a cow with its horns tangled in a hawthorn tree. Single hawthorns are sacred to the sidhe and so the fairies now regarded the cow as their property. Foolishly, he freed the animal, and incurred the anger of the fey. When he arrived at his home, he found that the fairies had taken his daughter to the bottom of the lough. The girl was allowed to return to let her father know that she was safe in the fairy kingdom, but she could only return from then on in order to warn of impending death in the family by keening. Maeve is a very old Irish name, found in the oldest sagas, and appears more in keeping with the apparent antiquity of the banshee myth. The ending -een is a common diminutive in Irish, an affectionate twist on a name that would seem to reinforce the story that the banshee was originally a daughter of the house.[166]

The O'Neill demesne borders Lough Neagh, which has been traditionally associated with the healing powers of the Little People, and might be the lake to which Maeve O'Neill was spirited away. The surname O'Neill carries a strong link to both the world of the fay and kidnapped offspring, making it an exceedingly fitting family name for the lead characters of *The Hole in the Ground*.

The film opens with the protagonist and her young son playing in a carnival or amusement park funhouse. She watches tenderly as her son makes funny faces into a mirror purposefully designed to distort its reflection. After sharing a laugh they exit the amusement park, cotton candy in hand, heading towards their car that is parked in an empty lot. The funhouse has a large sign on top reading '*Road to Hell*,' a statement that aptly sets up the next shot.

The scene changes to an overhead view of a car travelling towards a rural Irish town, set between two hills and surrounded by a large, dark forest. The camera's point-of-view quickly flips upside-down, strongly signaling a shift in reality, as the car travels towards a liminal space and time, carrying two people in a transitional stage of life. This scene has been touted as a nod to Stanley Kubrick's classic horror film *The Shining*, which also heralded a family's move towards an in-between existence.

Fairies are encountered in liminal places at the threshold between worlds. Appropriately, the family's journey begins at an urban amusement park or fair, a place that is often impermanent, moving around from town-to-town. They are also places of illusion, specifically the funhouse, which is where the O'Neills' story begins: as they leave behind an old life, they unknowingly progress towards the very edge of another world.

As another fairy motif, I found the 'Road to Hell' sign with its devilish image of additional interest, since some Christian-based folklore describes fairies' origins as demonic, perhaps even fallen angels. As Christianity swept through Western Europe, minor pagan deities and spirits of the land were rebranded as demons. The link between devils and fairies is further exemplified in the literary and folk character of Robin Goodfellow, otherwise known as Puck; Goodfellow is commonly depicted as satyr-like, complete with horns and cloven hoofs, attributes closely associated with devils.

This multiple layering of liminality found within the film's setting is established very early on. Sarah and Christopher move into a rental or temporary home, in need of renovation, located between the town and a forest. However, it's not just the setting that is liminal, but the lead characters' lives that are at a point of transition too.

"Fairies earned a reputation as liminal figures by virtue of their reputation in the popular consciousness with life transitions," writes Regina
Buccola, Professor of English at Roosevelt University in Chicago.[167] In
folk belief, people are far more likely to be vulnerable to the influence of
fairies during periods of life alteration such as marriage or divorce, the
birth of a child, and at times of illness and death.

Early on we learn that Sarah has recently separated from Chris's father, who was likely violently abusive towards her—there are a few scenes
where she hides a scar on her forehead, which she is reluctant to fully
explain to others. This deepens the complexity of Sarah's character: she is
in a transitional point in life, newly separated, moving from an urban setting to rural life, starting a new job, becoming a single parent, and coping
with the trauma of spousal abuse. On the other hand, Chris is a young
child coping with the stress of moving away from a familiar home in the
city, having to make friends in a new school, and missing his father who
he may only be vaguely aware is not following them to this new rural life.
Both Sarah and her son are at points in their lives that would make them
vulnerable to the influence of the Little People.

Another clue suggesting the O'Neills fled a toxic environment comes at
a pivotal point in the film when Chris becomes angry that his mother will
not kill a spider for him like his dad would. This establishes Sarah's gentle
character in comparison to her ex-husband, and her dismay when her
son purposefully steps on the female spider, which she has just released
outside. It is clear at this point in the movie that she has not been fully
truthful with her son about their separation from his father, and hints
to the viewer that Christopher may have inherited some aggressive traits
from his dad. This scene with the stomping of the spider sets the stage
for the horror enfolding the rest of the film.

On the drive from Chris's school to their new house the O'Neills encounter a strange, hooded woman who suddenly appears in the middle
of the road. Sarah swerves to avoid hitting her, nearly crashing their car
and breaking one of the side view mirrors. The woman stares vacantly at
Christopher, whispering some unintelligible words, and Sarah gets out of
her car to see if the stranger is injured. The woman is reminiscent of the
old hag or hooded bean sidhe seen along the roadside in folklore. Despite
her unnerving appearance and odd mumbling, she appears unharmed.

After ascertaining there was nothing physically wrong with the strange
woman and retrieving the broken mirror, the O'Neills proceed to their

house, which they have only just moved into a short time before. This incident on the road clearly traumatises them both, and serves as a portent to the fate of the boy. Now home, we see the isolated rental house the O'Neill family moves into has an added layer of liminality: it is in need of renovation. Sarah starts the process by gradually replacing the wallpaper with a design reminiscent of the famous interlocking carpet pattern of *The Shining*'s Overlook Hotel—clearly another subtle homage.

Chris is seen seated at the table playing aggressively with his action figures and being picky with his food. He is obviously unhappy with their new house and country life. After discovering a spider, one of many in the kitchen, he screams out for his mom, setting up the spider killing scene mentioned earlier. The child is frightened and upset that his mother would set the spider free, and begins questioning her about his father. When Christopher realizes Sarah has likely lied to him about his dad coming to live with them in the new house, he runs off towards a forest behind their ancient house.

Sarah chases after her boy, afraid he will become lost in the woods. It is there she first encounters the gigantic crater from which the movie takes its name. Fearing the worst, Sarah turns away from the hole only to discover Chris standing right behind her. They both stare into the gaping hole, and he asks her what she thinks the hole might be. Sarah, visibly shaken and disturbed, blows off this question, saying, "It's *nothing*," and they leave the forest.

The inspiration for the story of this film came from a real life tragedy involving a sudden sinkhole that opened up under a Florida house, leaving a family homeless and at least one person dead.

"There was a particular news story I saw about—this was a long time ago—a man in Florida was watching TV in his armchair in his sitting room and a small sinkhole opened up beneath him," recalled Lee Cronin, writer and director of *The Hole in the Ground*. "He was unable to be rescued, he fell down into the earth and I thought that was horrific."[168]

While I was researching sinkholes in preparation for this essay, I came across some gardening information indicating that the early stages of sinkholes can appear like rings in the ground caused by fungi, also known as fairy circles. I noted this as another possible synchronicity because the havoc a sinkhole can wreak upon persons and property much resembles the chaos of fairy rings. Entering a fairy ring can have terrible consequences such as being cursed or abducted into Fairyland. However, the obvious tie-in between a hole in the ground and fairies is the popular belief that the fay are seen as magical beings that come from under-the-ground.

"Their habitations were universally believed to be underground, in dimly lit regions, with the entrance to them under a sod, near one of their circles, by some ancient standing stone, under the bank of a river, away on the open moor hidden by bushes, or in the ruins of an old castle," wrote Reverend Daniel Parry-Jones, folklorist.[169]

In the next scene we are introduced to Sarah's new friends the Caul family, which is another interesting name choice. A 'caul' is the amniotic membrane enclosing a fetus, and in some superstitions a baby born with an intact caul is considered gifted with 'second sight' or other psychic abilities. The Cauls in the film give Sarah some insight and information on the strange woman that she and Chris encountered in the middle of the road. Sarah learns that the lady's name is Noreen Brady, and that she has a very tragic past, involving the death of her son, James, when he was still a child. The Cauls tell her how Noreen would show up at her son's school, ranting that he was "not her son." Police had to restrain Noreen, who was now considered to have a psychiatric disorder. James was consequently taken out of the school, and was murdered later that year after his mother was released from her mental institution. Noreen had purposefully run him over with her car.

Later in the film, Sarah and Chris come across Noreen in the middle of the road again, this time in front of her own house. Noreen's husband Des Brady is standing outside, and when Sarah goes over to talk with him, Noreen approaches the side of the car where Chris is sitting inside. She starts screaming, "He is not your son!" and bashes her head against the car window. Des gently takes his wife back into their home, and Sarah drives away in horror.

Noreen's behaviour is disturbing, but she does have many characteristics of a fairy doctor. These were almost always older women who had specific knowledge and abilities to see past fairy deceptions, and remedies to thwart them. In this scene we see Noreen bleeding from the cut she sustained by beating her head against the car window. According to Irish superstition, as noted in *Ancient Legends, Mystic Charms, and Superstitions of Ireland* by Lady Jane Francesca Wilde, the fairies have an aversion to blood, which makes Noreen's actions seem far more purposeful than the mere random act of a madwoman.

Several days later Sarah decides to visit the couple to find out more about what happened with Noreen. When she arrives at the couple's house she is shocked to find that Noreen had been murdered the night before in a very gruesome way: her body was found in the yard, pecked by crows, with her head completely buried beneath the earth. In Celtic folklore crows are associated with the fairies, and in 18th century Scotland and Ireland, shepherds would make offerings to the fae, *to keep the crows from attacking their flocks.*[170]

There is much death in this film, which is to be expected in a horror movie. There are the literal deaths of the spider, James, and his mother Noreen. There are also symbolic deaths in the ending of Sarah's relationship with her partner, the transformation of the O'Neills' lives, and the many other losses that can come with the breakdown of a family.

Fairies in general are not considered murderous, but the belief that fairies come from deep within the earth, underneath hills, and inside caverns extends itself to the idea that their origin is associated with the dead. As Patricia Lysaght wrote, "Irish belief in fairies is often intertwined with beliefs about the dead—both like to visit houses in the night and both like to find a clean, warm kitchen with a supply of fresh water on arrival; if they do not find these things, both tend to create mischief." Ghost lore and fairy lore share many similar motifs, and there are numerous stories of the dead appearing alongside the fairies.[171]

Sarah attends the wake of her neighbor Noreen, held at the Brady's home. She notes that there are an unusual number of mirrors hanging on the walls of the different rooms. They are all completely covered by black cloth, which is customary during periods of mourning, and she decides to ask Des about them. He explains that his wife had become convinced that their son James was an imposter, whose true form was only revealed in the reflection of a mirror.

Mirrors are commonly found in folklore and superstitions in all cultures around the world, and they are featured heavily throughout this film. The movie opens with Chris playing around with a mirror in the amusement park's funhouse. The broken car mirror early on is a portent of things to come, and is later used by Sarah to establish Chris's true identity. Noreen was obsessed with mirrors even after her son James's tragic death, and the closing scene of *The Hole in the Ground* is filled with mirrors of varied types and sizes.

Mirror images in various traditions and beliefs are considered gateways of the soul, which is why in folklore vampires cannot cast a reflection, i.e. vampires have no soul. Mirrors are also believed to be entry and exit points to other worlds. *Through the Looking-Glass,* Lewis Carroll's 1871 novel and sequel to *Alice's Adventures in Wonderland,* is perhaps the most famous fictional use of a mirror serving as a supernatural doorway. This may have been what influenced director Lee Cronin's liberal use of them in telling this story.

"I've got my own mythology that I built using existing lore."
– The Hole in the Ground director Lee Cronin, Bloody Disgusting,
January 2019

In the case of the imposters in this film, mirrors are used as a device to see past the illusion of their appearance, like those created by *fairy glamour*. A fairy can use glamour in order to hide their true identity by appearing as something completely different from what they are, or by making an object appear as something it is not. In the case of Noreen's son James, she believed her son's imposter was using a similar type of magic, and employed numerous mirrors throughout her home in order to reveal this.

Following the scene where Chris runs off into the sinister forest behind their house, the relationship between mother and son begins falling apart. Although Sarah is slow to realize that something is very wrong with her child, viewers who are knowledgeable in fairy lore will have guessed at this point he is actually a *changeling*.

Changelings are the most sinister of all folklore associated with the Fair Folk because it taps into one of our most primal fears: the loss of our children. Fairies are universally notorious for kidnapping human babies, children, and sometimes young adults, replacing them with one of their own kind. These stories of fairy changelings are a part of a group of motifs that have been recorded in the Aarne-Thompson folklore index:

> The basic premise of these motifs is that the faeries, through supernatural means, are capable of abducting babies from humans, whilst replacing them with one of their own, usually a wizened old faerie who would proceed to eat and drink voraciously, and maintain a surly silence. With external advice, the parents are usually advised of how to rid themselves of the changeling and restore their own baby from the faeries.[172]

After the Cauls tell Sarah about Noreen and the fate of her son there is another incident that same evening with Chris and the forest. While in bed, Sarah hears a strange sound coming from downstairs. Upon investigating, she finds the backdoor leading from the kitchen into the yard wide open, slamming in the wind. She grabs a flashlight and begins searching around the yard, going up to the edge of the forest and calling out for Christopher. There is a very eerie moment when it appears someone or something is hiding behind a tree, but when she very cautiously investigates she sees no one. Thinking Chris has run away again, she returns to the house to call the police, only to find Christopher standing in the doorway of his bedroom. He tells her that he was home the entire time.

A few days later while jogging in the forest, Sarah finds Christopher's favourite action figure lying discarded under a tree. During their evening meal, Chris—sitting at the table voraciously eating a giant plate of spaghetti Bolognese, a dish he previously said he hated—denies going into the woods when his mother confronts him about the toy's location. After Sarah says she does not believe him and has proof that he was lying, he becomes enraged and, in a fit of unnatural super-strength, shoves the large, heavy kitchen table at her. Christopher's surly behaviour, super strength, and voracious appetite are all traits of a changeling according to fairy folklore, and it is these behavioural changes that arouse Sarah's suspicions.

One evening while taking a bath, Sarah hears strange noises coming from Christopher's bedroom. She silently creeps up to the closed doorway and observes her son through the gap between the door and the floor chasing, catching, and eating a spider. Sarah is visibly disturbed and frightened, and sneaks back into her bedroom so that Chris does not know she was there. The next day she takes him to the doctor who assures her that it is normal behavior for a child. She is not convinced (and, frankly, neither would I be if this were my kid). Sarah decides to put a hidden camera in her son's bedroom so she can monitor his nighttime activities.

The next day Chris is taking part in a school assembly in front of his mother and the other students' parents. He has joined the choir and made several new friends, including a boy he had previously told his mother he did not like. The children sing an old Irish folk song, *The Rattlin' Bog,* and as Christopher begins to sing his part he intensely focuses on Sarah and begins speaking his lines in a distorted and emotionless voice. Sarah runs out of the performance, and later away from Chris when he is walked back to her by his teacher.

The Rattlin' Bog song continues the fairy motif within the movie. The way the lyrics describe a "nesting" motif, to me at least, also describes the climax of the film… You could easily rewrite it as, "the boy in the mud in the cave in the hole in the ground in the woods…."

There is a rich body of geographical lore related to real or imaginary hazards found within bog landscapes. Bogs are often perceived to be mysterious and bottomless, and they are home to *ignis fatuus* or will-o'-the-wisps, a type of light phenomenon closely associated with fairies—and, in some traditions, fairies themselves.[173]

Before the school event, Sarah (along with the viewers) can dismiss the plot's horrific and mysterious events as the result of a mother's anxiety and the family's breakdown. Sarah is plagued with strange dreams of Chris, and violent hallucinations of him breaking the arm of their neighbour during an arm wrestle. She is taking anti-anxiety medication, and is clearly under a lot of stress.

This assumption finds support when Des Brady mentions Capgras syndrome—"a psychological disorder that can cause someone to believe that someone they love, a person close to them, has been replaced by an imposter, a duplicate"—to Sarah at Noreen's funeral.[174] When they discuss why Mrs. Brady had so many mirrors around their house, Des says that having a name for her delusions did not help the situation.

Sarah returns to the house where she retrieves the hidden camera and takes it to her neighbour Des. What she shows him on the camera shocks them both, and he smashes it on the ground. Sarah tells Des she does not believe Noreen was crazy, nor is she, and that both James and Chris were replaced by imposters. Des reluctantly admits he cannot deny what she is saying.

Sarah decides to confront the changeling, but first drugs him with her anti-anxiety and sleeping medications. She mixes it in with his spaghetti Bolognese and grated parmesan cheese—which the real Chris called "cheese dust," another reminder that the changeling has a very different appetite and taste. I view this act as a reversal of the fairy lore that cautions against eating or drinking any food offered by the Fair Folk. The food and drink offered in hospitality by the fairies is usually not what it appears to be, and is in fact a trap. To partake of fairy food meant to be trapped in Fairyland forever.[175]

When Christopher begins showing visible signs of the drug taking affect, Sarah administers one final test by invoking a favourite game she and her son liked to play, which of course the imposter knows nothing about. "You're not my son!" she declares.

Sarah confronts the changeling, which attacks her violently with a brute strength that knocks her unconscious. When she awakens the imposter is preparing to bury her in the same manner as Noreen was found. Before he can finish the job, however, the drugs Sarah tricked it into ingesting take effect, and the changeling falls into a deep sleep. Sarah manages to free herself from the dirt hole, and carries the thing back into the basement of the house. She uses the discarded, broken car mirror to break the spell of the creature's glamour and sees its true form. This wakes the changeling up, and after further struggling with it, Sarah manages to knock it unconscious again. She flees the basement, locking the changeling inside.

Ironically, considering the subject matter, a lot of what you see in this film is real in the sense that computer-generated imagery was barely used, including in the scenes where we see the changeling in its true form. The following quote is from the *Bloody Disgusting* interview with writer and director Lee Cronin that I mention previously:

> In terms of practical elements, it's actually a contortionist performer in prosthetic, Cronin told us. It's a European co-production. It's Irish, Belgian and Finnish. Some of the casting came from Finland so there are some great circus performers in Finland actually so I leant on my Finnish producer and put the call out. We found this guy, Miro Lopperi; he was just so game for it. We only really had a day with him to get what we needed but he was all over it and he brought a lot of value to it as well.

> Okay, maybe it's not 100% Lopperi, but it's mostly him. There's not a lot of a creature in the movie, not a lot of monster, but what you do see, I would say 90-95% of it is real, Cronin said.[176]

The film does not explain how Sarah O'Neill knows that her real son is inside the gigantic and very sinister hole in the ground. We could envision this as a symbolic descent, but for the purpose of this chapter I would like to think it is a mother's deep bond with her child, and Sarah's own psychic intuition, that leads her to her real son's location.

Sarah allows the hole to swallow her up, and she finds herself in an underground cavern, which, as already discussed, is a typical setting for Fairyland. Once inside she shines her flashlight on several skeletons and bone fragments of unknown origin. The bones, including skulls, appear humanoid, lending support to theories that fairies are actually the dead or related to death. This theory is fleshed out (forgive the pun) in Janet Bord's book *Fairies: Real Encounters with Little People*, along with other speculations as to the origin of fairies. In Irish lore, people who died were sometimes considered to have been taken underground by the fairies, and could therefore potentially return or be retrieved, similar to Sarah's rescue mission inside the hole.

Sarah finds Christopher alive and seemingly in a deep sleep in an earthen bed or cocoon, which is covered with dirt. By the time he is found he has been away for several days, presumably without food or water, yet he does not appear outwardly suffering because of it. This might lend itself to the thought that Fairyland has a different time-scale than the one in our human world. In tales of Fairyland, the passage of time may occur either more slowly or quickly than it does here above ground in reality.

When Sarah and Chris flee towards the cavern's exit, they are pursued by creatures that look like hobgoblins—presumably the fairies that *The Hole in the Ground* has been alluding to throughout the film. Robin Goodfellow, mentioned earlier, was sometimes described as a type of hobgoblin or "ugly fairy." These bad-tempered, trickster-like, humanoid creatures are said to dwell inside caverns and underground passageways.

When one of the subterranean creatures grabs Sarah, she turns around and is shocked to see that it has transformed itself into an exact duplicate of her own face and upper body. This moment calls into question who else may have stumbled upon the fairies' lair—is the entire town being replaced by changelings like in *The Invasion of the Body Snatchers* (another film filled with Fair Folk motifs)?

Sarah manages to escape the hole with the unconscious Christopher in her arms and runs back to their house. Once there she finds her car keys still inside the kitchen, and leaves Chris outside beside the car while she re-enters the house one last time. Grabbing the keys off the countertop, Sarah glances over to the basement door and hears the changeling crying out for her in Chris's voice. Unsympathetic, Sarah sets the house on fire with the changeling still trapped inside, and she and Chris watch the smoke and flames rising from their home.

118 | FAIRY FILMS

This scene is an eerie reminder of the lore surrounding the burning of changelings, which inspired real historical murders. The power of the fairy faith was so strong throughout Ireland and the rest of the British Isles that the changeling belief persisted well into modern times. Changelings were tortured by fire because it was believed that fairy parents would hear the changeling's cries and come to rescue it, immediately restoring back to the mortal world the kidnapped human being who had been held captive in Fairyland.

One case from the turn of the last century is particularly chilling.

"It is not my wife!" – Michael, husband of Bridget Cleary

Bridget Cleary was an Irish dressmaker and egg-seller living in County Tipperary. On March 15th, 1895 her husband of five years burned her to death because he believed she was a fairy imposter—at least that was his defence for murdering his wife. According to accounts from that period, Bridget had fallen ill after delivering eggs to a place that contained a fairy fort, or fairy ring. The town physician had diagnosed her with bronchitis, but her husband and neighbours felt differently.

Michael Cleary became convinced that his wife's illness was caused by the fairies, and he, along with their neighbours, attempted to force feed her various herbs, demanding she identify herself either as Michael's wife or as something else. Not satisfied with the results of this abuse, Cleary doused his sick wife with lamp oil and set her on fire. He had said at the time he expected the real Bridget to be delivered back to him via the chimney—a common point of fairy egress—as the smoke of the burning imposter went out. Needless to say, this did not happen.

Bridget was reported missing, and by the time her badly burned corpse was found, nine people including her husband had been charged with her murder. Michael Cleary was found guilty of manslaughter and, after serving 15 years in prison, immigrated to Canada. Charges against several of the co-accused were dropped and others were given very light sentences, given the circumstances.

Newspaper reports in the aftermath wrongly stated that Bridget was the last witch who had been burned in Ireland. There was neither a witchcraft accusation nor trial in her case; Michael Cleary killed his wife because he believed she was a changeling, and his neighbours assisted him because of their strong belief in the fairy faith.[177]

More than a century later in the fictional landscape of *The Hole in the Ground*, Sarah and Chris O'Neill watch as their house burns down, and the changeling trapped inside goes up in smoke. We, the viewers, are left guessing its eventual fate… no fairy parents are shown trying to rescue this imposter.

Once again the O'Neill family is on the road, this time driving in the opposite direction. The film concludes with the family returning to an urban neighbourhood. Sarah is seen taking in a university lecture, something she was unable to pursue before, due to the birth of her son Christopher. The boy is obviously much happier in these familiar surroundings, too.

Sarah, however, is unable to fully escape the events of before. While Chris rides his bicycle outside, she peers outside of their flat's window, camera firmly in hand. She begins taking pictures of her son whose face, unlike the other objects in the frame, is blurred. The point-of-view shifts to a wider angle of their new urban home's interior, revealing that Sarah has lined the walls with mirrors and a standing looking glass. A very brief glimpse of her is reflected within one of them, reassuring us that, while Christopher may be changed once more, the real Sarah managed to escape the subterranean Otherworld of the fay.

When the O'Neills exited the hole in the ground I have to admit that I questioned whether or not they were both imposters. In the literature a parent venturing to Fairyland, rescuing a child, and returning is exceedingly rare, and certainly not without the fae controlling the situation, like they did with the return of the historical O'Neill daughter as a banshee. Christopher's blurred face in the closing scene's photographs strongly suggests that this is not the real boy at all. Maybe the child she found in the hole in the ground was an extension of the changeling she burned in the fire, or yet another imposter? In any event, it seems Sarah failed in her rescue mission, much like Michael Cleary failed in his attempts to retrieve his wife from Fairyland, with horrific real life consequences.

The Hole in the Ground has a haunting musical score throughout, but as the credits roll, we are treated to an Irish children's folk song called *Weile Weile Waile*. Its lyrics are deliciously disturbing, and speak of a woman living in a forest who commits infanticide by a river. This is a very a common way to restore a changeling. One grandmother was acquitted after drowning her grandchild in a river; her defence was that she wished to "put the fairy out of it."[178]

The purpose of these types of songs, and traditionally gruesome fairy tales, were to frighten children from wandering off into scary places like the dark forest that Chris ran into, and presumably where James had played 30 years before. Both boys were kidnapped, and later switched with imposters.

During my research I came across an interesting connection between writer and director Lee Cronin's last name and another ancient folk song. 'Cronin' is a variation on the old Irish surname 'Cronan,' meaning 'little dark one,' which naturally hints at the mysterious Little People. However, what I found most intriguing is an old Gaelic lullaby that was sung from the Fae point of view, called *Cronan na Eich-mhara,* and its purpose was to comfort a baby abandoned in the woods because it was suspected of being a changeling.[179]

> *Avore, my love, my joy*
> *To thy baby come*
> *And troutlings you'll get out of the loch*
> *Avore, my heart, the night is dark,*
> *wet and dreary.*
> *Here's your bairnie neath the rock.*
> *Avore, my love, my joy, wanting fire here,*
> *wanting shelter, wanting comfort*
> *our babe is crying by the loch.*
> *Avore, my heart, my bride*
> *My gray old mouth*
> *touching thy sweet lips,*
> *and me singing old songs to thee.*

The Hole in the Ground is a film that has been marked by the Fae, both overtly and knowingly, by its writers and director… and perhaps far more subtly and mysteriously than its makers had realised.

You Can't Spell Frank-N-Furter Without F-A-E: Fairy Lore of The Rocky Horror Picture Show

Patrick Dugan

Most of my fun stories begin with, "So this one time when I was drunk…" and *The Rocky Horror Picture Show* (1975) was no different. It was eye-opening, to say the least. A couple of friends (you know who you are) dragged me to see it at the Palace Theater in Syracuse, New York and it changed me forever in a good way… I think.

I'd spent my early years as a science fiction geek watching *Battlestar Galactica, Star Wars, Buck Rogers in the 25ᵗʰ Century*, and a slew of other shows and movies as fast as I could get my hands on them. Growing up in a middle-class family in the suburbs hadn't prepared me for the wild ride of *The Rocky Horror Picture Show* (RHPS). In my "experience" there was nothing else like what I saw on the screen in the pre-internet world.

The film begins with Brad (Barry Bostwick) and Janet (Susan Sarandon) at a friend's wedding. On their way to see Dr. Everett Scott (Jonathan Adams) on a terrible stormy night, they have a flat tire and are forced to walk to the spooky "castle" or manor house they passed. Once there, they meet Riff Raff (the handyman played by *RHPS* creator Richard O'Brien) and his sister Magenta (a domestic played by Patricia Quinn) who inform them their master is having a special event that evening. Before they know it, Brad and Janet, two wholesome kids, are whisked into Dr. Frank-N-Furter's (Tim Curry) party where he is unveiling his creation, Rocky Horror (Peter Hinwood). Before the big reveal, motorcyclist Eddie (Meat Loaf) emerges from cold storage to seduce Columbia (a groupie played by Nell Campbell), but Dr. Frank-N-Furter kills him instead. Once Rocky is brought to life, he is more attracted to Janet than his creator. In the end,

Riff Raff and Magenta kill Dr. Frank-N-Furter and return to their home planet of Transsexual in the galaxy of Transylvania.

Mainstream media has lots of great representations of fairies, so why pick *Rocky Horror* instead of *True Blood* or *The Dresden Files* series or even *The Eisteddfod Chronicles*? After all, these stories revolve around a version of the fae and their interactions with humans. Stories of the fae are as old as mankind itself.

By now you're probably asking yourself, "How is *this* movie inspired by stories of the fae?" At its heart, *The Rocky Horror Picture Show* is a tale of the fae cross-dressing as science fiction. From the time Janet and Brad step through the front doors, we are in the realm of the fae, with its wonderful, whimsical characters, odd behaviors, and "pleasures unimagined." But also, lurking beneath the surface is danger and unrevealed truths awaiting our stranded motorists. As with all good fairy tales, there are lessons to be learned from these strange folk.

Allow me to serve as your narrative guide through this thinly-disguised fairy tale. Hopefully, your eyes will be opened to what has been hiding in plain sight, much like Dr. Frank-N-Furter. The main areas of exploration are the fairy tale nature of the story, the fae courts, and their rules, traditions, and magic. I was surprised to find the sheer number of ways you can draw parallels between the two.

So, let's take a jump to the left, and a step to the right, and dive into the wild, wacky, wonderful world of *The Rocky Horror Picture Show*!

"Once Upon A Time...."

Classic fairy tales usually begin with some form of "Once upon a time." Tales of the fae were traditionally spoken with a narrator adding in colorful bits and baubles to enhance the story. As more of these tales were written down, narrators took a more central role, replacing the storyteller. *Rocky Horror* starts with a pair of red lips singing to the audience, a nod to the oral traditions of fae storytelling. When the narrator soon appears, pulling out a large tome, he takes over and guides us through our tale.

In general, narrators provide a framework for the larger story to unfold. Our narrator, the Criminologist (Charles Gray, not inconsequently designated as the expert), provides a trusted voice to deliver context to the movie and add insight into the motivations of the various characters as the film progresses, along with leading us through "The Time Warp." This echoes how a traditional fairy tale unfolds in its telling. For example—though unrelated to the fae—in 1987's *The Princess Bride*, Peter Faulk reads the eponymous story to his sick grandson, interjecting along the way, building tension, or adding a comic touch where necessary.

Through the construct of reading us a story, the Criminologist gives us details about the characters we wouldn't have known, but are necessary to tie the plot together. By describing Eddie (an ex-delivery boy captured by Dr. Frank-N-Furter) as "a no-good kid," we are granted not only a reference to his interaction with Dr. Frank-N-Furter, but also gain insight into Dr. Everett Scott as his concerned uncle. Equally important, Dr. Frank-N-Furter admits he knows Dr. Scott and thinks Brad and Janet were sent by him. Without these important details, the story falls apart with no connections bringing its players (all dressed in corsets and stockings) together for the final conflict at the end of the movie.

The other service our erstwhile narrator provides is adding a human perspective to events that are abnormal for the audience. He explains the intricacies of the story that might be missed otherwise, especially as he reveals the details of Dr. Frank-N-Furter and his companions, Riff Raff and Magenta. By doing so he is holding up a mirror to our humanity and allowing us to see the difference, both good and bad, between two societies.

In written folklore, the narrator as the trusted storyteller is more than a character in the proceedings. The Italian fae story "The Three Fairies" by Giambattista Basile (1634) tells the story of Cecella, who is tormented by her stepmother until one day the girl throws her basket down a cliff. The storyteller goes on to describe how the three fairies befriend Cecella and help her to free herself from her predicament.[180] This would be an example of an omniscient narrator. In the 2003 film *Big Fish*, narrated by Albert Finney, the protagonist shares his wild exploits through the weird and wonderful world he's created; the narrator is an active character in the story, telling his tale to the audience to explain the marvelous wonders he experienced. The movie *Stranger Than Fiction* (2006) merges the omniscient narrator with a character in the film when it is revealed the narrator is the author who is writing the story. The main character can "hear" the author as she writes, and is bewildered by what is happening.

In each of these cases, the narrator describes and clarifies strange events so their importance is understood by the audience. As you can see, the role of the narrator is as critical in these modern-day stories than in the oral tradition. It is interesting to see how well modern stories tie back to the traditions of original fairy tales.

Crossing the Veil

In fairy lore, a veil exists between the lands of humans and the fae. Most humans cannot see this veil, and only through bad luck or happenstance do they find themselves in Fairyland. Celebrations around the world speak to the thinning of the veil between the lands of the living and the dead (Día de Muertos) or the lands of the fairy (Samhain/Beltane). On these days, it is believed the dead or fairies can more easily cross into the world of men, the "weakened" veil also allowing humans to pass over into the Otherworld.[181] Pathways into the unknown are commonly fraught with peril; whether demanding the Goblin King steal your baby brother, stepping through a wardrobe, following a shooting star, or merely falling asleep and awakening in a magical kingdom, the ways protagonists arrive in Fairyland are as varied as the stories themselves, each holding a central theme of crossing into the unknown on an adventure.

Tales of storms, floods, full moons, war, and other natural and man-made disasters were used in these fae stories to explain trips into the unknown. Prior to the Scientific Revolution, natural events were associated with gods or other supernatural beings of power, including the fae. In Japan, typhoons are described as "divine winds": Fūjin, Shinto God of the Wind or a spirit of immense power, was said to become visible during such tempests.[182] In Norse mythology Thor, God of Thunder, brought the storms. Around the world, each culture has its own explanations for natural events. It only makes sense that they would be tied into the activity of the unseen realms which mortals rarely see.

The inclusion of a storm in *Rocky Horror*'s opening alludes to its fairy tale legacy, as storms commonly marked the crossing from one world into another. It is a dark and stormy night in which we find our lost couple, Janet and Brad. Motorcycles pass them in the middle of nowhere as they search for the way home. An unfortunate flat tire sends them in search of a phone and ultimately to the door of Dr. Frank-N-Furter's mansion, itself a strange and fanciful place. The two wayward travelers have no idea what is in store for them or what they will face as they step through the mansion's front door and out of reality.

The next few lines—from Magenta's portion of "The Time Warp"—further mythologize this connection between the two realms.

In another dimension / With voyeuristic intention / Well secluded, I see all....

As in fairy lore worldwide, these lyrics suggest the Transylvanians have the ability to watch without humans knowing they exist, bringing up the idea of separation that "the veil" implies. We can therefore infer Magenta possesses the talent to hide from normal humans, just as the fae would in legend; perhaps Brad and Janet only found the manor because they were hunted and *called* by magic. Normal humans can't see the world of the fae; similarly, Brad and Janet wouldn't have found the mansion without being led through the supernatural tempest.

Given such strong ties between the fae, bad luck, and natural events, it is implied that both the massive storm and the flat tire aren't mere coincidence. As the couple approaches the house, Riff Raff is in the upper window—a folkloric point of entry and exit for malicious spirits—awaiting their arrival.[183] When Brad and Janet cross the threshold, they are no more prepared for what they find than when Belle agrees to stay at the Beast's castle in France's "Beauty and the Beast" (*La Belle et la Bête*) or when the Prince meets the maiden in Estonia's "The Gold-spinners."[184] Instead of a hideous beast or a witch, however, Brad and Janet find themselves in a much different situation.

We've established the presence of a veil separating realities. As with most walls, you need an entrance to access the other side. Portals are a very common form of entering and exiting different dimensions. From Alice's looking glass to the doorway into the Other of Neil Gaiman's *Coraline*, these portals are what facilitate transportation from reality into the strange and uncharted regions of these new worlds. In *Rocky Horror*, the portal is actually the front door of the mansion; while not as overly imaginative, it still functions as the crossing point from the plain old world into the realm of the Transylvanians. Once through the portal, what are our adventurers to do? They are in a new land, know nothing of the place or its creatures, don't understand the rules or the customs.

If we stay within the well-established patterns of a fairy tale, a guide should appear to lead our lost travelers; enter Riff Raff and Magenta. Not all guides are good or helpful in fantasies. In *The Lion, the Witch and the Wardrobe* Mr. Tumnus, a benevolent *faun* guide, meets the young Lucy and helps her to return to her world, but only after abandoning his original plan to turn her over to the White Witch. Similarly, in *Through the Look-ing-Glass*, Alice's initial contact after stepping through the mirror and into an alternative world is with the Red Queen. Certainly, these are not the best characters to guide our protagonists.

Why is the guide so important other than helping humans acclimate to the Otherworld? For one thing, they deliver exposition to both the audi-ence and main characters. The guide also provides a metric by which the viewer/reader can gauge just how different the world they now inhabit is from their own. When Wendy and her brothers alight in Neverland, for example, Peter Pan warns them of the dangers of his world and especially about Captain Hook.

In *Rocky Horror*, the storm has driven our unsuspecting pair into the lair of Dr. Frank-N-Furter. First seen in the window of the ominous man-sion, Riff Raff now lets our hapless travelers enter the house and explains to the wary couple they have arrived on a very special night, as the Master is having a fête, the Annual Transylvanian Convention. Brad's request for a phone goes unanswered (pun intended) as they are led deeper into the mansion.

Riff Raff describes what is happening at the castle that very night and who their host is. Magenta, the domestic and Riff's sister, enters the story. Each lends their voice to the situation at hand and warns, in their peculiar way, of the events to come. Once they've given their cautions they launch into "The Time Warp," a song which in itself reveals the time paradox Brad and Janet are entering. At this point, the audience has a launchpad for the upcoming events. With a bit of knowledge and a lot of apprehen-sions, Brad and Janet join the party.

Seelie, Unseelie

What would a fairy tale be without a colorful and strange troop to illus-trate the differences between the "real" world and the land of the fae? The soaked duo of Brad and Janet are chased into the Annual Transylvanian Convention and encounter a host of oddly-dressed party-goers. "The Time Warp" is key to Brad and Janet experiencing a huge shift in their reality as they step into Fairyland. Gaily attired and dancing around—as fairies often did—the partygoers are quite a shock to our "normal" pair. (We won't even get into "elbow sex.") While credited as "Transylvanians" in the film, the partygoers in the original stage production were called

"Phantoms," echoing the manner in which fairies would cavort with the dead in legend.[185]

How does it tie this story to the land of the fae? In order to illuminate the subject, let's jump into the lore behind the Fairy Courts. Depending on the region, fairies were ascribed various identities: they were the Tuatha Dé Danann, demoted pagan gods, nature spirits, the dead, the original occupants of the British Isles, etc. In late medieval, Renaissance, and Elizabethan retellings of Celtic mythologies, the fairies were ruled by Queen Titania and King Oberon.[186] In some stories, after an uprising, the fae were split into two courts, the Seelie and the Unseelie. The fae who stayed with Oberon and Titania (as named by William Shakespeare) became the original Seelie Court.

As an example, *Peter Pan*'s Tinker Bell might constitute a member of the Seelie. In some literature, members of the Seelie court follow a strict set of rules about interacting with humans, which makes them more honorable, but just as deadly as their Unseelie court foes. The Seelie tend to be more "benevolent" toward humans, though still dangerous in their own right.

In the Irish story "Teig O'Kane and the Corpse," a spoiled young man is confronted by the fairies and forced to carry and bury a corpse as punishment for all the bad choices he's made. The corpse refused to be buried and he was forced to continue carrying him all night long until he found the right spot. After such an extreme punishment, he went home and married the girl he loved and never caused trouble again.[187] Tales like these show the power of the fae and the righteousness of the Seelie.

Some consider the Unseelie "evil" fairies who actively seek to harm humans. These are the fae who wish to restore their place on Earth by ridding themselves of humans. The Irish Dullahan, the infamous Headless Horsemen, are excellent examples of the types of fae associated with the Unseelie Court: the Dullahan call out to a person whose spirit is then stolen, leaving them dead.[188] Mischievous English Boggarts could be considered another member of the court, haunting families who have wronged them.[189] These Fae live in a survival-of-the-fittest mode.

In modern times, Disney's Maleficent character is an example of the Unseelie, cursing Sleeping Beauty over a supposed insult. In Jim Butcher's *The Dresden Files* series, Harry Dresden deals with both courts and things don't always go as planned—these fae are touchy, violent, and, to the human mind, evil. They represent the unknowable aspects of nature, the unpredictability of the storm, the deadliness of the typhoon. Fear and warnings abound when the Unseelie Court is represented in tales.

Just like the two Courts of the Fae, there are two factions in the mansion. Dr. Frank-N-Furter is the embodiment of the Queen (or is it King?) of the Seelie Court. He welcomes Brad and Janet to his kingdom, invites them to stay, and accepts their "offerings" as payment for staying in this incredibly strange world. When Eddie emerges from the freezer, thus breaking their agreement (a.k.a. "strict set of rules"), Frank-N-Furter kills him. As with the Seelie Court, while Eddie was taken in, he was dispatched when necessary. As in the tradition of the Unseelie, there is an uprising. Riff Raff and Magenta rebel against Dr. Frank-N-Furter, thus creating their version of the Unseelie Court. They want to return to their homeworld, Transsexual in the galaxy of Transylvania, and are willing to kill any and all who stand in their way.

After Riff Raff murders Rocky and Dr. Frank-N-Furter, Magenta asks him why he killed them; he responds, "He never liked me." This is all the rationale a capricious Unseelie Court ruler needs to kill off another. The most amazing part is Riff Raff allows Brad, Janet, and Dr. Scott to live, but only after they agree that Riff Raff was justified in murdering Dr. Frank-N-Furter and Rocky.

The Magical Nature of the Fae

The Rocky Horror Picture Show opens at a small wedding with the bride and groom getting their pictures taken. Brad and Janet pose with some of the church's workers in the background. Look closely and you'll see Dr. Frank-N-Furter, Riff Raff, and Magenta all looking like plain folk. All through the song "Dammit, Janet," the trio is setting up for a funeral. You might wonder if this was this on purpose? Were these doppelgängers impersonating our travelers from the planet Transsexual? To my thinking, this is a direct tie into fairy illusions and other magics, and this isn't the only example. Let's look at the history of the fae and their magic.

For example, in Arthurian legend, the magic of Morgan le Fay ("Morgan the Fairy") is prominent. She has been portrayed as fae, a witch, and a sorceress as the legends have changed over time. Morgan is one of nine magical queen sisters, each capable of shapeshifting, flying, and other magical feats according to *Vita Merlini* by Geoffrey of Monmouth. After

Arthur battles Mordred and dies, Taliesin convinces her to bring Arthur back to life, though Morgan warns it will take a long time to revive the fallen king.[190] In *The Rocky Horror Picture Show*, we see "fairy magic" employed in the form of glamour and "science" to take advantage of Brad and Janet, even turning them to stone.

The scene at the church illustrates the use of magic by Dr. Frank-N-Furter, Riff Raff, and Magenta to appear as normal people (a common fairy tactic of shapeshifting), hunting their next targets to attend the party that very evening. As noted, the arrival of the storm beckons back to the concept of fae manipulating nature to push their targets where they want them. The question becomes who cast these spells to bring Brad and Janet to the mansion?

Dr. Frank-N-Furter would seem the obvious choice for who is luring the unexpecting couple into his grasp, being the King (or Queen) of the visitors from Transsexual. His ego alone might demand outside witnesses to his incredible feat of bringing Rocky to life. Dr. Everett V. Scott is also a rival scientist, so stealing away two people close to him might be seen as a blow against his foe. All of these things seem possible, but are they the "true story"? Seeking adoration and worship from humans would be very much in-line with the Seelie Court fae, Dr. Frank-N-Furter's contingent of the Transylvanians. There is no malice toward Brad and Janet on his part. He welcomes the couple and invites them to witness his achievement. Is this enough motivation to entice the unwitting Brad and Janet to his mansion on such a night?

Riff Raff and Magenta, wishing to return to their planet, could also have summoned the pair simply to throw a monkey wrench into Dr. Frank-N-Furter's plans. Indeed, when Brad and Janet approach the mansion, recall how Riff Raff is sitting in the upstairs window waiting for them. With the knowledge of the impending reveal of Rocky, did they bring the innocent Janet there as a temptation for Dr. Frank-N-Furter's creation? The other obvious motive was to bring Dr. Everett Scott to the house to find his nephew Eddie and stop Dr. Frank-N-Furter from completing his plans and forcing a return to their homeworld. This would be the type of motivation we would expect from the Unseelie court Fae, and by extension, Riff Raff and Magenta. Using a third party as a weapon would ensure Riff Raff and Magenta weren't in danger and, as the movie shows, they wait until the proper time to spring their trap and eliminate

Dr. Frank-N-Furter and return to their homeworld. In my mind, this is the more likely scenario.

The Seduction of the Fae

Folklore from almost every culture has some form of the seducer in their myths. In Greek culture, it was the sirens. Contemporary Egyptian mythos has the *El Naddaha* who lure men to their deaths in the Nile. In his *Fairy and Folk Tales of the Irish Peasantry*, W.B. Yeats described the *Leanhaun Shee* (or Fairy Mistress), a fairy lady who "seeks the love of mortals. If they refuse, she must be their slave; if they consent, they are hers, and can only escape by finding another to take their place." He also describes a male seducer called the *gean-cānach* (love-talker) who preys on shepherdesses and ruins their reputation.[191]

The bedroom scenes with Brad and Janet fall into this classic case of using magic to seduce or confuse the victim. Another example of this fae magic is the Irish fairy tale "The King of Erin and the Queen of the Lonesome Island," where a king swims out to sea pursuing a black pig, only to discover an island where he is fed, without seeing who is bringing him food. On the third night, the Queen explains she was the pig and brought him to her island because she needs a son to rescue her and sends the king back in a boat the next morning. When the King is attacked, the Queen sends her son by magic to defend the King and drive out the invaders.[192]

The fae can perform magic and use it on themselves and humans alike. In *The Rocky Horror Picture Show*, we see multiple uses of magic and its effects on the humans involved. Eddie is "frozen" but emerges fully functional, if somewhat beat up. Later in the story, Dr. Frank-N-Furter uses glamour to trick Brad and Janet into having sex with him while in the disguise of their significant other. This is very emblematic of fae seducing men or stealing women to produce children.

Another piece of the puzzle is the Transylvanians' attempt to use Brad and Janet in their plot to overthrow the Doctor and return to their homeworld. Magic is one of the cornerstones of fairies in folklore and an equally large part of *The Rocky Horror Picture Show*—though it is called "science" to disguise such folkloric parallels.

Fae Bargains

One thread running through all of these stories involving the fae is there are no gifts, only bargains. Anything can be acquired for a price, though the unsuspecting often find the price far higher than they ever thought possible. In *Rumpelstiltskin*, a maiden ends up promising her first born to an imp through a series of escalating transactions; in Hans Christian Andersen's "The Little Mermaid," the mermaid trades her voice to a sea witch for human legs; in 1986's *Labyrinth*, Sarah unwittingly gives her little brother to the David Bowie's Goblin King. In a more straightforward, less carnal parallel, the German fairy tale of "The Elves and the Shoemaker" tells of two Little People who make shoes to help a beleaguered cobbler. When the shoemaker crafts beautiful shoes for the pair in gratitude, they leave, but the shoemaker remains prosperous from then on.[193] In the German legend of Dr. Faust, he willingly trades his soul to the devil for unlimited knowledge.[194] The story led to the term "Faustian Bargain" which definitely applies to dealing with the fae in their many guises, including the Transylvanians; unlike Faust, Brad and Janet seem unaware of the bargain they are accepting.

In *The Rocky Horror Picture Show*, offerings—another hallmark of fairy interaction—are made in the bedroom in exchange for staying in the manor. Dr. Frank-N-Furter visits Janet and Brad individually and "accepts their offering" after using glamour to make them think he is their partner… at least at first. When the glamour breaks, they still continue amorously, with the promise not to tell their significant other.

Of course, Magenta and Columbia are watching on a screen (shades of fairy clairvoyance) and a wandering Janet sees Brad and Dr. Frank-N-Furter together in bed. Depending on your viewpoint, this might not have been such a bad bargain.

Rocky the Changeling

Another common theme in tales of the fae is exchanging a human child with a fairy changeling. The legend states that fairies substitute something—a beglamoured dummy, an ill fairy infant, or an elderly fae—for a victim who is often but not always a human baby. In one German story, a woman's child is kidnapped by elves and a changeling left in its place. When the woman boils water in two eggshells, the changeling begins laughing at her, an act that forces the elves to return her child.[195]

I would venture that Rocky, the creation of Dr. Frank-N-Furter, is actually a changeling and not a human man as he appears. Yes, he looks human, but that is the danger of dealing with changelings. While the classic comparison drawn to Rocky is that of Frankenstein's monster (Frank-N-Furter's name alone makes this apparent), Rocky is fully in control of his faculties, though limited in intelligence. He is an "adult" and can speak and think whereas Frankenstein's Monster, at least in most cinematic adaptations, is unable to do these things despite its human brain. Given the legends around an elder fae replacing a child, it stands to reason that Rocky is far more advanced than a newly created individual.

The use of Eddie's brain to animate Rocky also echoes Walter Evans Wentz's theory that changelings could be explained by "soul-wandering" or "demon-possession," i.e. that a child's consciousness could vacate its body and be supplanted by that of a fairy. "When a child has been changed by fairies, and an old fairy left in its place, the child has been, according to this theory, dispossessed of its body by an evil fairy…" he wrote in *The Fairy-Faith in Celtic Countries*. "… The leaving behind of the old fairy accounts for the changed personality and changed facial expression of the demon-possessed infant."[196]

Another reason that Rocky could be a changeling is his inherent fear of fire. In Irish folklore, putting a changeling in a fire would cause it to jump up the chimney and return the stolen human child. In German lore, putting a changeling in an oven would accomplish the same thing.[197] Given the consistent fear of fire changelings exhibit, is it any wonder that Rocky pulls away from the fire that Riff Raff taunts him with? This is consistent with legends of changelings. Why would Rocky be so afraid of the fire as to break free and try to escape? This is more than just a basic fear of being burned.

As soon as Rocky is brought to life, he sings about the "Sword of Damocles," referencing the peril of those in power and the threads of destiny. In this case it is more an allegory for "heavy is the head that wears the crown." If Rocky was newly-formed, how would this be his concern? The reason is Rocky is an elderly fae replacing the "baby" that Rocky was. Comprehending the situation that the characters find themselves in, at this level of sophistication, far surpasses Rocky's mentality. Dr. Frank-N-Furter even refers to Rocky as a "baby," though maybe not in the same way as a literal infant. (It could also be argued that Rocky is wearing a diaper, but that's a different topic.)

Another piece begging comparison to changelings comes when Riff Raff shoots Rocky at the end of the movie, the energy bolts bouncing off him as he climbs the radio tower with Dr. Frank-N-Furter. The blasts harm Dr. Frank-N-Furter, which means Rocky's immunity isn't a factor of him being from Transsexual Transylvania. This "immunity" leads me to think that Rocky is more than a mere person and has enhanced abilities, even magic, to protect himself just as a fairy would.

Given the similarities between Rocky and fae legends of changelings, I feel that there is a strong connection between the two. In fact, replacing the mummy in Rocky's birth tank with a changeling is one of the more compelling arguments we can muster.

The Nature of the Fae

The last aspect of the fae pertinent to our discussion revolves around feasts, time, and immortality. Since the earliest stories, venturing into Fairyland produces unpredictable results for the humans involved. Examples include Rip Van Winkle's drinking rum that causes him to sleep for twenty years and Alice's desire for treacle in *Through the Looking-Glass*.

Consumption of otherworldly food has always demanded caution. In "Goblin Market" by Christina Rosetti (1862), two sisters living by the river hear the call of goblin merchants. One of the sisters, Laura, stays late with the creatures and, after offering "a precious golden lock" of hair and "a tear more rare than pearl" in exchange, feasts on their forbidden fruit. The next day she can no longer hear the goblins, but her sister, Lizzie, can. As Laura wastes away, Lizzie takes a silver penny to buy more. When she refuses to eat, the goblins attack her, but she flees with several pieces of the fruit. Laura eats the fruit and in the morning is fully restored of health.[198]

The dinner scene from *The Rocky Horror Picture Show* embodies the fairy food taboo, where to partake of fae food is to remain trapped in Fairyland forever. Given the earlier offerings both Brad and Janet make, this could be considered the sealing of their fate. Columbia even confronts Dr. Frank-N-Furter about how she was tossed away for Eddie, who is in turn replaced by Rocky; the Doctor presents a repetitive behavior of bringing new conquests into the manor with the intent of trapping them forever. Eddie features prominently in the dinner scene, albeit in an unexpected manner. His note to Dr. Scott warns of Dr. Frank-N-Furter's "evil deeds" and it is revealed that, in fact, the roast they are eating is the recently departed Eddie, confirming the guests' worst fears. This is a theme repeated in many other fairy stories where things aren't quite what they seem to be, a variant on the widely-held belief that fairy food is a sham—consisting of worms, leaves, twigs, dirt, and other detritus—cloaked in glamour to only *seem* appealing.

While dinner parties are interesting, we learn even more from the film's most famous song, "The Time Warp," which kickstarts the festivities early in the story. "The Time Warp" provides several connections to the fae—for example, Columbia (my favorite) sings:

> *Well, I was walking down the street / Just having a think / When a snake of a guy / Gave me an evil wink / He shook-a me up / He took me by surprise / He had a pick-up truck / And the devil's eyes / He stared at me / And I felt a change / Time meant nothing / Never would again....*

Columbia's lyrics tie in directly to stories of the fae. There are a multitude of stories about people realizing something is "off" about a person. "Among the many beliefs held about the fairies, there is one strand which describes them as beautiful in appearance, but with a deformity which they cannot always hide," wrote Katharine Briggs in 1976's *An Encyclopedia of Fairies.*[199] In the words of John Gregorson Campbell, the fae, like Middle Eastern *djinn,* possess "some personal defect... by which they became known to be of no mortal race."[200]

In one such tale, a pair of brothers plowing a field happen upon a "maiden" who offers them food and drink. One brother accepts and is healthy until the end of his days, while the other—who refused the food because he could tell she was a fairy—withered and died before the year was out. The fact that Columbia knew Dr. Frank-N-Furter was "different" mirrors this story. Although in *The Rocky Horror Picture Show*, sexual deeds are the standard fare exchanged, rather than the milk and mead of tradition.

Fairy stories commonly involve a supernatural lapse of time out of alignment with the mortal realm. In the Celtic Otherworld of Tír na nÓg, time moves either at a snail's pace compared to the human world or alarmingly fast. Days seem like minutes, years like days; many a traveler to the Otherworld emerges only to find the entire landscape changed, their families and friends long since passed away as a result of this "time warp."[201] This phenomenon is not exclusive to the West—in one Japanese fable, the fisherman Urashima Tarō visits the undersea kingdom of Ryūgū-jō. When he returns after three days, three hundred years had passed in his world.[202] Another example are the stone circles and phantom islands of Scotland and Ireland, which only appear at certain times of the year. Humans may use these doorways to pass into the lands of the Sidhe, often never to be heard from again.

When Columbia sings, "Time meant nothing / Never would again," she is likely referring to becoming immortal since she met Dr. Frank-N-Furter. In fact, Eddie sings:

> *Whatever happened to Saturday night / When you dressed up sharp / And you felt all right… / It don't seem the same since / Cosmic light / Came into my life and I thought / I was divine.*

This is a direct reference to the time manipulation of the fae. What Eddie sees as "cosmic light" could be a number of things, all related to the fairies. It is possible this represents time slowing in the fae realm. How else would being shut into a deep freeze not affect him? The gash on his forehead may be symbolic of the blood sacrifices sometimes required to contact the Otherworld, or payment for the bargain a human has reached with the fae.

Equally, Eddie's "cosmic light" could represent the anomalous lights seen throughout sacred sites, which share a longstanding association with fairies. In the modern UFO era, contact with these glowing orbs can commonly led to spiritual insights or "divine" revelations. The fairy-UFO connection brings us neatly around to our manor's inhabitants, who are explicitly extraterrestrials.[203]

Conclusion

It's astounding we've made it this far. Any of these pieces alone wouldn't represent a strong argument connecting fairies to *The Rocky Horror Picture Show*—but taken together, very strong parallels between the fae, Dr. Frank-N-Furter's mansion, and the other Transylvanians emerge.

As with most stories of the fae, we are not left with a tidy, happy ending. The arch-enemy, Riff Raff, kills Dr. Frank-N-Furter and returns to Transsexual Transylvania with Magenta. As in many fae stories, *The Rocky Horror Picture Show* advises caution around these strange beings, whatever they call themselves. Like the fae, the denizens of house Frank-N-Furter think themselves beyond human cares, human woes, human lives. As the Narrator reminds us at the film's close, we are simply "crawling on the planet's face, some insects called the human race… Lost in time, and lost in space … and meaning…."

Close Encounters of the Third Kind: A Faerie Story of Liminality and Individuation

Dr. David Floyd

I

Steven Spielberg's *Close Encounters of the Third Kind* was released on 14 December 1977, to date having earned a cumulative worldwide gross approaching $300,000,000. While skillfully executed, balancing several subplots along with the primary storyline, and featuring compelling special effects and iconic visual images, the film is somewhat of an anomaly among its contemporaries in the broadly-defined science fiction genre.[204] It is in no way the kind of beloved romance of *Star Wars* (1977), nor the violence-fueled existential enterprise of *Blade Runner* (1982), nor the endearing family fare of *E. T. the Extra-Terrestrial* (1982).

One may even go as far as to say that *Close Encounters* runs a bit longer than necessary, keeps a rather slow pace, is unevenly or self-consciously humorous, and is certainly cerebral by popular standards. Andrew Gordon calls it a "solemn and mawkish" affair, peopled by "paper-thin characters" who are "extremely sketchy and difficult to care about."[205] Indeed, it should be noted from the outset that in the hands of a lesser actor, the film's protagonist, Roy Neary, might easily come off at best as dysfunctional and at worse irritatingly self-absorbed. Arguably, however, Richard Dreyfuss brings to the role the same endearing vulnerability he exhibited in *Jaws* (1975), where, as Hooper, he balanced Roy Scheider's baffled everyman, Brody, and Robert Shaw's ribald loon, Quint.

In light of these considerations, one may question what exactly appeals so to audiences about *Close Encounters*. Certainly, post-Vietnam American society, traumatized by various forms of social upheaval, demonstrated a notable escapist enthusiasm for alternate realms and the otherworldly, whether supernatural, extra-terrestrial, or otherwise.[206] Subject matter, however, does not a classic make, for countless other films of the period dealing with alien life-forms and secondary worlds appeared, only to be relegated to the outer darkness of VHS obscurity. *Close Encounters*, however, offers something more, something beyond the typical two-hour filmic escape or savvy pandering to a given cultural zeitgeist, and that is the universality of its protagonist's developmental arc.

Initially, Roy, husband to Ronnie (Teri Garr), father to three boys, and lineman for an Indiana electric company, embodies the normative standards of late-twentieth-century middle-class American society. This normality, his role as an average fellow who is in no way particularly remarkable, of course, affects his relatability. Much in the same way the moisture famer, Luke Skywalker, or the leisurely, unambitious hobbit, Bilbo Baggins, are at first cloaked in culturally-defined anonymity, Roy is as ordinary as any hypothetical theater-goer. It is not simply the recognizable normalcy of its protagonist, however, upon which the appeal of *Close Encounters* is contingent. Additionally, it is this common, mundane individual's glimpse of, aspirations towards, and arduous journey into something exceeding his immediate paradigmatic boundaries, and, indeed, something beyond himself. More to the point, Roy's is an archetypal journey of individuation, that annihilation of the former self only by which the higher self might be attained.[207]

Any mention of the archetypal journey, individuation, or the self must evoke psychoanalyst Carl Gustave Jung and mythologist Joseph Campbell, both of whom did much to elucidate the prevalence of certain images and motifs throughout human storytelling and the psychological implications thereof. The former's *The Archetypes and the Collective Unconscious* (1959) endeavored to identify and define figures such as the hero, supernatural helpers, the wise old man, and others, so intrinsic to the human experience as to appear within narrative traditions extraneous of temporal or geographical contexts, and to suggest what Jung called the collective unconscious.[208] Jung's "On the Phenomenology of Fairy Tales" most directly examines the "symbolic folkisms" relevant to this chapter's focus, and more specifically alludes to the kind of narratives wherein faerie beings appear.[209] Similarly, perhaps more than any academic immersed in Jung's theories, Campbell not only helped to articulate the former's concepts for a more popular audience, but codified the basic structure of what he termed "the hero's journey," clarifying the template by which narratives tend to be constructed. Arguably a more accessible path to a similar destination, Campbell's *The Hero with a Thousand Faces* (1949) is a conflated study of mythology, legend, folklore, and other genres, and while not every tale includes every element to which his study refers, the ubiquity of his provided structure is undeniable. Like Jung, Campbell asserted psychoanalytical reasons for this recurrence, a shared repository of racially remembered elements that comprise the essential components of the hero's journey.

Mired in the perceived meaninglessness and dehumanizing prescriptions and demands of his cultural context, the hero first appears in a situation that is fixed, predictable, and familiar, but particularly unpromising.[210] His summons to something different is initiated by the insinuation into this world of "the herald," embodied, in Roy's case, in the ship he encounters while out in his service vehicle. This is an unprovoked, mysterious, sometimes terrifying mechanism that challenges the hero's paradigmatic inertia and compels him out of complacency. The implications of accepting this proposal are inherently dire, promising dramatic alterations the daunting nature of which frequently result in the hero's hesitation, if not outright refusal of the call. Indeed, several of the most crucial, emotive scenes depict Roy's being pulled in opposing directions, one of marriage, fatherhood, and social responsibility, and the Other, following the mysterious, unrelenting summons to abandon the rational.

Having begun his quest, the hero often receives assistance in the form of supernatural phenomena, magical helpers, and such, as exemplified in the enchanted inanimate objects that tend to Belle in the Beast's castle, or the crafty and sentient mice who assist Cinderella in the making of her gown. In Roy's case, such assistance lies less in physical creatures and more in supernatural, perhaps telepathic, provocation and inspiration. At some stage, the hero encounters a mentor, typically a wise elder, who imparts wisdom and instruction, but this teaching is not easily acquired, for the mentor speaks in riddles and haunts places not easily trod.[211] As addressed below, Claude Lacombe (François Truffaut), the enthusiastic French scientist who is some stages ahead of Roy in the pilgrimage toward a similar place, serves this capacity.

Throughout, the hero encounters several pivotal junctures, thresholds the crossing of which marks crucial stages in the journey, and which serve as defining moments in his development. Beyond these thresholds lie the unknown, various obstacles, and promises of trial.[212] The threshold is a liminal space frequently guarded by "the watchman," who warns of the outcomes of transgression, and whose admonition represents popular opinion, the status quo, or consensus reality.[213]

In *Close Encounters*, such opposition is embodied in military and other administrative voices that endeavor to scrutinize and quell the inquiries from Roy and others who seek the truth. At some point, the active, rational, and yet incomplete hero encounters the maiden, the feminine, the anima, who embodies emotional depth, artistic expression, and openness to the implications of metamorphosis. Without their union occurring on some level, the hero's quest, in fact, his development entirely, cannot be accomplished. The quest takes many forms, but is always characterized by two vital aspects. The first involves the diverse trials that compel the hero to access theretofore untried capacities and tests of endurance, physical, psychological, or otherwise. The other necessitates the shirking of former ways, a process only by which the individuated self is realized.

This is the essential structure foundational to human narrative regardless of the trappings of a given genre, the universality of which makes Roy's experience so pertinent across demographics, and makes *Close Encounters* such a poignant artistic statement. Critics' assertions notwithstanding, Roy is indeed an amiable everyman, in whom most can discern a part of themselves, and in whose journey there is a vested interest, because it is our journey.

Oh, and it's facilitated by faeries.

The provocative alien entities of *Close Encounters* are remarkably similar to faeries in such a sufficient number of ways as to recommend reading the narrative less as a work of science fiction and more as a faerie story. One of the most unsettling aspects of the Other is its potential for establishing its own paradigm, a capacity to re-chart traditional considerations of the world and even human experience extraneous of conventional frames of evaluation and interpretation, thereby deforming or reproducing.[214] The entities, who have initiated and facilitated to various degrees Roy's journey towards individuation, recall the fey who, in Cirlot's estimation, are "personifications of stages in the spiritual life."[215] Likewise, Jung regards dwarves, for instance, as guardians of the threshold of the unconscious, and asserts that the invisible spirit may be represented in either "grotesque gnome-like figures or talking animals."[216]

Apropos of the ambiguity of fey engagement with humanity, the complexity of the entities' actions problematizes clear delineations of intent or plan. Indeed, one of their more peculiar aspects is the paradoxical variations of their conduct. Fey behaviors are as diverse as the historical accounts that preserve them. Elves, for instance, were feared as malicious to both people and animals, but also were subjects of enchanting feminine beauty. Beings such as fauni or the spirit Puck led travelers at best astray and at worse into pits, mires, and bogs, while others might bestow blessings or magical powers upon those "favored or canny" humans to whom they felt some affinity.[217]

On one hand, the entities at the film's conclusion appear benevolent, even bumbling and humorous. On the other hand, their abduction of Barry in the first act approximates a scene from a horror film, evincing no consideration for Jillian's (Melinda Dillon) terror or loss. This seemingly capricious nature mirrors that exhibited by the fey, whose activities range from assistance with household chores to unrelenting harassment and even destruction of property. Ernest Warren Baughman's folktale index, for example, notes such altruistic behavior as that found in F491.2 "Will-ó-the-Wisp lights people to their homes," which contrasts dramatically with that of F491.1 "Will-ó-the-Wisp leads people astray."[218] That the entities in Close Encounters at times appear benign, peaceful, and amusing, and at other times effectively instill terror in witnesses with unapologetic resolve and unsettling if not destructive chaos echoes the abstruse dimensions of fey nature and behavior.

Such complexity is demonstrated in the various manner to which faeries have been referred. Wayland D. Hand describes "kindred species of the wee folk," including elves, dwarves, brownies, and other "kindred denizens" of what he calls "lower mythology."[219] This "spirit race",[220] "willful, capricious child-spirits of the world"[221] are referred to as half-fallen angels,[222] "malignant phantoms,"[223] spirits of the prematurely departed, or even the last descendants of a distant Celtic race.[224] That the euphemism the "good people" is frequently employed in reference to them belies their less desirable attributes, which result in their being described as "magical and traditionally malevolent" as well as "mischievous and vain,"[225] even if they represent "the least malignant of monsters."[226] The demographics of the faerie world, indeed, are as amorphous as their activities.

Etymological aspects do little to diminish these discrepancies. Early on, there was a notable lack of specificity and ambivalence in regards to the identity of such anthropomorphic yet non-human creatures, faeries, and their similars, and vague notions of their respective identities.[227] While later endeavors sought to categorize faerie beings, there seems to have been resistance to placing them within a necessarily theological taxonomy, scholars being content with or resolved to merely assuming them to be unexplainable mysteries. The term *fairy* arrived in Britain via the French in the high and later Middle Ages, previous British reference to such beings having been "elves," a term no less rife with multiple meanings.[228] Though denoting a hostile "nocturnal sprite," the fourteenth-century *goblin* was nevertheless a somewhat indefinite term as well.[229] Further complicating linguistic matters is the fact that *fai* or *fay* more frequently functioned as a verb meaning the making of something magical or strange, while in English, prior to the fifteenth century, *faierie* referred to anomalous phenomena rather than a kind of being.[230] Not until the thirteenth century does there emerge what Ronald Hutton calls "a comparable range of entities," and not until the mid-seventeenth century was it that "the standard characters and associations of fairyland were established in the British literary imagination," after which they remained largely unaltered.[231]

II

A notable aspect of the faerie phenomenon, liminality, plays an integral role in *Close Encounters*, particularly in regards to social isolation and spatial dissociation. While Roy's home seems a fairly typical American domestic space, it is quickly established as oppressive, overwhelming, and ultimately unwelcoming to the jarring realizations with which he begins to grapple. This conflict is suggested in Roy's first appearance, where he amuses himself with a train set, the locomotive of which, meeting an upraised bridge, topples into a ravine.[232] This bears several implications regarding Roy's increasing isolation.

On one hand, one could flippantly infer this as a metaphor of Roy "going off the rails," as his preoccupation incrementally disengages him from his family.[233] More so, however, it serves as an analogue of the routine normalcy of Roy's predictable middle-class existence being absolutely upended, the familiar compromised by the intrusion of the anomalous. Indeed, it is Roy's dissociating shift from one paradigm to another, a process initiated and facilitated by faerie intervention, which forms the basis of the story. In notable contrast to the inhibiting and distracting claustro-phobia of his domestic situation, as well as the frenetic but unproductive character of his workplace, Roy is a notable anomaly, not only perceptive of but open to the provocations and implications of his encounter.

Indeed, when his access to the faerie world quickens his consciousness, its effect, if initially baffling, ultimately develops into visionary obsession drawing him from typical parameters. Such unconscious phenomena as that typified by Roy's visionary obsession tend to manifest themselves, in Jung's terms, in "fairly chaotic and unsystematic form," which, due to their characteristically "decentralized congeries of psychic processes," are perceived otherwise as psychotic ideas, which have the capacity "to draw the ego into their system," and essentially overwhelm the individual.[234] Campbell similarly refers to such notions, as those to which Roy is increasingly vulnerable, as "a disintegration of consciousness,"[235] one of the primary results of which is the individual's eventual isolation. The implications and evident demands of this paradigmatic adjustment prove at odds with his now outmoded reality.

Roy is frequently visually delineated from those around him. When first summoned to his place of employment, he is surrounded by co-workers robotically shouting about routines and protocols, and dressed in tan, khaki, and otherwise unremarkable tones, calling to mind Campbell's assessment of the majority of modern humanity, where "men who are fractions imagine themselves to be complete."[236] Roy, on the other hand, wears orange, an autumnal color not only associated with change and transition, but emblematic of the disaffecting passion and enthusiasm he will eventually exhibit. This is also the color with which he and Jillian are marked by their respective encounters, and which visually conveys their shared, if alienating, experience.[237]

Other chromatic implications of estrangement can be seen in what could be considered Roy's final mental break. As he begins assembling a facsimile of Devils Tower in his living room, garbed in an earth-toned housecoat that visually associates him with the detritus of his yard and the project with which it is constructed, his estranged family and neighbor-hood onlookers are notably in yellow, a color that in superstition is com-monly associated not only with various forms of "infamy or wickedness," but cowardice, envy, jealousy, spite, malice, guile, deceit, heresy, faithless-ness, as well as sickness and death.[238] Throughout the rest of the film, Roy wears a nondescript jacket, as though to convey his loss of belonging. It is not until he joins the group slated to leave with the entities that he again wears orange, his jumpsuit demonstrating his assimilation into the kind of social construct from which he has heretofore been ostracized.

Liminality is conveyed in other ways throughout *Close Encounters*. In a narrative wherein the protagonist struggles to comprehend and articulate the implications of an experience that increasingly isolates him from others, one of the film's foundational themes is the lack of communication. This theme affects allusions to one of the more pervasive characteristics of the fey, the endeavor, at times endearing, at others, capricious and even malicious, to communicate with human beings.

The sandstorm of the opening scene is complemented by attempts to locate a French translator in Mexico, a scenario that appropriately concludes with the storm absolutely consuming the scene before fading to black. The following scene in the radio control tower is a cacophony of air traffic controllers speaking over one another, while interested onlookers are incrementally introduced into a more and more audibly and visually crowded space.[239] Indeed, practically every scene, from Roy's degenerating attempts at communicating with Ronnie, to the assemblage of bewildered scientists awaiting the entities' arrival, is convoluted by children arguing, a television playing, radio chatter, foreign languages, or various overlapping concurrent conversations. This recurrent theme of hindered communication provides consistent commentary to the bewilderment Roy endures as a result of his experience. Indeed, the vision he has that he cannot understand can only properly be comprehended by his dislocation from familiarity to a space conducive for reception of and cooperation with the entities' summoning.

Accordingly, therefore, the few instances of proper communication are facilitated by the entities, alluding to Baughman's F262, "Fairies make music,"[240] as well as Lady Wilde's assertion that "music and poetry are fairy gifts."[241] Towards the film's conclusion, in the notably liminal space of Devils Tower, it is fitting that, both the musical exchange between the mothership and the musician at the keyboard, and the entity's Kodály hand signals[242] with Lacombe, immediately precede Roy's entrance into the mothership, and what may be assumed to be his moment of enlightenment, assimilation, and understanding.[243] It seems appropriate that the animatronic puppet that served as the entity that bade farewell at the film's conclusion was nicknamed "Puck" by cast and crew.[244]

The disturbance, and, in effect, liminality of the domestic space, too, is a central theme of the film, one not unrelated to the faerie phenomenon. Spielberg's successful infusion of folkloric elements into contemporary settings, in fact, has been applauded by critics. Citing the director's use of the familiar domestic space of middle-class sensibilities in *Close Encounters, Poltergeist* and E. T. *the Extraterrestrial,* Andrew Gordon calls Spielberg the "wizard of the suburbs, transferring tract homes into fairy-tale cottages."[245] While faeries typically inhabit rural, natural, and otherwise remote areas, there are those whose primary aim is to infiltrate, intrude, and attach themselves to domestic spaces. One of the primary characteristics of the Other, faerie and otherwise, is a potential for intrusion into perceived safety and sanctity of normative spaces, domestic, cultural, psychological, or otherwise.

The folkloric origins of the medieval epic, *Beowulf* (ca. 900), for instance, lie in ancient Germanic tales of monstrous entities' ever threatening encroachment into a civilized space. As Keala Jewell writes, though the Other seem to hail from some other place, they "seem ever pressing nearer."[246] The primary function of some fey species, in fact, appears to be intrinsically bound with specific places. William Thornber, for example, asserts that there are faeries "whose existence was once accredited by selecting for haunts certain places."[247] Baughman's entry, F480, refers to "House spirits."[248] Compelling linguistic implications of this notion are the German *bahrgeist*, "spirit of the beir"; *burhgast*, "town sprite"; and *bargheist*, "gate ghost,"[249] which indicate the boggart as an entity inhabiting, if not haunting, a particular site. There was, according to Thornber, "no village, or ancient mansion, escaping reputation of being infested by its 'Boggart.'"[250] There was scarcely an old house or hall of any considerable age in Lancashire, claim John Harlan and T. T. Wilkinson in 1873, "that cannot boast of that proud distinction over the houses of yesterday, a ghost or boggart."[251] As far back as 1691, in *The Secret Commonwealth*, Robert Kirk notes that the fey "in some barbarous Places as yet, enter Houses after all are at rest."[252] In his 1869 account of various boggart haunts, Edwin Waugh likewise writes of one site, for instance, "a lone and desolate-looking house indeed; misty and fearful even at noon-day," positioned near a gorge that went by the name "the glen of the hall of spirits."[253] Clearly the sanctity of the domestic space is in no way invulnerable to the intrusion of the Other, be it alien, faerie, or otherwise.

Roy's domestic space is increasingly disturbed, perhaps as dramatically if somewhat indirectly, by the entities' psychic presence. After his initial encounter with the craft that serves as "the herald," Roy bursts into the house, waking his sleeping family, his unrequited enthusiasm devolving into bewildered depression, and finally a conflation of visionary inspiration and evident delusion. In her 1859 article, "Our Fairy Lore," lamenting the tendency of science and practicality to erode man's fascination with mysteries, Mrs. Feitchte asserts that "the imaginary world will only come at the call of the dreamer or thoughtful enthusiast."[254] As though his encounter with the entities endows Roy with the capacity of wonder to which Feitchte refers, he is compelled to a consideration of initially impenetrable possibilities and concepts the intensification of which incrementally distance him, first psychically then physically, from the staid predictability of his bourgeois existence, and toward that "imaginary world." Indeed, Baughman includes D1723 "Magic power from fairy,"[255] which asserts that, should they choose to do so, the fey can bestow upon a chosen individual the gift of clairvoyance.

As is often typical of the burgeoning hero figure, initially, Roy expresses no inclination toward or aspirations of exceeding his provincial context. The entities, however, regard him otherwise. Roy's encounter is followed by several instances of precognition, envisioning Devils Tower in a handful of shaving cream, an upturned pillow, and a serving of mashed potatoes.[256] Thus, at one point, an overwhelmed Roy inquires of Lacombe, "How come I know so much?"

Beyond the threshold, the hero enters into a period of interiority, a site necessitating the self-annihilation incumbent upon him. This requires not only a dismantling of the world, but of the hero's place in it, the ruins from which is realized a reconstructed self. Such rites of passage are characterized by often severe "exercises of severance" through which the mind is dislocated in a profound way from the normative patterns, assumptions, and predispositions that must be abandoned in order to facilitate metamorphosis.[257] This marks a time fraught with danger, engagement with the dragon, or, in Roy's case, disgrace among his fellow men, where the hero encounters previously unknown depths. Only upon Roy's retreat from the world, detachment from the familiar, from the limitations of his locality and specific historical context, is he able to engage with the depersonalized, universal archetypes. This is the labyrinth, the cave, the dark forest, where ogres lie in wait.

Ultimately, his home is displaced, his wife and children abandoning him as he insinuates his vision into the home with sticks, dirt, bricks, and other yard debris through a shattered kitchen window. In a scene depicting the metaphorical death of Roy's former self, it may be of some benefit to note that, according to folkloric superstition, on the occasion of someone in the house nearing death, a window should be opened so as to permit his or her soul free passage from the house.[258] The hero's descent into the earth, what Ruth S. Noel calls "descent sequences," wherein the hero literally or figuratively descends into "the deep places of the world," are nearly always characterized by "an unreal, dreamlike quality," an experience typically accompanied by either perceptions of incredible dread, engagement with a threatening supernatural creature, or, as in Roy's case, an unforeseen achievement of great value.[259]

In regards to faerie encroachment into the domestic space, Jillian's farmhouse is the site of the entities' greatest physical disturbance.[260] Their initial visitation, while unsettling, is somewhat innocuous, as Barry's toys are animated and food is dispersed throughout the kitchen. In numerous cases, less malicious faeries merely exhibit a similar "larking propensity,"[261] drumming on or knocking about furniture, smashing pots and dishes, moving sleeping babies during the night, or removing stones or scaffolding from churches.[262] One account from a dell near Manchester called "Boggart Ho' Clough" tells of a boggart whose "invisible hand" would snatch children's bread and butter from their hands.[263] The fey were known to "upset milk pans, or move people's furniture around to suit themselves."[264] Old Red Cap, the boggart of Uppermill, was known to sit in cellars atop barrels of ale, wherefrom, upon someone entering to partake, blew out the candle.[265] W. S. Weeks reports of various incidences of "Goblin builders," such beings as witches, faeries, invisible beings, and even supernatural pigs with a penchant for disrupting the construction of buildings, particularly churches. In some cases they disassemble or reposition the masons' previous night's work, or remove the building's foundations to another site altogether.[266]

One notable aspect of the entities' first interaction with Jillian's house is its similarity to numerous accounts of fey interaction with children. The notion of woodland spirits' proclivity to lure children was common in high-medieval France and Germany, and by the early-sixteenth and mid-seventeenth centuries had been introduced into English and Scottish lore, respectively, though Ronald Hutton does note an ancient British tradition of indistinct otherworldly entities stealing children.[267] The animation of Barry's monkey, record player, toy vehicles, and other inanimate objects, are sufficient to draw his attention, while unseen to the audience, what are implied to be the entities themselves, then usher him out toward the woods. Baughman's entries, F261.5 "Fairies appear in house, offer to dance with child" and F310 "Fairies and human children,"[268] allude to a fey interest not only in interaction with, but the possible abduction of children. There are more ominous aspects to faerie interaction with the young which extend beyond mere antagonism. S. A. Caldwell notes that the boggart "delights in terrifying children,"[269] while the titular entity of Boggart-Hole was known for "frightening the poor children."[270] Tellingly, one Welsh word for faerie, *cipĕnaper,* derives from the root meaning "to snatch, to whisk away," indicating their proclivity for kidnapping. Pixies, as well as the Old English Mara, were known for nocturnal theft of sleeping children.[271] Sir Walter Scott wrote of faeries "carrying off their children, and breeding them as beings of their race."[272] That Barry alone sees the entities is somewhat notable, as one source claims that, while adults can discern its rattling around, only children can actually see the boggart.[273]

In addition to these implications of child abduction, the entities' second visitation indeed resembles fey activity of a more disquieting nature, as alluded to in Baughman's references, F473.1(g) "Spirits throw furniture and crockery about, often destructively," F473.5 "Poltergeist makes noises," F473.5(a), and "Knockings and rappings that cannot be traced."[274] In Boggart-Hole, the "unembodied troubler" of one George Cheetham's farm house was known for "scaring the maids, worrying the men, and frightening the poor children."[275] The boggart of Well Hall is said to be often heard moving around the house, "working the spinning wheels," "moving heavy pieces of furniture about," or "pulling the bed clothes off people."[276] The doors of a house near Edisford Bridge refuse to remain locked and closed.[277]

A chaotic conflation of deafening sound, disorienting light, and the seemingly supernatural disruption of the house's contents, the scene of Barry's abduction is indeed a harrowing and traumatic insinuation of apparently faerie phenomena, against which Jillian's locking the door and bolting the windows proves effective only until the bemused Barry crawls through the dog door, facilitating his abduction. While certain boggarts clearly inserted themselves into the home of their choice without impunity, there were in some cases restrictions on faerie agency. Though there is indication that the entities appear to Barry within the house in the first instance, their apparent inability to enter Jillian's home to abduct her son seems to allude to folkloric superstitions that certain beings could not enter a home without an invitation.[278]

III

Frequently, encounters with the fey occur in the outskirts, the rural, and the isolated, as the Other typically inhabits the borders of civilized space, such as the moors, forests and environs just beyond the community.[279] As one theory indicates, driven out by a heartier human population, faerie beings retreated to liminal areas, and most often occupy forests, hedgerows, solitary trees, bushes, mountains, moors, and swamplands, or interstitial sites like graveyards and crossroads, their homes typically subterranean, within mounds, caves, and the like.[280]

Indeed, "few sombre or out-of-the-way places, retired nooks and corners, or sequestered by-paths, escaped the reputation of being haunted."[281] Trolls and gnomes, too, inhabited the woods, caves, and mountains beyond the civilized space.[282] Fear of the dead was embodied in elves, beings who inhabited the hills, barrows, and other burial sites. The dead of All Hallows were reported to come "over the wild mosses, and marshes, and waste inland, and down the lonely roads from the far-off towns, and most of all, in from the washing waters of the sea beneath the cliffs beyond the church."[283] As James McKay notes, "this brow, that pool, yonder thick plantation, were all reputed to be haunted by boggarts."[284] In their description of Boggart Hole Clough, Harlan and Wilkinson state that it is "in yonder dark corner, and beneath the projecting mossy stone, where the dusky sullen cave yawns" that the boggart is suspected to lurk.[285] Similarly, in "The Grave of the Grislehurst Boggart" (1869), Waugh writes, "When one gets a few miles off of any of the populous towns in Lancashire, many an old wood, many a lonesome clough, many a quiet stream and ancient building, is the reputed haunt of some local sprite, or 'boggart,' or is enveloped in an atmosphere of dread by the superstitions of the neighborhood," and "particularly so in hilly parts," and furthermore "frequently the case in retired vales and nooks lying between the towns," where still survive "their ancient characteristics," as being "the resort of fairies, or 'feeorin.'"[286] The belief in the fey dwelling within dark, remote spaces was not limited merely to lore, but animated everyday behaviors. In his 1869 *Sketches of Lancashire Life and Localities*, Edwin Waugh relays an account of a fellow named Robin, of the Peancock Farm, who told of his habit "to advance his lantern and let it shine a minute or two into the 'shippon'" prior to entering, "due to the presence of 'feeorin' within." Such beings, Robin asserts, would then flee, as they "couldn't bide leet."[287]

Such in-between areas indicate the intersection of the peopled and unpeopled regions, of the known, unknown, and unknowable. In Jason Marc Harris' estimation, these geographically removed areas provide "topographical tensions," in that they are "reminiscent of folk legends," where supernatural beings dwell in the space "between wild and civilized locales."[288] Jarlath Killeen likewise discusses the "hesitation" and "quali-fication" proposed by narratives that are "populated by liminal creatures and dramatize liminal states of identity."[289] Indeed, there often seems in faerie stories a requisite either temporal or spatial severance from the rel-ative normalcy of day-to-day experience, a detachment from materialist expectations and rational criteria for factual probability that allows for the introduction of the anomalous.[290]

Spatial liminality, therefore, also figures prominently in Close Encoun-ters, where it is exclusively in isolated areas that the entities make their presence known. Baughman's inclusion of F235.2 "Fairies visible only at certain times [Note: fairies are invisible at all times unless special condi-tions prevail]"[291] suggests that their appearance generally occurs with their approval. *Close Encounter's* opening scene, in the Sonoran Desert, Mexico, is a desolate landscape of disused buildings cloaked by sandstorms, re-markable only by the appearance of the missing Flight 19 planes, but otherwise foreboding and inhospitable. Here, Lacombe, Laughlin, and their entourage enter through an unhinged gate.[292] Given the boggart's appellation as *bargheist*, "gate ghost," an entity that perches upon entranc-es, it seems noteworthy that in the film's opening scene, Lacombe and company must pass through the gate to access the first instance of the entities' intrusion into human reality and its attendant assumptions and preconceptions. In Gordon's terms, the entities are "the good fairies" who "possess not science, but *magic*."[293]

The initial account of the appearance of Flight 16 harkens back to the notion that the fey have the capability, as J. E. Cirlot puts it, to cause "peo-ple, palaces, and wonderful things to appear out of thin air."[294] The site of the film's only demonstrated abduction, Jillian's farmhouse in Muncie, Indiana, is notably rural, with no apparent neighbors in the immediate vicinity. Jillian's son, Barry, ventures out into the woods in pursuit of the mysterious visitors, who seem to summon him in a manner discernable only to him, indicative of Baughman's S240(a) "Fairy gets child by trickery."[295] Newfoundland folklore similarly asserts that children lost in the woods have been led astray by the fey, and being "pixie-led" is common in British folklore.[296] After leaving his home and receiving his orders from the power plant, Roy finds himself at a railroad crossing on a lonely country road where his encounter occurs. Accordingly, Campbell notes one of the various contexts for the call is "the dark forest."[297] Not only are faeries reported to assemble at crossroads,[298] but superstition holds that such places are regarded as "an ominous location" and a likely place to encounter a ghost.[299] As fog and mist intensify around him, consulting a map, Roy exclaims, "Help! I'm lost!" a phrase of increasing resonance throughout the film.[300] Indeed, his journey to wholeness appears to require both his physical and spiritual disorientation.

Ultimately, the narrative shifts away from occupied suburban areas entirely to the evacuated and daunting environs of Devils Tower. The mothership's location above Devils Tower alludes to medieval emblems, where the mountain, an emblem of salvation, is often complemented by a topping image, including a star, lunar crescent, crown, or circle.[301] Moreover, and appropriately, however, the mothership provides a technological analogue for the fairy castle, which were said to be made of gold and silver, and ornamented with pearls, jewels, and precious stones.[302] Baughman's list includes F215.1, "Fairyland in sky" and F215.2, "Fairyland in a cloud."[303] The circular form of Devils Tower is also likened to faerie hills or forts, circular stone formations that serve either as faerie dwellings or, as in this case, portals to another world. The Irish speak of the *Siodh-Dune,* or the "Mount of Peace," which Wilde calls "a favourite resort of the fairies."[304] Baughman includes in his list of motifs F0, "Journey to otherworld" and F150, "Access to otherworld."[305] Noel refers to Faerie as "a remote, inviolable land of indescribable beauty."[306] By most accounts, the fey could easily access the human realm, while human encroachment into the faerie land was typically accidental or the result of carelessness.

While an obvious choice for an iconic visual moment of cinematic history, this imposing geographical feature also serves as a profound archetype, the culmination of Roy's journey towards individuation. On a physical level, the mountain embodies the temporal and spatial matter pilgrims must surmount "in order to divest themselves of their worldly characteristics."[307] Certainly it is here that Roy's previous existence is absolutely abandoned in exchange for what is arguably a renewed sense of self. Appropriately in a narrative where entities from elsewhere seek some form of interaction with humanity, the mountain also represents the point of contact between heaven and earth, or the relationship between different worlds. Thus, J. E. Cirlot's assertion that the mountain's shape transposes "the notion of ascent to the realm of the spirit."[308] Representing the goal of the pilgrimage and the aspiration of spiritual ascent, as Jung argues, the mountain likewise bears "the psychological meaning of the self."[309] Similarly, Ania Teillard links the mountain with the interior loftiness of the spirit.[310] Western tradition in regards to the mountain includes the Grail legend, where Montsalvat, or "the mountain of salvation," like the center of the labyrinth, is notably "always inaccessible or difficult to find."[311] Jung writes of the folkloric young swineherd whose climbing the world-tree, "symbolizes the ascent of consciousness, rising from almost bestial regions to a lofty perch with a broad outlook."[312] Upon this ascent, having left the animal world and risen into "the upper world of light," the swineherd discerns the captive anima, who "symbolizes the ascent of consciousness."[313]

The path of spiritual fulfilment, in Jung's estimation, is "ambiguous, questionable, dark, presaging danger, and haphazard adventure," and "a razor-edged path" that is "without assurance and without sanction."[314] Certainly, the quest toward the summit is never easy. In "Queen Bee, or Little Tom," for instance, the protagonist is warned to remain quick and steady, lest he fall prey to the witches there that lasso those who attempt to attain the magic fountain there. In *Close Encounters*, Larry Butler, a third individual called to the site, escapes with Roy and Jillian in an attempt to ascend Devils Tower. Unable to keep this pace, however, he is overcome by the sleeping gas employed by the military to prevent their ascent. His collapse and the subsequent image of his inert body on the mountainside provides an image of the death of the former self, the former incarnation which Roy must leave behind in the process of ascent.

Consideration of mountain symbolism may also include that of the wise old man archetype, for it is often that this mysterious source of wisdom is engaged with only after ascension of the mountain upon which he often presides. Like the center of the labyrinth, or the summit of the mountain, this archetype and the knowledge he embodies may only be obtained with great effort on the pilgrim's part. Jung notes that this figure provides "insight, understanding, good advice, determination, planning, etc."[315] which are necessary but inaccessible given the limited capacity of the pilgrim.

Often, as in Roy's case, the hero actually possesses knowledge, but lacks the wisdom to apply it. Furthermore, the wise old man speaks in riddles, or answers one question with another, initiating in the hero the ability to articulate matters himself. When asked, "What did you expect to find?" Roy answers, "An answer. That's not crazy, is it?" Fittingly, when Roy is interviewed by Lacombe and translator, the former speaks in French that must be interpreted. This is compounded by Roy's four times repeated and notably unanswered question, "Who are you people?"

The wise old man is embodied in various forms of authority such as that occupied by Lacombe, who has achieved the individuation for which the pilgrim strives.[316] His position on the mountain prior to Roy's ascent positions him as the wise old man figure. Though a source of wisdom, of course, part of the wise old man's wisdom is his acknowledgement that one's journey develops but never really ends. Therefore, open to the implications of the situation around him, and thus less distressed than the initiate Roy, Lacombe occupies the role of the wiser elder, enthusiastically, but calmly, pursuing a new, arguably more enlightened paradigm to which only the individuated may be more calmly accepting.[317] Only when gaining the mountain top and consulting with the wise old man, is the pilgrim, in this instance Roy, permitted the full vision of the entities and his subsequent entrance into their enchanted space. Lacombe's interaction with Roy is notably almost completely silent, for it is when the hero "beholds the face of the father,"[318] that there is what Campbell calls atonement and the former receives the blessing of the latter.

The physical ascent of the mountain, of course, represents the deeper journey, psychological, spiritual, or otherwise, the aspiration of which is attainment of at least enlightenment or higher consciousness, if not dramatic transformation. The fulfillment of this endeavor, however, necessitates the union of the masculine animus with the feminine anima, the conflation, respectively, of male conviction, assertion, and action with sensitivity, intuition, and artistic expression.

Thus, Roy's ascent of Devils Tower is necessarily accompanied by the artist, Jillian, whose shared experience with the entities facilitates their union, and Roy's eventual individuation. The hero's encounter with the feminine, who represents "the totality of what can be known," the mother, bearer of children, creative artist.[319] While "she can never be greater than himself," she nevertheless "can always promise more than he is yet capable of comprehending."[320] While she is just as baffled as Roy, their shared experience and her attentiveness and relatability propose the possible fulfillment of his journey.[321]

IV

In that they "illuminate the way" and in that "their 'magic' still attracts us," we sense that the lore of faeries, asserts Jack Zipes, "can help us reach our destiny."[322] Zipes further argues that the writer of a faerie story is "a seer of the future,"[323] in that there is within such narratives the aspiration to either romantic individual development or a utopian societal vision. There is, however, in Stephen Spielberg's *Close Encounters of the Third Kind* a kind of nested historicity, appealing to the most essential elements of the human experience, despite its futuristic implications of a new millennial paradigmatic shift. If Roy Neary's journey is one from a restricting, suffocating, and uninspiring life of dead ends to a new, presumably off-world stage shared with non-human entities, it is also, on a deeper, arguably more accessible level, an archetypal quest from inhibited spiritual stasis to a redefining realization of a higher self. It is the hope that the present author's exploratory, if necessarily concise, investigation of Spielberg's film, contributes in some appreciable manner to discerning what Clyde Kluckhohn calls "detectible trends"[324] within various genres, or what Claude Lévi-Strauss refers to as "mythical thought"[325] within even the most contemporary of narratives. Furthermore, as seems inarguably demonstrable, that faerie beings and the lore that preserves them and their characteristic behaviors and attributes, by no means disappeared in the lapse of time since our ancestors accounted of them in the most ancient of orally transmitted stories. Rather, as much a part of our modern landscape as the foundational psychic elements of which humanity is comprised, and even if clothed in the trappings of our modern perception, the 'feeorin' nevertheless "seem ever pressing nearer."

Bibliography

Achen, S.T. (1978). *Symbols Around Us*. New York, NY: Van Nostrand Reinhold Company.

Bascom, W.R. (1965). Four functions of folklore. In A. Dundes (Ed.), *The Study of Folklore* (pp. 279-298). Englewood Cliffs, NJ: Prentice-Hall, Inc.

Baughman, E.W. (1966). *Type and Motif-index of the Folktales of England and North America*. The Hague, NL: Mouton & Co.

Bildhauer, B. and Mills, R. (2003). Conceptualizing the Monstrous. In B. Bildhauer and R. Mills (Eds.), *The Monstrous Middle Ages* (pp. 1-27). Toronto, CA: University of Toronto Press.

Briggs, J. (1977). *Night Visitors: The Rise and Fall of the English Ghost Story*. London, UK: Faber.

Campbell, J. (1949). *The Hero with a Thousand Faces*. 3rd ed. (2008). Novato, CA: New World Library.

Clarke, K.W. (1963). *Introducing Folklore*. New York, NY: Holt, Rinehart, and Winston, Inc.

Cirlot, J. E. (1962). *A Dictionary of Symbols*. (J. Sage, Trans.). New York, NY: Philosophical Library.

Danielson, L. (July 1979). Folklore and Film: Some Thought on Baughman Z500-599. *Western Folklore* 38(3), pp. 209-219.

English, L.E.F. (1955). *Historic Newfoundland*. St. John's, Newfoundland: Newfoundland Tourist Development Division.

Enright, D. J., ed. (1994). *The Oxford Book of the Supernatural*. London and New York: Oxford University Press.

Farmer, S.B. (July-September 1894). Folklore of Marblehead, Mass. *Journal of American Folklore* 7(26), pp. 252-253.

Feitchte, Mrs. (March 1859). Our Fairy Lore. *Cosmopolitan Art Journal 3*(2), p. 59.

Georges, R.A. & Jones, M.O. (1995). *Folkloristics: An introduction*. Bloomington and Indianapolis, IN: Indiana University Press.

Gordon, A. (November 1983). 'E.T' as Fairy Tale. *Science Fiction Studies 10*(3), pp. 298-305.

Guenon, R. (1950). *Le Roi du monde*. Paris, FR: Les Editions Traditionnelles.

Hand, W.D. (1981). European Fairy Lore in the New World. *Folklore 92*(2), pp. 141-148.

Hardwick, C. (1872). *Traditions, Superstitions, and Folklore (Chiefly Lancashire and the North of England)*. Manchester, UK: Ireland & Co.

Harlan, J. & Wilkinson, T. T. (1873). *Lancashire Legends, Traditions, Pageants, Sports, Etc*. London, UK: George Routledge and Sons.

Harris, J.M. (2008). *Folklore and the Fantastic in Nineteenth-Century British Fiction.* Burlington, VT: Ashgate.

Hume, R. (March 1969). Gothic versus Romantic: A Revaluation of the Gothic Novel. *PMLA 84*(2), pp. 282-290.

Hutton, R. (December 2014). The Making of the Early Modern British Fairy Tradition. *The Historical Journal 57*(4), pp. 1135-1156.

Jewell, K. (2001). Introduction: Monsters and Discourse on the Human. In K. Jewell (Ed.), *Monsters and the Italian Imagination* (pp. 9-24). Detroit, MI: Wayne State.

Jones, E. (1965). Psychoanalysis and folklore. In A. Dundes (Ed.), *The Study of Folklore* (pp. 88-102). Englewood Cliffs, NJ: Prentice-Hall, Inc.

Jung, C.G. (1959). *The Archetypes and the Collective Unconscious.* (R. F. C. Hull, Trans.). Princeton, NJ: Princeton University Press, 1990.

Kardiner, A. (1939). *The Individual and His Society.* New York (NY): Columbia University Press.

Killeen, J. (2014).Introduction: Remembering Bram Stoker. In J. Killeen (Ed.), *Bram Stoker: Centenary Essays* (pp. 15-36). Dublin, IE: Four Courts Press.

Kirk, R. (1691). *The Secret Commonwealth of Elves, Fauns, and Fairies.* London, UK: David Nutt (1893).

Kluckhohn, C. (1965). Recurrent Themes in Myths and Mythmaking. In A. Dundes (Ed.), *The Study of Folklore* (pp. 158-168). Englewood Cliffs, NJ: Prentice-Hall, Inc.

La Barre, W. (1948). Folklore and psychology. *Journal of American Folklore* 61(242), pp. 382-390.

Lévi-Strauss, C. (1955). The Structural Study of Myth. *Journal of American Folklore 68*(270), pp. 428-445.

Métraux, A. (1946). The ethnographic approach. *Journal of American Folklore 59*, pp. 504-506.

Musgrave, W.R. (1999). The Politics of the Monstrous in Burke and Kant. In P.G. Platt (Ed.), *Wonders, Marvels, and Monsters in Early Modern Culture* (pp. 271-293). Newark, DE: University of Delaware Press.

Nicholson, H. (Autumn 1998). Postmodern Fairies. *History Workshop Journal 46*, pp. 205-212.

Noel, R.S. (1978). *The Mythology of Middle Earth.* Boston, MA: Houghton Mifflin Company.

Pickering, D. (1995). *Dictionary of Superstitions*. London, UK: Cassell.

Platt, P.G. (1999). Introduction. In P.G. Platt (Ed.), *Wonders, Marvels, and Monsters in Early Modern Culture* (pp. 15-23). Newark, DE: University of Delaware Press.

Prichard, J.C. (1813). *Researches into the Physical History of Mankind*. 4th ed. (1998), 4 vols. London, UK: Sherwood, Gilbert, and Piper, pp. 1837-1841.

Taylor, J.B. & Shuttleworth, S. (Eds.) (1998). *Embodied Selves: An Anthology of Psychological Texts, 1830-1890*. Oxford, UK: Clarendon Press, pp. 352-56.

Rogers, W.S. (Spring 1953). Irish Lore Collected in Schenectady. *New York Folklore Quarterly 8*(1), pp. 20-30.

Saunders, C. (2010). *Magic and the Supernatural in Medieval English Romance*. Cambridge, UK: Cambridge University Press.

Scott, W. (1831). *Letters on Witchcraft and Demonology*. 2nd ed. London, UK: John Murray.

Sedgwich, P. (1974). *Mythological Creatures*. New York, NY: Holt, Rinehart, and Winston.

Spencer, K.L. (Spring 1992). Purity and Danger: Dracula, the Urban Gothic, and the Late Victorian Degeneracy Crisis. *ELH 59*(1), pp. 197-225.

Tatar, M. (Winter 2010). Why Fairy Tales Matter: The Performative and the Transformative. *Western Folklore 69*(1), pp. 55-64.

Teillard, A. (1951). *Il Simbolismo del Sogni*. Milan, IT: Fratelli Bocca.

Thornber, W. (1837). *An Historical and Descriptive Account of Blackpool and Its Neighborhood*. Poulton, UK: Smith.

Vrettos, A. (2002). *Victorian Psychology*. In P. Brantlinger & W.B. Thesing (Eds.), *A Companion to the Victorian Novel* (pp. 67-83). Oxford, UK: Blackwell.

Waugh, E. (1869). *Sketches of Lancashire Life and Localities*. London, UK: Simpkin, Marshall, & Co.

Weeks, W. S. (1888). *Some Lancashire Legends. Transactions of the Burley Literary & Scientific Club 6*, pp. 25-35.

Wilde, F.S. (1887). *Ancient Legends, Mystic Charms & Superstitions of Ireland with Sketches of the Irish Past*. London, UK: Chatto & Windus (1902).

Williams, N. (1997). *The Semantics of the Word 'Fairy'*. In P. Narvaez (Ed.), *The Good People* (pp. 457-478). Lexington, KY: University Press of Kentucky.

Wells, H.G. (1898). *War of the Worlds*. Leipzig, DE: Bernhard Tauchnitz.

Woods, B.A. (July 1958). *The Norwegian Devil in North Dakota. Western Folklore* 17(3), pp. 196-198.

Yeats, W.B. (1888). *Fairy and Folk Tales of the Irish Peasantry. London, UK: Walter Scott.*

Zipes, J. (1979). *Breaking the Magic Spell: Radical Theories of Folk and Fairy Tales.* Austin, TX: University of Texas Press.

Scary Fairies: Bogeymen of Yore

Allison Jornlin

I n our modern world, we are largely detached from the dark primordial forests of our collective pasts. An elevated perspective, from bright, rarefied, technological peaks, has lifted us from the foggy bogs and misty hollows of history, or so it usually appears. In reality, we are just a heartbeat from the smallest things that can still drag us screaming back to earth. It is that realization, lingering in the liminal spaces, barely in view, that incites such profound horror. Filmmakers play on these fears. Many of us tune into and feel such instinctive reactions triggered when horror movies grab us in the deepest, most visceral way. It's as if bogeymen from the ancient past still find a way to seize us, or at least capture our imaginations.

Trypophobia, the so-called fear of holes, is one contemporary example of an ancient dread that still grips many today. Merely observing clusters of small holes, like those presented in a honeycomb or the bumps of a skin rash, arouses extreme revulsion. Some with trypophobia even recoil from Swiss cheese and sourdough bread with fear and loathing. Holey moley!

Psychologists acknowledge that this overactive disgust response ('trypophobia' is an unofficial name, as it is not classified as a true phobia) may originate with some deep-seated ancestral memory of dangerous creepy-crawlies emerging from similar-looking holes or, even more likely, exposure to disfiguring diseases, both perhaps common in prehistoric environments. Such revulsion is not uncommon and may have protected our ancestors from infection. According to a 2020 article about the phenomenon in *New Scientist*:

> Many of the most unpleasant diseases—leprosy, smallpox and typhus among them—produce circular shapes on the skin or irregular clusters

of pustules. It makes sense that early humans would have benefited if they avoided people with those marks.

Innate reactions like this one and *haemophobia*, fear of the sight of blood, may be evolutionary safeguards. So, perhaps, other visceral responses harken back to a time in human development when such reflexes were a matter of survival. Some of these powerful cues, easily stimulated by horror movie imagery, may represent instinctual responses that are still deeply engrained. Although supernatural beings including the fae are thought to dwell underground in many traditions, and no one knows for sure what crawled out of those primeval holes that gave us such a scare, trypophobia is only indirectly related. The holes presented by humanity's concealed fears are metaphorically subterranean. They lie just below the surface of our waking consciousness. If we dig a little deeper, we may find their roots. My point is to suggest that we look a little closer at such quizzical, instinctual fears to see what forgotten truths they may reveal. This is also our opportunity to descend into mysterious rabbit holes of such inquiry!

THREATS OF THE BOGEYMEN

Over the centuries and across cultures, certain fears persist, remain potent, and may not be entirely imaginary. What follows is an analysis of the fear provoked by the invisible, elemental forces of nature and the suspicion that 'hidden people' exist among us. Is this fear still reflected in culture? Is there some evidence of an occult ecosystem that still occasionally interacts with humanity? Do fairies and elves actually exist? Even in these skeptical times, many modern Irish, Icelandic, and other citizens cannot bring themselves to totally disavow this belief… If they are real, can these beings reach out and touch us?

In the Icelandic sagas, one such hidden creature is the *troll*. However, unlike today where we have a well-defined image of the troll as a huge, daft, misshapen monster, to the Vikings it was an open, umbrella term. The Online Etymology Dictionary notes that troll:

> … seems to have been a general supernatural word, such as Swedish *trolla* "to charm, bewitch;" Old Norse *trolldomr* "witchcraft"… The old sagas tell of the troll-bull, a supernatural being in the form of a bull, as well as boar-trolls. There were troll-maidens, troll-wives, and troll-women; the trollman, a magician or wizard….

To a Viking, a troll was anything sufficiently otherworldly and threatening. A troll could be a ghost or a witch or some other supernatural aberration. The purpose of such tales, according Dr. William R. Short, an expert on Viking lore, was to record such peculiarities for posterity. In *The Troll Inside You: Paranormal Activity in the Medieval North*, author Ármann Jakobsson imparts a relevant message for my readers as well:

> The first thing readers… must do is refrain from imagining that they know precisely what a troll is. While in the nineteenth century Icelandic trolls were taxonomized, an endeavor worth returning to below, in a thirteenth-century narrative a troll has no such clear identity, not even within the human psyche. Trolls do not constitute a race or a species. The first step when considering the troll sighted on the ridge is to avoid the idea of a clearly demarcated group. Thirteenth- and fourteenth-century textual evidence from Iceland makes it clear that a witch is a troll but so also is a ghost or vampire, a demon, a possessed animal, and a mountain dweller. The evidence does not suggest that any one of these groups held primary claim on the term… The troll is danger; what is not dangerous and feared cannot be a troll… Danger turns the world on its head. Like death it intrudes into the established order, snatches all imagined control from the humans who have set themselves up to be the protagonists of their own lives. Danger becomes an abyss, into which one can feel themself helplessly falling. As an image of danger, the troll cannot be but terrible. Its very appearance is ominous… there is no shortage of attacking trolls in medieval Icelandic literature… [these stories are] not about the troll but about the men who encounter it… There is here an abundance of anthropomorphic otherness… signifying the impossibility of total separation between us and them; what we are faced with instead is a shared uncanny relationship… Uncanny otherness is perhaps the most potent of human threats, an attack on all notions of humanity and on order itself.

Like trolls, fairies (no matter how you refer to them—fairy' or 'faerie' or 'fair folk' or 'fay' or 'fae' or 'elves' or 'elementals') are non-human intelligences, the ultimate Other. Like *homo sapiens*, they have the capacity to be kind or monstrous. There are as many different names for these truly unknowable creatures as there are cultures who recognize their presence. The fae are legion, as anyone who has ever browsed through a fairy dictionary knows. There are supposedly many different varieties and tribes, but all this terminology, accumulated over centuries, has failed to bring us any closer to the essence of what these creatures actually are. To complicate matters, the pervasive imagery we've grown up with, of tiny, winged Polly-Purehearts, bears little resemblance to the complicated nature spirits of ancient legend.

In modern films, the purpose of similar tales involving the interactions between humans and other, stranger forms of life is arguably solely to thrill an audience. But what is the origin of this thrill? Perhaps in our attempt to avoid confronting the possibility that we are the only intelligent life in our world, we invented other intelligences and personified the forces of nature. Nature's tendency to give generously, but then take brutally, does bear a certain resemblance to the fairies of folklore, who bless your harvest one day and then blind your daughter the next.

However—in the Ireland of the near-past at least—interactions with the fairy realm appeared to be so commonplace in the country that they went beyond casual imaginings, impacting daily life, including such serious undertakings as building practices. The placement of homes and other buildings was determined by a site's relation to fairy forts and fairy thorn trees, storied sanctuaries of the fae. Great care was taken to avoid these areas and to prevent the obstruction of the invisible fairy paths that allegedly connect them. Oversights still occurred, of course, but sometimes tragedy could be averted by demolishing the offending part of the home. At other times, such diplomacy failed, resulting in ill-fated outcomes for the inhabitants of such structures. Poltergeist activity, illness, bad luck, and even death were blamed on such incursions into fairy territory. As a result, offending corners were cut from homes by stone masons, additions were demolished, and whole properties were abandoned. According to Paul Devereux, author of *Fairy Paths & Spirit Roads*, "There are numerous homes in the western counties of Ireland with their corners modified, supposedly in order to correct problems resulting from encroachments onto fairy paths." In modern times, even the spectacular failure of the DeLorean Motor Company has been attributed to the destruction of a fairy tree when the factory was being built.

Similar inhibitions still affect road construction and other projects in Ireland as well as additional places in the world. For those who live closest to territorial supernatural beings, it may well be that all the extra hassle involved in careful site selection is preferable to the extreme consequences for meddling in the fairy domain. Perhaps such cases are more analogous to Hollywood's most malignant fantasies than we'd like to admit.

Over the ages, fairies have provided a convenient scapegoat. They have been blamed for everything from devastating tragedies like Ireland's deadly potato famine to the most common and minor irritations like tangled hair and the everyday enigma of that accumulating pile of unmatched socks. Of course, movies only portray the most sensational examples of fairy treachery, their most vicious attacks, and heinous acts.

The belief in such powerful, invisible intelligences, which at first glance may seem scarce today, was once prevalent in most cultures around the world. The conviction that fairies could inflict illness was so deep in Europe that several common words to describe these frightful maladies still hide in plain sight in the English language. However, we have long since forgotten the supernatural heritage of these common terms.

The word 'blast,' meaning a gust of wind, shares its origins with the word 'blister.' Blister derives from a Teutonic variation meaning 'breath' or 'spirit.' It seems an odd association until you realize that many Europeans believed that fairies travelled in the wind and would sometimes afflict unsuspecting, unlucky bystanders with blisters, boils, sores, or bruises.

In another example, we use the word 'stroke' to describe a paralytic seizure accompanying a blood obstruction in the brain. According to Patricia Monaghan's *The Encyclopedia of Celtic Mythology and Folklore*, the term is originally derived from 'fairy stroke,' meaning a sudden, severe paralysis and insensibility brought on by the malevolent touch of a fairy. Much earlier, such sanction by the fairies was known in Gaelic as *poic sidhe*, the fairy poke, and was dealt in response to the cutting down of certain trees, cultivation over fairy rings, or other forms of trespass.

Countless cultures, including Inuits on the top of the world, warn about paralysis resulting from contact with such otherworldly foes. In one story, an elder related how, as a child, he was stricken with paralysis on one side of his body after accidentally attracting the attention of a nature spirit. His grandfather was compelled to enlist the help of a spiritual practitioner to save his life.

Monaghan asserts:

> The full or partial paralysis that we now know to be caused by an interruption of blood to the brain or a clot therein was believed, in the past, to be punishment for offending the fairies, who would "stroke" the offender in punishment.

Later, when Christianity challenged the Fairy Faith, the term was re-framed as 'the stroke of God's hand.' The malignant effect of the fairy's touch is also evidenced in the phrases 'touched in the head' and 'away with the fairies,' each employed to denote someone gone insane, a common side-effect of interacting too much with these unfathomable beings.

THE HALLOW: THE FAIRY BLAST

In the 2015 horror film *The Hallow*, a young family who has recently re-located to a new forest home is afflicted by a grotesque den of hostile fairies in yet another painful and gruesome way. Adam and Claire Hitchens, along with their baby Finn, take up residence deep in an Irish forest recently sold for development. The sickly-looking fairy creatures occupying this woodland, one of the last in Ireland, infect human invaders with a fictional strain of the *Cordyceps* fungus.

Adam, a conservationist, stumbles upon this discovery only to succumb to it later in the movie. Like the actual *Ophiocordyceps unilateralis*, which spectacularly disfigures afflicted ants, a human infected by the movie fungus erupts with hideous tendrils of fungal growth. In reality, *Cordyceps* affects the behavior of infected ants, causing them to move to areas conducive to fungus growth, earning them the nickname 'zombie ants' in popular culture.

After one of the mutated, infant-like creatures injects its fungus into Adam's eye with a needle-like finger, he begins his horrific metamorphosis. However, even though infected humans in the film presumably transform into fairy creatures, the fungus's mind-control seems ill-equipped to conquer Adam's will. (Perhaps the fungus only incapacitates adults, but transforms children?) His changes seem largely cosmetic as extra fungal appendages burst from his head and shoulders.

Although Adam's transformation strongly resembles the mutant *Cordyceps* enemies in the videogame (and HBO series) *The Last of Us*, this film is not actually about fungal zombies. Instead, it's a slapdash amalgam of fairy tropes: lethal fairy touches, changelings (where fairies replace stolen, healthy, human children with sickly facsimiles), and the use of iron to deter the fae all play a role in the film.

According to Richard Sugg's *Fairies: A Dangerous History*, the households of true fairy believers featured "routine precautions aimed to prevent child theft… a very common one involved putting fire tongs over a cradle, because of the fairies' well-known antipathy to iron." In the *Encyclopedia of Wicca & Witchcraft* by Raven Grimassi, the author reiterates this belief and provides a possible explanation:

> Some folklorists feel that this legend is symbolic of the use of iron to plow fields and fell trees, all of which addressed the power of humans to assault Nature. To the fairies iron was an abomination.

There is also a compelling prop in *The Hallow*, a dusty old book given to the family as a warning by a foreboding neighbor. Filled with creepy illustrations and cryptic Gaelic text, the book somehow fails to make a significant impression, and the family clearly doesn't get the message. However, the reference is fun for fairy fans, as there is an actual ancient tome called *The Book of Invasions*.

The Book of Invasions, or *Leabhar Gabhála*, is supposedly an ancient history of Ireland and tells of the god-like inhabitants called the *Tuatha Dé Danann*, who were eventually conquered by the ancestors of the present-day Irish. The defeated race surrendered the world above and disappeared into the underworld, becoming the fairies. The notion that fairy tales represent folk memories of an actual population of people displaced by conquerors in early Ireland still proliferates in popular culture. This idea appears to have originated as early as 1894 with a professor of John Rhys named A. C. Haddon, whom he credits in his seminal *Celtic Folklore*, published in 1901. This still-popular, scientific-sounding explanation for the persistence of the belief in fairies speculates that fairy sagas grew from the Iron Age interpretation of events in prehistory. Similar justifications are also bandied about to explain away tales of Menehune in Hawaii and even Orang Pendek in Indonesia.

Unfortunately, the movie prop for *The Hallow* is *The Book of Invasions* in name only, the presented text and illustrations in the film have nothing whatsoever to do with the actual text or true historical events. The quote opening the film does not actually appear in the real *Leabhar Gabhála*: "Hallow be their name, and blessed be their claim. If you who trespass put down roots, then Hallow be your name." This fictional epigraph only serves to foreshadow Adam's infection.

Although *The Hallow*'s sinister fairy creatures are clearly bent on stealing children and babies, their motivations are not entirely clear. Cora, a little girl kidnapped by the fairies, is transformed into one herself. However, when little Finn is taken and replaced with a look-alike, the protagonist's baby is unharmed and remains uninfected, ultimately allowing him to be saved. This clouds the motivation of our little antagonists, but it's a plot hole that allows the movie a somewhat-happy ending.

While *The Hallow* explores the changeling narrative for horrific effect, perhaps a more thoughtful treatment of the fae's possible motives can be found in *Border*. This 2018 Swedish fantasy film concerns the realistic struggles of a troll couple dealing with the aftereffects of humanity's prejudice and cruelty. In the mythos of this movie, set in modern times, a troll transforms an unfertilized troll embryo into the likeness of a human child, switching it with a baby for revenge and financial gain. The changeling exchange ultimately ends with the sale of the baby to human sex traffickers. The character Vore explains his actions thus: "Humans are parasites that use everything on earth for their own amusement. Even their own offspring. The entire human race is a disease...."

The Hallow, though, finds novel ways for its fairies to infect humans. This reflects the surprising methods fairies allegedly harmed humans with in traditional folklore. The deformities that twist Adam's body in the film, at least in spirit, echo the truly alien nature of fairy afflictions of old. The destructive winds of the aforementioned 'fairy blast' inflicted sudden, severe pain and horrendous carbuncles, swellings filled with nonsensical items including thorns, moss, rags, and bits of pottery. One of the most unusual examples, described in a study of fairy blasts by Barbara Rieti, was filled with extraordinary lengths of string, which piled upon the floor as the sore was let. The victim's wound required draining of all the pus and removal of all the foreign objects before healing could begin.

Although fairies often provided convenient scapegoats for all the world's ills—and the fae arguably aren't all bad—their first recorded appearance in literature does not portray them in the best light. According to the *Encyclopedia of Wicca & Witchcraft*, "the first mention of fairies appears in the Anglo-Saxon Chronicles" circa 800 A.D. The entry describes charms used against 'elf-shot,' a condition similar to the 'fairy stroke.' In this method of affliction, fairies or elves or some such supernatural entity attacked by firing invisible projectiles like darts or arrows at victims.

In one of his contributions to the collection *The Good People: New Fairylore Essays*, Peter Narváez recounts a story from Newfoundland related by a witness named Patrick Shea about a neighbor who took an ill-advised shortcut through fairy property:

... he kept down below in this marsh. And halfway across he got a jab in his left leg... It felt troublesome... And 'twas beginning to protrude, expand, turn black up to the knee and down to the ankle, and they got a doctor in. And the doctor cut this open and out comes little bunches of grass and little splinters of wood, out of this man's leg. There was so much damage done, they cut the man's leg off up to the knee.

Such an experience makes quite an impression, enough to swear off shortcuts through the bush for a lifetime. In the same publication, Rieti presents additional accounts from Newfoundland cataloging a wide array of mysterious foreign objects seeping from these angry boils including sticks, stones, feathers, hair, bones, rags, moths, teeth, rusty nails, porcelain shards, needles, clay, and bits of comb or knife blade.

A folk-medicine practitioner called a 'fairy doctor,' allegedly possessing special powers or influence with the fairies, was the one often ministering to these patients. It is always possible, where financial gain is involved, that some slight of hand and fraud could account for such strange contaminants, as in the similar, widely discredited practice of psychic surgery. However, such charlatanism becomes less likely when similar manifestations appear across time and cultures, are witnessed by medical doctors, and appear on X-rays. The quizzical miscellanea found deep inside some patients are even more difficult to explain than the fragmentary metal removed from alleged alien abductees.

In movies, the closest we come to the absurd and ridiculous array of foreign objects oozing from fairy blasts is the strange vomit spewing from the mouths of the possessed or bewitched. Adam's transformation in *The Hallow*, featuring hideous eruptions of fungal fruiting bodies, is consistent with the gory reality of Cordyceps infection for flies and ants, yet somehow is not as weird as the kitchen-sink-menagerie afflicting victims of demons and witches. In the 2015 film *The Witch*, magical treachery ensues when a character expels a bloody apple from his throat before dying. In the television series *Salem*, a man under the spell of the witches is forced to swallow (and later purge) a frog, a familiar spirit, which controls his behavior from within. From the notorious pea soup projectile vomit in *The Exorcist* to the vomiting of pins and nails in lesser movies about demonic possession, the devil also inspires unthinkable upchuck. The late Vatican exorcist Father Gabriele Amorth wrote in his autobiography *An Exorcist Tells His Story* about such weird items discovered in actual cases of possession, "... we find the strangest objects, such as nails, pieces of glass, small wooden dolls, knotted strings, rolled wire, cotton thread of different colors, or blood clots. These objects may be expelled naturally, often by vomiting." Cultures around the world abound with tales of bodily violation via the supernatural implantation of cursed objects.

In the far-flung culture of the Hmong, originally from the mountains of Laos, there exists an unlikely analogue to the fairy blast also implanted by a hidden, supernatural being. In traditional Hmong belief, certain people possess the power to tame an evil spirit and send it to do their bidding. According to Bruce Thowpaou Bliatout's *Hmong Sudden Unexpected Death Syndrome: A Cultural Study*, an evil spirit is sometimes sent to "implant a foreign object into a victim's body" to make them sick. Enemies may also employ these spectral creatures to suck "the victim's blood and life away".

Victims of this type of attack usually exhibit signs similar to European fairy blast symptoms, although reported hundreds of years later and thousands of miles away. The victims experience "acute and violent pain and often lose consciousness suddenly." Like the fairy doctors of European cultures, only special people, Hmong shamans, have the power to cure the patient by removing the foreign objects or stopping the evil spirit from draining away the victim's essence or life-force.

I classify these Hmong evil spirits alongside fairies because some folklorists in the United Kingdom claim fairies are actually evil spirits visiting our world at night. For many, fairies in the days of yore were god-like, mercurial bogeymen, capable of strange and unusual cruelty. In fact, the word 'bogeyman' is itself a fairy term, as detailed in *Spirits, Fairies, Gnomes, and Goblins: A Encyclopedia of the Little People* by Carol Rose:

> A class of frightening goblin or bugbear in English folklore. These spirits may be called by the following variations of the name: Bog, Bogge, Bogey, Bogy, Boguey, Bogie Beast, Bogyman, Bogeyman, Booger Man, Booman, and Budge Fur... The Bogie is also used frequently as a nursery Bogie to frighten children into good behavior. In other countries the following spirits equate with the activities of the Bogie: The German Bumann or Boggelmann, the Irish Bocan or Puca, and the Bubak of Bohemia.

Whatever name we give these ethereal fauna, anyone can see they were often up to no good.

According to the *Encyclopedia Britannica*, even the ancient South American nomadic peoples of the Gran Chaco region, occupying a four-corner area crossing Brazil, Paraguay, Bolivia, and Argentina, held similar beliefs. Just like the fairy blasts and Hmong evil spirits, these people believed terrible illnesses were often precipitated by mysterious foreign objects which had magically penetrated the body. It was the Chaco shaman's task to suck out the foreign object and effect a cure. Some of these nomadic hunters and gatherers still survive, maintaining much of their original culture in areas not yet contacted by Westerners.

A 2001 *African Oral Literature: Functions in Contemporary Contexts* essay entitled 'The Role of Oral Literature in Yoruba Herbal Medical Practice' reveals similar spiritual impurities in the bodies of the Yoruba people of West Africa. Author Albert Olawale presents additional modern evidence for cross-cultural fairy blast phenomenon, referencing the work of a Dr. Kiniffo, who has encountered some remarkable afflictions in Nigeria and Benin. He reported foreign objects that had entered the victims' bodies through some mysterious means: "This has included such objects as, for example, a needle, a dry leaf (*ewe gbigbe*), a small medicinal gourd (*ado*), a pebble, etc."

In one case, "fish hooks, cowries, and snapped-off tips of scissors" were extracted from the arm of a patient who complained of a sharp pricking sensation. However, sometimes X-rays revealed foreign objects that later "seemed to have mysteriously disappeared. The operation may even be carried out several times without the object ever being located." In other cases, surgeons may manage to locate and remove these objects, only to have them reappear later. Still other scenarios see doctors attacked by the mystical forces besieging their patients. "The only way to remove the object permanently is to ensure that the person or gods whom she has offended are appeased."

Olawale points out that Dr. Kiniffo's colleagues at the University of Ibadan agreed these purely surgical interventions could prove disastrous. "They noted that some of them have had to carry out similar operations sometimes with unfortunate consequences." Olawale further says:

> It is generally believed that such foreign objects are best expelled from the body by herbalists. This is largely because they are the only ones who understand how the objects manage to enter the body in the first place... To treat a problem such as this, the doctor first performs all the necessary divinations, and then gives the patient a decoction intended to induce vomiting. It is therefore not too strange in Yorubaland to hear

of a person who vomited toads, snakes, dry leaves, needles after taking a traditional purgative.

To Western eyes, such claims seem suspect, but in these instances doctors appear positioned to financially gain by practicing Western medicine, unhindered by traditional beliefs. The traditional herbalist, on the other hand, may benefit from flim-flam and sleight of hand as in cases of Celtic fairy doctors before the turn of the century.

Newfoundland and Western European descriptions of wounds drained of all manner of strange things—snips and snails and puppy dog tails—resemble the 'psychic surgery' shams of the 1970s. Although some accounts state that fairy doctors never took money for their craft, there was a loop-hole: they could accept gifts from their clients. Financial interests inevitably corrupt and there were some well-documented cases of fraud. There are also verified accounts of people world-over who have faked vomiting toads and so-called *bosom serpents* for attention or some vague prospect of fame and fortune.

Reports of fairy blasts aren't as frequent in recent years, at least in Western countries. However, perhaps they have just taken on other labels. An alleged medical condition called Morgellons Disease (MD) bears a striking resemblance to the fairy blast of old, as first recognized in a 2018 blog entry by Joshua Cutchin, the editor of this book. Morgellons is a terrifying affliction where the victim believes that her skin has been infected by bugs or, like in some fairy blasts, string; experiencers commonly report that their lesions spew fibrous protrusions. Morgellons is unrecognized by medicine, the general medical consensus reducing the 'string' claims to abrasions that accidentally collect fibers from clothing.

However, this verdict may be changing. A 2016 study in the *International Journal of General Medicine* reads:

> Although MD was initially considered to be a delusional disorder, recent studies have demonstrated that the dermopathy is associated with tick-borne infection, that the filaments are composed of keratin and collagen, and that they result from proliferation of keratinocytes and fibroblasts in epithelial tissue.

Although Morgellons appears to be a modern phenomenon, at least one bewitched victim in the 19th Century displayed almost identical symptoms. A sickly young man, Carl Siege of Watertown, Wisconsin, was plagued by ill-health, and was eventually granted the Catholic Rite of Exorcism by a visiting Milwaukee bishop. Before that, however, he visited a doctor, who administered powerful herbs and drawing plasters on his shoulders. When the plasters were removed they "were found to be covered with bristles of various colors, from a half to three inches in length," according to *The Indianapolis Journal* from December 3, 1869. "Strange things to come out of the young man, and no one could account for it."

From the preceding examples, it is apparent an ardent international belief persists regarding foreign objects penetrating victims by supernatural means. A multitude of tantalizing anecdotal reports, as well as medical documentation, exists. That alone warrants further study. These beliefs usually involve extraordinary and invisible fauna of unknown variety, crossing over into sorcery in some folklore. Whether the perpetrators are labelled fairies or not seems immaterial; we still have no idea what these afflictions and their causes truly are. We only know that their preferred headquarters are lonely, untamed regions of the world.

As *The Hallow* concludes, the audience is put in the uncomfortable position of nearly cheering on the loggers who have come to chop down the cursed forest. *The Hallow* may suggest that we accept the loss of our old growth forests, proposing that the concrete jungles of our present and future are preferable alternatives to the beautiful, yet deadly forests of our collective pasts. Is the loss of natural habitats a necessary evil when faced with the fae threat? The final scene reveals a legion of lumbermen clear-cutting the woodland home of the wretched fairy creatures… but of course with the fungus contaminating some of the logs being harvested, just in case the film was popular enough to warrant a sequel!

DON'T BE AFRAID OF THE DARK: FAIRY MURDER

In the horror film *Don't Be Afraid of the Dark*, the protagonists are besieged by a multitude of tiny, yet horrific goblins intent on perpetuating their existence by emerging from their subterranean hole and transforming a human into one of their own. In both the 1973 original and the 2011 remake, the greedy little demons exhibit a single-minded purpose to find someone to replenish their ranks. In 1973, the object of their desire was a young wife. In the 2011 update, their intent was revised. The creatures take a page from the long history of child abduction narratives in folklore and focus their efforts on stealing the family's child. In the meantime, the little trolls attack the handyman, an 'accident' nearly resulting in his death by a thousand cuts, eventually revealing the goblins.

Can similarly unaccountable accidents or deaths in real life be attributed to the fae? On November 17th, 1929, 33-year-old occultist Netta Fornario set out into the wilderness of Iona, an island off the western coast of Scotland. She intended to make contact with the spirit of a fairy burned at the stake centuries before by Christian monks. On that night, locals witnessed blue lights flashing in the woods near the fairy mound.

Two days later, Netta was found dead on the fairy mound. She was naked except for a long, black robe. There was no evidence of foul play, but in her hand she held a silver dagger, and around her neck she wore a large silver cross, both blackened by tarnish. Cuts covered the bottoms of her feet, but not her heels; other strange scratches were found all over her body.

Netta's friend Dion Fortune—famed magician and author of the well-known guide to protection spells, *Psychic Self Defense*—recalled that Netta was "especially interested in the Green Ray elemental contacts, too much interested for my peace of mind." 'Elemental,' of course, is a Theosophic word for a nature spirit, or fairy. In lieu of anything more specific on Netta Fornario's death certificate, the cause of death reads "exposure to the elements"... or should that read "elementals"?

Fellow ceremonial magicians, however, contended there was a more plausible explanation: Netta Fornario died from a long-distance psychic attack by an unknown sorcerer. Others thought that perhaps she was taken by the fairies. After all, she was found dead on top of a fairy mound in an area notorious for fairy lore—and this wasn't the first time someone had been discovered dead under such circumstances.

Robert Kirk, the minister, Gaelic scholar, and folklorist who authored *The Secret Commonwealth of Elves, Fauns and Fairies*—the guy who literally wrote the book on fairies!—supposedly went out the same way. The book, a compendium of folklore collected between 1691-1692, was published posthumously in 1815 by the famed historian and novelist, Sir Walter Scott.

We are told the story of Kirk's eerie demise in the introduction of the book. Kirk is said to have enjoyed wandering around the Scottish fairy hills by night. On the evening of May 14, 1692, he went out in his nightgown, and was found unconscious on Doon Hill, a fairy site near his house in Aberfoyle.

Kirk was carried to his bed by loved ones, but died soon after without regaining consciousness. His wife was pregnant, and in a well-known legend, on the night before his child was born, a kinsman named Grahame of Duchray dreamt that Kirk appeared to him. In his dream Kirk claimed he was not dead, but had been carried away to Fairyland. If his child was christened in his house, he would have the power to return, but only if at his appearance during the baptism, Grahame hurled his dagger over the apparition's head. Kirk's apparition appeared as promised, but Grahame was so surprised he failed in his task and Kirk was seen no more. To this day, others believe that Kirk's soul is imprisoned in a tall Scots pine atop Doon Hill in the village of Aberfoyle. (If you visit, ask locals to direct you to the Minister's Tree or the Fairy Tree.)

These stories are provocative, but largely unsubstantiated. More impressive are the multitude of unexplained disappearances worldwide amassed by David Paulides in his series of books entitled *Missing 411*. The well-documented frequent vanishings in Alaska are equally compelling and fantastically explained in hundreds of years of terrifying native fairy lore. However, scant records exist of the victims' experiences prior to their disappearances. Documentation of their perceptions leading up to their deaths or disappearances may provide valuable insight.

In my own community of Milwaukee, Wisconsin, I found such a case, one of a little boy possibly led to his death by supernatural forces. As reported in *The Milwaukee Sentinel* on May 22, 1920, nine-year old Raymond Naatz was a normal little boy whose demeanor had suddenly changed, as if he was already 'away with the fairies.' His mother had uncharacteristically, for the time, separated from his father who had custody of Raymond. On his last visit with her, he seemed paralyzed by fear, his eyes constantly roaming the room. She recalled that Raymond refused to speak to her except for repeating that a 'white shadow' was following him.

As Raymond's father walked him home, the boy refused to walk alongside him, instead remaining several steps behind. When they returned home, Raymond sat silently in the corner until past his bedtime. When his father demanded he go to bed, Raymond begged not to be left alone.

"All the way home that white shadow crept right along behind me," Raymond explained. "Something is going to happen, I can feel it."

Later that night, Raymond's father heard him talking in his sleep. He laughed out loud and cried, "You're only fooling me, you can't get me." When awakened, Raymond told his father, "I dreamed that I was down in the water playing with the fishes, Daddy, and it was so nice."

The following morning when his father left for work, Raymond, who had been left in the care of a neighbor, snuck off to Lake Michigan. His cap and fishing pole were later found on the lakeshore, his body near the foot of Pryor Avenue. Raymond's watch had stopped at 8:45 a.m. The timeline of events led investigators to accept that Raymond never intended to go fishing at all; in fact, upon arriving at Lake Michigan, Raymond immediately dropped his fishing pole and walked into the waters, directly to his death.

But what about strange deaths with irrefutable medical documentation? Are there murderous monsters among us as horror movies would have us believe?

Unfortunately, there may be. A fate similar to the tragedy of Raymond Naatz, as well as the ongoing mystery deaths of other young Asian men, inspired Wes Craven to pen 1984's *Nightmare on Elm Street*. From a 2014 interview with Craven in *Vulture*:

> I'd read an article in the *L.A. Times* about a family who had escaped the Killing Fields in Cambodia and managed to get to the U.S. Things were fine, and then suddenly the young son was having very disturbing nightmares. He told his parents he was afraid that if he slept, the thing chasing him would get him, so he tried to stay awake for days at a time. When he finally fell asleep, his parents thought this crisis was over. Then they heard screams in the middle of the night. By the time they got to him, he was dead. He died in the middle of a nightmare.

In *Sudden Unexpected Nocturnal Death Syndrome among Hmong Immigrants: Examining the Role of the "Nightmare,"* medical anthropologist Shelley Adler examines the mysterious deaths of Hmong men from 1977-1985. Over 130 young, healthy men were ostensibly killed by their nightmares. This fatal phenomenon gained widespread attention in 1981 when the first report about Hmong immigrant deaths was submitted to The Centers for Disease Control. The resulting press crossing his desk was just too incredible to pass up, according to Wes Craven in an interview with *Cinefantastique*.

> [It] was a series of articles in the *L.A. Times*, three small articles about men from South East Asia, who were from immigrant families and who

had died in the middle of nightmares—and the paper never correlated them, never said, 'Hey, we've had another story like this'... It struck me as such an incredibly dramatic story that I was intrigued by it for a year, at least, before I finally thought I should write something about this kind of situation.

The horrific manner of death in these all-too-real cases gives one pause. Sleeping victims suddenly cry out in their sleep and struggle, as if in distress, or under attack, before suddenly dying. Gurgling, gasping, foaming at the mouth, and labored respirations were also reported in some cases—a terrible spectacle for family members or friends to witness. It's even more alarming that the victims' culture attributed these deaths to savage creatures much more fae-like than the hideously burned form of child-molester Freddy Krueger. The media attention attracted international interest, yet this was hardly the first time such ephemeral villains had attacked unexpecting victims in the night.

According to *The Ashgate Encyclopedia of Literary and Cinematic Monsters*, "Throughout recorded history, elves have often been linked with the demons… and the similarly unpleasant figure of the mare, female supernatural beings who crush people in their sleep…." In her *Sleep Paralysis: Night-mares, Nocebos, and the Mind-Body Connection*, Shelley Adler reports on her investigation of Sudden Unexpected Nocturnal Death Syndrome (SUNDS) cases as well as other possibly-related parasomnias experienced internationally, like 'Old Hag' encounters. Normally explained away as mere 'sleep paralysis,' experiencers world-over regularly view these incidents as nocturnal attacks. By all accounts, such encounters are uniformly terrifying, perceived as a frightful presence of various descriptions that is always determined to cause the victim harm. In many cultures, fairies or other supernatural denizens are blamed.

A 2011 study in the journal *Forensic Science International* described SUNDS as follows:

> Sudden death is one of the major concerns in forensic medicine. Especially when the deceased is a young subject without significant history, the case will be of major interest to the authorities. Sudden unexplained cardiac death has been known as Pokkuri Death Syndrome (PDS) in Japan, Lai Tai in Thailand, "Bangungut" in the Philippines, "Dream Disease" in Hawaii, and "Sudden Unexpected Nocturnal Death Syndrome" among South Asian immigrants in the USA.

Although deaths like these were first recorded in 1917 by a Spanish language medical journal in the Philippines, the modern medical history of SUNDS begins with medical examiners in Hawaii who were the first to make their puzzling findings public in the English language. In March 1955, medical examiner Dr. Nils P. Larsen published 21 case histories of Filipino immigrants to Hawaii who had died from what he termed 'Sudden Unexplained Nocturnal Death Syndrome.' Newspapers, magazines, and tabloids soon ran sensational articles about 'Nightmare Death.'

Between 1946-1955, SUNDS claimed at least 107 men of Filipino blood on Oahu. Most of the victims were able-bodied workers on the sugar plantations of the era. All of the victims were male, outwardly healthy, and in the prime of their lives. Autopsies revealed no obvious cause of death.

According to an article Dr. Larsen wrote about the phenomenon for *The Saturday Evening Post* in 1955, the mysterious deaths among the Filipino population were nothing new and "medical men in the islands have tried to find what causes them, but the main result has been only to find out what does not cause them." Everything from deliberate and accidental poisoning, to parasitic infection, to simply overeating were considered and eliminated as possible causes. Furthermore, in his book *The Men with Deadly Dreams*, chronicling the 21 cases of SUNDS he studied, Larsen uncovered one survivor story: the lucky man credited friends who had awakened him with saving him from a 'little man' who was strangling him in his sleep.

The phenomenon is robustly described throughout eastern Asia. In the Philippines, SUNDS is labelled '*bangungut*' from '*bangon*' which means 'to rise' and '*ungol*' which means 'to groan' in Tagalog. The perpetrator is believed to be the *Batibat*, a corpulent female spirit who once inhabited the trees before they were cut down to make beds and houses. To enact her revenge, Batibat smothers sleeping men by sitting on their faces or chests, identical to European 'Old Hag' traditions.

In Japan, it is named Pokkuri Death Syndrome; '*Pokkuri*' translates as 'surprise.' In Thailand, it is called '*lai tai*' and is believed by the common people to be the wicked work of widow ghosts seeking men to mount in the night. Wives hoping to protect their husbands from these spirits dress them in drag before bed. (This is reminiscent of the Irish practice of dressing both boys and girls for bed in red flannel petticoats until the age of twelve. This trick to fool the fairies, who favored stealing boys in particular, was employed until at least the 1930s.) Additional Thai attempts to outwit these deadly fiends feature sexy scarecrows placed outside in the yard. Each figure is fitted with a log, shaped and painted to resemble a giant, erect penis, intended to keep widow ghosts busy and away from a village's sleeping men. This would be a comical practice if the stakes weren't so high.

According to Mak Koon Hou's *Understanding and Preventing Sudden Death: Your Life Matters*, when *lai tai* deaths suddenly surged among Thai construction workers in 1984 in Singapore, these frightened young men took similar measures:

> … they believed that "widow ghosts (*phi am*)" may be searching for a husband, and stealing their spirits. So to mislead and avoid being chosen, they painted their fingernails red and masqueraded as women by wearing women's clothes and cosmetics.

The Hmong people call the fatal phenomenon '*tsog tsuam*' and the monstrous being that attempts to suffocate sleepers the '*dab tsog.*' It is the role of one's ancestors to protect the Hmong family from these dangerous creatures and the head of the household's responsibility to thank their ancestors by providing regular offerings.

However, when the Hmong people took refuge in the United States after the Vietnam War, their ability to perform traditional duties was disrupted. It's easy to imagine the difficulty involved in sacrificing live chickens and other livestock in a cramped apartment in the middle of Minneapolis or Los Angeles. These immigrants suffered as a result. In her survey of nightmare deaths, Adler observed that all surveyed SUNDS victims were men except for one woman, who—atypically—was head of the household and, as such, assumed all responsibility and blame for not properly appeasing her ancestors.

According to John Michael Greer's *Monsters: An Investigator's Guide to Magical Beings*, "Surveys have shown that an extraordinary 50 to 60 percent of the Hmong population in America have undergone at least one [so-called] Old Hag experience of the classic variety," which involves suddenly awakening to the sensation that you are paralyzed and a malevolent presence is compressing your chest in an attempt to suffocate you. That rate of experience is "two to three times that of the general population." Among Hmong immigrants who have converted to Christianity, the rate is even higher, "72 percent, according to one study, which would give Christian Hmong the highest rate of Old Hag Experience of any known population anywhere." Thankfully, now that the Hmong have largely re-settled in rural areas and been able to resume their sacrifices and other ceremonial duties, SUNDS deaths which "had climbed steeply from 1977-1981—have decreased steadily ever since."

Meanwhile in Newfoundland—a hotbed for fairy blast afflictions as previously discussed—anthropologist David Hufford discovered abundant reports of nocturnal attacks by the 'Old Hag' as well. In his seminal 1982 study, *The Terror That Comes in the Night: An Experience-Centered Study of Supernatural Assault Traditions*, Hufford found that nearly 25% of respondents who reported attacks claimed they had never heard of the 'Old Hag' or any equivalent bedtime ordeals.

Although other anthropologists label such experiences as culture-bound, Hufford's study concluded that 'Old Hag' encounters occurred regardless of cultural influence, i.e. sufferers worldwide experienced a waking paralysis with the sensation of chest pressure and a non-human presence. Hufford refutes the popular cultural source hypothesis and argues for the experiential source hypothesis, proposing that these extraordinary experiences—rather than being *caused by* belief—may in fact be the *causes* of belief.

> Countless articles and books on supernatural belief have stated that such belief is irrational and, sometimes even by definition, not empirically grounded. I think that the present study has amply demonstrated that at least some apparently fantastic beliefs are in fact empirically grounded and that the empirical data have been dealt with rationally by those who have assimilated these experiences to their world views.

Back in the U.K., official death records uncovered from 1656-1663 in Lamplugh, Cumbria by archivist Anne Rowe attributed four deaths in the community to being "frightened to death by fairies." Who is to say this is not what is happening to victims of SUNDS? Certainly, prior to their deaths, at least some victims of SUNDS strongly believed they were under attack by supernatural foes.

In 2002, medical researchers first noticed a correlation between SUNDS and Brugada Syndrome, a condition causing heart arrhythmia. However, this connection doesn't explain why greater incidences of SUNDs appear at particular times for certain populations rather than a more regular distribution. Why do the deaths sometimes come in waves like the periodic feeding cycle of a horror movie monster? Why is the incidence of nocturnal death among females virtually non-existent?

The *U.S. National Library of Medicine Genetics Home Reference* maintains "researchers have determined that SUNDS and Brugada syndrome are the same disorder." At the time of this writing, the website also contends Brugada Syndrome may also be responsible for another nocturnal medical mystery: "This condition may explain some cases of sudden infant death syndrome (SIDS), which is a major cause of death in babies younger than one year. SIDS is characterized by sudden and unexplained death, usually during sleep."

Perhaps, in essence, fairies still carry off infants in the night. What other evidence of their continued presence might hide in plain sight?

QUATERMASS AND THE PIT: THE UNCANNY VALLEY

In the 1967 fictional film (adapted from an earlier BBC television production) *Five Million Years to Earth*—originally named *Quatermass and the Pit* in the U.K.—scientific researchers make a startling discovery. Workmen uncover an ancient proto-human skull while building near the fictional Hobbs Lane in Knightsbridge, London. After examining the remains, Paleontologist Dr. Matthew Roney believes they are evidence of the 'missing link,' an undiscovered hominid, pivotal to our understanding of human evolution. Roney reconstructs a dwarf-like humanoid he believes was a primitive man predating any other hominid at 5,000 years old. The revelation is set to rewrite prehistory when wackiness ensues.

Additional digging reveals more age-old skeletons and a large metal object, which is initially deemed an unexploded missile from World War II. Surprisingly, it's actually a prehistoric alien spaceship filled with giant locusts which turn out to be ancestral Martians! Resulting resonances from the ship and/or the ghosts of the dead Martians within awaken dormant psychic powers in some people. These new abilities and old prejudices trigger a race war, pitting regular old humans against the genetically enhanced descendants of those ancient Martians.

So how are the fairies involved? Well, it turns out fictional Hobbs Lane has a history of unexplained occurrences well before the WWII era. Continual poltergeist activity and sightings of non-human apparitions caused the near-total abandonment of houses along the street. A trip to the archives unveils documentation recording similar encounters dating back to medieval times. The strange manifestations are blamed on non-human creatures the people of the time labeled hobgoblins, a type of fairy. The grotesque faces of the Martian locusts call to their human descendants, their stubby antennas resembling the horns of the devil. The imagery is used to great effect in the television series and later the movie. The word 'hob,' as in Hobbs Lane, is even revealed as an ancient name of the Devil.

In actual fairy lore, fairies and elves often cross paths with witches and the Devil. The fae were thought to serve as familiars for witches, endowing them with magical powers and doing their masters' bidding. Even the Old English poem *Beowulf* records "elves among the monstrous races springing from Cain's murder of Abel," reinforcing this demonic identity. The Middle English hagiographies called the *South English Legendary* describes elves as angels that sided neither with Lucifer nor with God, thus banished by God to Earth rather than Hell. Lady Jane Wilde in her *Ancient Legends, Mystic Charms, and Superstitions of Ireland* maintains that for many, fairies are simply fallen angels in disguise:

> The islanders, like all the Irish, believe that the fairies are the fallen angels who were cast down by the Lord God out of heaven for their sinful pride. And some fell into the sea, and some on the dry land, and some fell deep down into hell, and the devil gives to these knowledge and power, and sends them on earth where they work much evil.

Five Million Years to Earth reveals yet another one of humanity's fears, that evil is actually somehow already within us, perhaps an inextricable part of our being, the ultimate hiding-in-plain-sight scenario. It also shows us that our labels for such liminal beings as fairies are based on our very limited view of reality, and as such can sometimes serve as formidable barriers to understanding. In the Quatermass mythos, humanity variously blames strange encounters at Hobbs Lane on ghosts, poltergeists, hobgoblins, and the Devil. Ultimately, these experiences reveal themselves to be manifestations of the same thing, Martian technology with its own alien motives.

There is a valuable takeaway here. A multitude of odd creatures have been cataloged cross-culturally throughout human history, each endowed with elaborate backstories and sometimes religious significance based on the culture recording their encounters. All we know for certain is that evidence suggests non-human intelligences exist and can do us harm.

Like trypophobia, which gives a glimpse into the prehistoric fearscape that shaped our current nightmares, there are other visceral reactions that provide clues about possible threats in our midst. Beyond the creepy crawlies that can get beneath our skin and wreak havoc, there are other dangers in our environment we seem programmed to avoid.

One mental landscape from which instinct repels us has emerged very recently, but may give us insight into humanity's curious past. 'The uncanny valley' is a term you may have heard, but like most of us you probably never questioned its usefulness. The concept was first introduced in the 1970s by Masahiro Mori, then-professor at the Tokyo Institute of Technology. In an essay for Japanese journal *Energy*, Mori wrote: "I have noticed that, in climbing toward the goal of making robots appear human, our affinity for them increases until we come to a valley, which I call the uncanny valley." Mori coined the term to describe his observation that as robots become more human-like in appearance, they become more appealing—but only up to a certain point, after which our positive reactions plummet. Like the terrible alien faces of the Martian locusts from *Five Million Years to Earth,* beholding such figures causes an involuntary descent into a feeling of strangeness, a sense of unease, and a visceral tendency towards revulsion and fear. But why should that be? Unlike the fearsome image emerging above a burning London beheld by Professor Quatermass' colleague, Dr. Roney, android visages don't transmogrify into the face of the devil. They don't represent an ancient evil awakening within us. So what about these almost—but not quite—human faces bothers us so?

Christoph Bartneck, an associate professor at the University of Canterbury in New Zealand, warns robot designers that the uncanny valley appears to be more of an uncanny cliff. "We find the likability to increase and then crash once robots become humanlike," he says. "But we have never observed them ever coming out of the valley. You fall off and that's it."

Though the uncanny valley was originally defined as a negative human reaction to encounters with humanoid robots, these uncomfortable reactions can also occur with exposure to other anthropomorphic non-human creatures like dolls, mannequins, ventriloquist dummies, wax figures, and even some animations.

"The 2019 live-action versions of the animated film *The Lion King* and the musical *Cats* brought the uncanny valley to the forefront of pop culture," according to the journal *IEEE Spectrum.* "To some fans, the photorealistic computer animations of talking lions and singing cats that mimic human movements were just creepy."

But why? If we are the only humanoids who exist, why would we harbor such strong, innate fears towards creatures who look like us, but are not human? What threat significant enough to provoke a visceral reaction akin to forementioned trypophobia exists here? If trypophobia is brought on by the fear of disease and/or poisoning, what comparable danger does the uncanny valley represent? Robots have presumably been built to help humanity and the colorful chimeras of the screen intend to merely entertain—so what is the basis for such deep-seated fear? Perhaps near-perfectly disguised interlopers in our prehistory could be to blame. Was humanity ever threatened by beings who looked human and acted human, but weren't human? Did they mimic us well enough to draw us in close enough, so they could attack?

Folkloric traditions from all points of the globe warn us of such imposters: the fairies. But certainly we've remade the modern world in our image and nearly removed all the dark and mysterious natural spaces. No longer do we need to fear the supernatural creatures that once inhabited the landscape. As the deforestation in the final scene of *The Hallow* implies, habitat loss may ultimately eliminate this threat.

THE LAST WINTER: FAIRY INTERFERENCE

In contrast, movies like the 2006 film *The Last Winter* predict environmental devastation will reach a tipping point, leading to our final judgement by these elemental forces. If such beings are as powerful as the bulk of humanity once believed, we could be in real trouble; it seems likely that, should their very existence be threatened with no means of escape other than self-defense, such god-like creatures will unleash hell, fighting tooth and nail until the very end. Humanity's drive to conquer every inch of our planet may finally flush out into the open other intelligent lifeforms once content to live on the fringes of our society or in the most remote landscapes.

In *The Last Winter*, humanity has finally encroached too far into the wilderness, and what was once hidden in ancient permafrost is revealed in the deadliest and most horrific of ways. Hoping to exploit the oil resources in Alaska's Arctic National Wildlife Refuge, an oil-drilling crew nearly succeeds in conquering one of the last pristine landscapes in the world, only to provoke resident entities in the process. Plagued by increasing equipment failure and other mishaps, the crew begins to feel as if they are cursed. However, their work continues undaunted... until members of the team begin dying mysteriously.

Gusts of wind precede each strange event, as in the aforementioned fairy blasts. Maxwell McKinder, the youngest member of the crew, perishes first, but not until after he is mysteriously spirited away in an earlier incident. His satellite phone fails to work, preventing communication with the base, and, as his team prepares to search for him, he suddenly reappears. He is physically unharmed, but psychologically transformed. His sat phone shows he has traveled an improbable 300 miles, recalling the vast distances over difficult terrain traversed by many victims featured in *Missing 411* cases. This anomaly is disregarded as simple equipment malfunction.

Gremlins, like those made popular in the 1984 film of the same name, were a tongue-in-cheek scapegoat for inexplicable equipment malfunction made popular during WWII by Royal Air Force pilots. Although there is scant evidence for the actual reality of the Gremlin phenomenon, there are modern day cases of strange accidents and equipment failure from Ireland and Iceland, and even Hawaii, that are far more compelling. Many such incidents are taken seriously enough by construction workers and local officials to delay projects, and development in areas historically considered off-limits due to the habitation of fairies and similar supernatural beings may even be rerouted.

In *The Last Winter*, station phones and email mysteriously fail, and, although returned, Maxwell seems as if he is still 'away with the fairies.' He refuses to eat and his new demeanor features a thousand-yard stare punctuated by cryptic outbursts. He pleads with environmentalist James Hoffman, recommending they abandon the project and station. The spirits of nature have apparently had enough of global warming and man's unrelenting march of progress. No one takes him seriously, even Hoffman, who has had his own suspicions about the strange nature of the events.

In response, Maxwell sneaks out into the night with a camera to get photographic proof that they are not alone, but unfortunately forgets his clothes. Barefoot and naked, he trudges into the snow out to the drill site, where the crew finds him frozen solid the next morning. Later examination of Maxwell's video footage seems to show him overcome by a spectral beast, but team leader Ed destroys the video before anyone can get a closer look. Willful disregard for the evidence will not eliminate the existential threat that has emerged from the not-so-permafrost.

Motivated by Maxwell's mysterious death and the strange behavior of the mechanic (nicknamed 'Motor'), James finally proposes they all evacuate the station. He speculates that sour gas (natural gas primarily containing hydrogen sulfide) may have leaked out as a result of the melting permafrost, provoking hallucinations and insanity in the group. The two token native Alaskan characters, Lee Means and Dawn Russell, mull over the possibility that the cause may be an evil spirit they label the 'Wendigo' (perhaps a reference to filmmaker Larry Fessenden's 2001 film about the subject).

This unfortunate allusion is incongruous since the Wendigo is, in actuality, an all-too-human monster closely associated with cowardice, frailty, and cannibalism during times of famine. The manifestations of *The Last Winter* actually seem more akin to nature spirits, as suggested by earlier caribou apparitions, the disembodied sounds of hoofbeats, and mysterious hoofprints.

A more accurate label for the spectral forms in *The Last Winter* would be the '*tuurngaq*' or '*tuurngait*,' an Inuit nature spirit. Some tuurngaq were monstrous and capable of inflicting misfortune as well as outright sabotage. A tuurngaq makes a compelling monster in season one of AMC's television program *The Terror*, although Dan Simmons, author of the novel the series is based upon, chose the alternate spelling '*tuunbaq*,' the creature is undoubtedly one of these ubiquitous non-human intelligences inhabiting the landscape of Inuit cosmology.

In *The Terror*, the tuurngaq takes a form that's almost indistinguishable from a native polar bear, but not quite. In the book its neck is a little too long, while the television adaptation presents the beast with human-like hands and feet, tantalizing clues to its otherworldly nature. Just like Hmong wild spirits performing a shaman's bidding, or European fairies utilized as witches' familiars, the tuurngaq can be controlled by an Inuit sorcerer known as '*angakkuq*.'

According to *Shamanism and Reintegrating Wrongdoers into the Community*, one of a series of books compiling the wisdom of Inuit elders, "Tuurngait will sometimes appear in human form, or in animal form, or in the form of a dog. Tuurngait are able to take on different shapes." Another elder recounts a time when he saw a strange fox climb a pole like a person, its legs wrapped around the length, and then sit at the top. When he blinked it had vanished, and it was at that moment he realized it had been no normal fox, but a *tuurngaq* in disguise.

Shape-shifting is a common ability in nature spirits, including fairies. In an interview I conducted with a man from Bhutan, he regaled me with the description of a creature the Bhutanese call the *'mirgula.'* "It looks like a rabbit," he said. "But it's not a rabbit."

In *The Last Winter*, the monsters take the form of giant beasts with caribou heads but the bodies of predators. In one of the final scenes, Ed and James are shoved off the top of a hill by unseen hands. As they struggle to rise, the strange creatures converge. James fires a flare gun into the air as a distress signal before one of the monsters spirits him away under its arm, another three moving in on Ed to tear him apart.

The Last Winter is uneven in its delivery, but remains interesting for the fairy tropes throughout—supernatural gusts of wind, mysterious travel over vast distances, unexplainable equipment malfunction, and encroaching insanity brought on by otherworldly contact. The possible involvement of hydrogen sulfide might also be a nod to the presence of sulfur in many paranormal encounters, discussed extensively in *The Brimstone Deceit* by Joshua Cutchin. The incidences of inexplicable equipment malfunction are arguably the most compelling, directly paralleling actual reports of modern-day interaction with elves and other supernatural beings.

Many populations in the world today still openly or tacitly acknowledge the existence of invisible nature spirits. Currently, there are fairy believers in our midst. Some may even be your next door neighbors.

Numerous polls from Iceland have revealed up to 80% of the population refuses to deny the existence of elves. Although a much smaller percentage claims an unequivocal belief in elves, the fact that so many hold open the possibility is as surprising as it is instructive. In an interview I recorded for YouTube, Magnus Skarphedinsson, headmaster of Reykjavik's Elf School, explains:

> 54% of Icelanders believe that elves do exist. This is normally three or four percent in other Western countries. There is a reason behind this. Everybody in Iceland knows some witnesses. Iceland is a small community, only 300,000 people... Everybody has heard dozens and hundreds of stories of people meeting elves and hidden people. A politician in Iceland who would stand up and say that elves and hidden people is nonsense [sic]... he would never be re-elected here... People know witnesses, witnesses that they trust. That is the reason why Icelanders believe so much in elves. These stories are so close to everybody here

in Iceland… I've met more than 900 Icelanders and 500 foreigners that have seen elves.

In fact, the international press continues to report interactions between elves and construction crews. As in *The Last Winter*, mysterious equipment failure often halts the unrelenting march of progress, at least in Iceland.

According to *Paranormal Encounters in Iceland 1150–1400*, edited by Ármann Jakobsson and Miriam Mayburd:

> Civilization has a tendency to spread into the space formerly claimed by the Wilderness. This usually presents no or very few problems, so long as the creatures of the Wilderness have the opportunity to organize their resettlement on their own terms. But when the proper forms are not observed, then things can turn ugly, as road builders in particular have experienced in Iceland down to the present day.

One particularly dramatic example comes from Iceland, although similar events have played out around the world. Near a city called Kópavogur, just south of the capital, there's a hill called Álfhóll, which literally means *elf hill*. The well-known yet incredible tale was retold in *The Guardian* in 2015:

> A rock known as Elfhill has caused disruption since the 1930s, when attempts to build a road through it were abandoned after a series of accidents. Plans to level the hill re-emerged in the 1980s, but problems recurred and workers refused to go anywhere near it. Even TV crews said their cameras failed to record anything when pointed at the rock. A road was finally built skirting round the protrusion—drive along it and you'll notice that the house numbers skip a plot, in deference to the invisible neighbours who ultimately had their way.

So what are we to make of all this? Some might automatically reject these claims as impossible and file them away with extant superstitions. Although irrational cultural fears—Korean fan death, or, at the opposite extreme, the Eastern European obsession with killer drafts, or even the American obsession with the elimination of the accursed 13th floor—have influenced businesses and individuals in similar, powerful ways, categorizing the phenomena examined here with those unfounded fears would be a misfiling. Icelandic elfin fears differ in two major respects: they are not limited by culture and offer significant documentation.

BOGEYMEN OF YORE, BOGEYMEN OF TODAY

Modern people from many countries and all walks of life have accumu-lated evidence of ethereal creatures—mysterious wounds, inexplicable equipment failure, and, most terrifyingly, mysterious disappearances and deaths. Accounts such as these would, and have, fueled some fantastic horror movies, but the reality of this phenomena is not so entertaining. In light of the available evidence, of which the preceding has been just a small sampling, the bogeyman of yore actually seem alive and well, here and now.

The latest study of SUNDS—"Sudden Unexplained Nocturnal Death Syndrome-- in Central China (Hubei)" in the journal *Medicine*, conducted in 2016 in Wuhan—recorded only 49 cases over 16 years. Those numbers don't seem congruent with cases as they played out in Hawaii and then later in the continental United States, where deaths spiked during a tighter time frame before plummeting to zero. Did these deaths represent a dis-proportionate increase?

Researchers at least hint at this, although they stop short of saying it directly. For the Hmong deaths, some researchers speculated that a grad-ually improving diet among the immigrants was the reason for the abrupt drop in SUNDS deaths—a reverse twinkie defense at best. There is no elegant explanation for this drastic, unexpected decrease in cases. When you consider other, more dramatic, SUNDS flaps, this explanation seems even less plausible. In light of the accepted figures for regular distribution of SUNDS cases, how do we explain the 11 Filipino deaths in one year (1960) at a single U.S. naval base in Guam, or the 407 Thai men, working in the construction industry in Singapore, who died of SUNDS between May 1984 and July 1994? This virtually-unknown affliction suddenly rose to become one of the leading causes of death… and then unexpectedly vanished.

This strange periodicity, distinguished by a dramatic spike and an equal-ly sudden full stop, resembles the suspicious drowning cases in the USA once considered to be the work of a network of serial killers. For example, La Crosse, Wisconsin reported a cluster of deaths between the late 1990s and early 2000s. Eight young men lost their lives in a string of drowning deaths in the Mississippi River off Riverside Park… then nothing. All the deaths were ruled accidental due to intoxication. The river has been quiet now for over a decade, yet La Crosse remains a college town where young men drink too much every weekend.

Irregular patterns like this call for statistical analysis. For now, such sudden upward trends of mysterious deaths resemble the periodic feeding of hibernating monsters. Stephen King and other storytellers use similar cycles to great effect. For example, Pennywise the Clown, the titular antagonist of King's novel *IT*, returns every 27 years to feast on human fear and suffering in Derry, Maine. King's inspiration was indeed very fairy. He imagined *IT* lurking in the sewers of Derry, as the modern-day equivalent to the troll under the bridge in *Three Billy Goats Gruff*.

An entry for a creature called "It" in Katharine Briggs' *An Encyclopedia of Fairies: Hobgoblins, Brownies, Bogies, and Other Supernatural Creatures* gives one pause. "It" was originally described in the book *Shetland Traditional Lore* by 19th Century folklorist Jessie Saxby as a shapeshifting creature that defies classification, appearing differently to each witness. Perhaps Stephen King gets at least some of his ideas from fairy lore!

The numerous fairy encounters recorded by cultures world-over including Iceland, the United Kingdom, Newfoundland, the Pacific Islands, Asia, and South America, as well as the Native American nations, point to an underlying cross-cultural animism. Waldorf Education, which claims 1,000 schools in 60 countries as well as public school programs in Milwaukee, Wisconsin and Detroit, Michigan, includes fairy study in their curriculum. The founder of Waldorf schools, Rudolph Steiner, wrote much on the subjects of fairies, elves, or elementals including the following: "There are beings that can be seen with clairvoyant vision at many spots in the depths of the earth... Many names have been given to them, such as goblins, gnomes and so forth."

Fairy believers have been in our midst all the while, we just had to know where to look. Fairies, elves, gnomes, goblins, trolls, monsters—it matters little what we call them. Our labels are only mental constructions based on mere glimpses throughout the ages, a very limited perception of these elusive creatures. By all accounts, there is an intangible quality about them so unlike us that we may never truly understand them.

The word 'monster,' from the Latin *'monstrum,'* literally means 'that which is revealed.' As our civilization invades the last refuges of wilderness, one wonders what concealed truths may finally be unveiled. While these stories might not make you a true believer in fairies, you may be persuaded to look at the reports with a less prejudiced eye. The sheer depth and breadth of actual cross-cultural accounts, as well as humanity's perennial collective fears and fascinations as reflected in film and real life, cannot help but draw the curious gaze of anyone paying attention. The dangerous possibility that our reality is permeable to harmful incursions of non-human intelligences warrants consideration. Hollywood has given us a template to explore such alternative perspectives.

Although today's fairy tales of the big and small screen are widely inaccurate in many respects, they are playgrounds where the mind can grapple with questions yet to be satisfactorily answered—for example, why did every culture in human history develop such animistic and shamanistic beliefs as those described above? Would humanity as a whole develop such beliefs, in conditions where pragmatism was absolutely imperative for survival, if there was no basis for those beliefs in reality? These and more such questions remain. The provocative quote below comes from a 1995 episode of the *Outer Limits*—yet, regardless of their source, these words remind us to not be overconfident in our understanding.

> Fairy tales are about the bogeyman… every culture seems to have one fairy tale about a creature who lives in the forest, under beds, in caves, and carries children away… Our world has been mapped, the oceans charted, animals and plants named and indexed… or so we believe. But there are still places grownups forget they've been….

Movies and television shows mine the forgotten hollows of the psyche, sometimes revealing surprising fears and truths. They suggest it is best to know and learn from our past, even when it presents us with something seemingly ridiculous like the enigma of universal fairy lore; for it is the curious and unexplained aspects of our past that will continue leading us to new discoveries about the world we thought we knew… or we can chuck the evidence into the burn barrel and declare that we know all there is to know, while the unknown quietly waits for us out on the dark ice or underneath the ground.

Bibliography

Adam, D. (January 15, 2020). Trypophobia: Why a fear of holes is real – and may be on the rise. Retrieved February 12, 2023 from https://www.newscientist.com/article/mg24532650-800-trypophobia-why-a-fear-of-holes-is-real-and-may-be-on-the-rise/

Adler, S.R. (2011). *Sleep Paralysis: Night-mares, Nocebos, and the Mind-Body Connection*. Piscataway, NJ: Rutgers University Press.

Adler, S.R. (Winter 1991). Sudden Unexpected Nocturnal Death Syndrome among Hmong Immigrants: Examining the Role of the "Nightmare". *Journal of American Folklore 104*(411), pp. 54-71.

Amorth, G. (1999). *An Exorcist Tells His Story*. (N.V. MacKenzie, Trans.). San Francisco, CA: Ignatius Press.

Aupilaarjuk, M., et al. (2002). *INUIT PERSPECTIVES ON THE 20TH CENTURY: Volume 4 - Inuit Qaujimajatuqangit: Shamanism and Reintegrating Wrongdoers into the Community*. Iqaluit, Nunavut, CAN: Nunavut Arctic College.

Bajkuša, D. (July 18, 2021). The Fault in The Uncanny Valley. Retrieved February 12, 2023 from https://medium.com/digital-reflections/the-fault-in-the-uncanny-valley-7f1254cffc3d

Biodrowski, S. (October 15, 2008). Wes Craven on Dreaming Up Nightmares. Retrieved February 12, 2023 from http://blog.cinefantastiqueonline.com/wordpress/wes-craven-on-dreaming-up-nightmares/

Bliatout, B.T. (1982). *Hmong Sudden Unexpected Death Syndrome: A Cultural Study*. Portland, OR: Sparkle Publishing Enterprises.

Briggs, K. (1976). *An Encyclopedia of Fairies: Hobgoblins, Brownies, Bogies, and Other Supernatural Creatures*. New York, NY: Pantheon Books.

Caballar, R.D. (November 6, 2019). What is the Uncanny Valley? Retrieved February 12, 2023 from https://spectrum.ieee.org/what-is-the-uncanny-valley

Chen, Z., Mu, J., Chen, X., & Dong, H. (March 7, 2016). Sudden Unexplained Nocturnal Death Syndrome in Central China (Hubei): A 16-Year Retrospective Study of Autopsy Cases. Medicine (Baltimore) 95(9):e2882. Retrieved February 13, 2023 from https://www.ncbi.nlm.nih.gov/pmc/articles/PMC4782858/

Coulter, P. (February 13, 2015). Fairy tales: Finding fairy bushes across Northern Ireland. Retrieved April 30, 2021 from https://www.bbc.com/news/uk-northern-ireland-31459851

Cutchin, J. (2016). *The Brimstone Deceit*. San Antonio, TX: Anomalist Books.

Cutchin, J. (n.d.). The Faerie Blast: An Analogue for Alien Implants? Retrieved February 12, 2023 from https://www.joshuacutchin.com/single-post/2018/08/23/the-faerie-blast-an-analogue-for-alien-implants

D'Evelyn, C. & Mill, A.J. (1956). *The South English Legendary*. London, UK: The Oxford University Press.

Devereux, P. (2003). *Fairy Paths & Spirit Roads*. London, UK: Vega.

Fortune, D. (2001). *Psychic Self Defense*. San Francisco, CA: Weiser Books. (Original work published 1930.)

Greer, J.M. *(2004). Monsters: An Investigator's Guide to Magical Beings*. St. Paul, MN: Llewellyn Publications.

Grimassi, R. (2000). *Encyclopedia of Wicca & Witchcraft*. St. Paul, MN: Llewellyn Publications.

Hufford, D.J. (1982). *The Terror That Comes in the Night: An Experience-Centered Study of Supernatural Assault Traditions*. Philadelphia, PA: University of Pennsylvania Press.

Indianapolis Journal. (December 3, 1869). An Individual Hell.

Jakobsson, Á & Mayburd, M. (2020). *Paranormal Encounters in Iceland 1150–1400*. Berlin, DE: De Gruyter.

Jakobsson, Á. (2017). *The Troll Inside You: Paranormal Activity in the Medieval North*. Santa Barbara, CA: Punctum Books.

Johnson, N. (n.d.). The Darker Side of Christmas. Retrieved February 12, 2023 from https://www.historic-uk.com/CultureUK/The-Darker-Side-of-Christmas/

Lang, A. (1893). Introduction. In R. Kirk, *The Secret Commonwealth of Elves, Fauns, & Fairies* (pp. ix-xlix). London, UK: David Nutt.

Larsen, N.P. (December 3, 1955). The men with deadly dreams. *Saturday Evening Post*, p. 20-21, 140-143.

Macalister, R.A.S. (1938). *LEBOR GABÁLA ÉRENN: The Book of the Taking of Ireland*. Dublin, IE: The Educational Company of Ireland, Ltd. Retrieved February 13, 2023 from https://archive.org/details/leborgablare01macauoft/

Mak, K.H. (2015). *Understanding and Preventing Sudden Death: Your Life Matters*. Singapore: World Scientific.

Marks, C. & Tannenbaum, R. (October 20, 2014). Freddy Lives: An Oral History of A Nightmare on Elm Street. Retrieved February 12, 2023 from https://www.vulture.com/2014/10/nightmare-on-elm-street-oral-history.html

MedlinePlus. (March 1, 2015). Brugada syndrome. Retrieved February 13, 2023 from https://medlineplus.gov/genetics/condition/brugada-syndrome/

Middelveen, M.J. & Stricker, R.B. (October 2016). Morgellons disease: a filamentous borrelial dermatitis. *International Journal of General Medicine 9*, pp. 349-354.

Milwaukee Journal. (May 22, 1920). Not Reconciled By Son's Death: Drowning of Boy Fails to Reunite Parents Who Seek Divorce.

Milwaukee Sentinel. (May 22, 1920). Boy Haunted By Shadow, Drowns: Body Of Raymond Naatz Taken From Lake After All Day Search: Saw Fishes In Dream: Leaves Home To Go Fishing After Acting As In Daze. Retrieved February 12, 2023 from https://www.marquette.edu/cgi-bin/cuap/db.cgi?uid=default&ID=1895&view=Search&mh=1

Monaghan, P. (2004). *The Encyclopedia of Celtic Mythology and Folklore*. New York, NY: Facts on File, Inc.

Mori, M. (June 12, 2012). The Uncanny Valley: The Original Essay by Masahiro Mori. Retrieved February 12, 2023 from https://spectrum.ieee.org/the-uncanny-valley

Nakajima, K., Takeichi, S., Nakajima, Y., & Fujita, M.Q. (April 15, 2011). Pokkuri Death Syndrome; sudden cardiac death cases without coronary atherosclerosis in South Asian young males. *Forensic Science International 207*(1-3), pp. 6-13.

Narváez, P. (1997). III. Physical Disorders: Changelings and the Blast. In P. Narváez (Ed.), *The Good People: New Fairylore Essays* (pp. 225-226). Lexington, KY: The University Press of Kentucky.

National Institutes of Health. (March 1, 2015). Brugada syndrome. Retrieved February 12, 2023 from https://medlineplus.gov/genetics/condition/brugada-syndrome/#references

Oberg, K. (January 25, 2007). South American nomad. Retrieved February 13, 2023 from https://www.britannica.com/topic/South-American-nomad

Olawale, A. (2001). The Role of Oral Literature in Yoruba Herbal Medical Practice. In R.H. Kaschula (Ed.), *African Oral Literature: Functions in Contemporary Contexts* (pp. 72-91). Claremont, SA: New Africa Books.

Online Etymological Dictionary. (September 25, 2018). troll (n.1). Retrieved February 12, 2023 from https://www.etymonline.com/word/troll

Rhŷs, J. (1901). *Celtic Folklore*. Oxford, UK: Clarendon Press.

Rieti, B. (1997). "The Blast" in Newfoundland Fairy Tradition. In P. Narváez (Ed.), *The Good People: New Fairylore Essays* (pp. 284-298). Lexington, KY: The University Press of Kentucky.

Rose, C. (1996). *Spirits, Fairies, Gnomes, and Goblins: A Encyclopedia of the Little People*. Santa Barbara, CA: ABC-CLIO.

Saxby, J.M.E. (1932). *Shetland Traditional Lore*. London, UK: Simpkin Marshall Ltd.

Steiner, R. (May 16, 1908). THE INFLUENCE OF SPIRITUAL BEINGS UPON MAN. Retrieved February 12, 2023 from https://rsarchive.org/Lectures/19080516p01.html

Sugg, R. (2018). *Fairies: A Dangerous History*. London, UK: Reaktion Books Ltd.

Wainwright, O. (March 25, 2015). In Iceland, 'respect the elves – or else'. Retrieved February 12, 2023 from https://www.theguardian.com/artand-design/2015/mar/25/iceland-construction-respect-elves-or-else

Weinstock, J.A. (Ed.). (2016). *The Ashgate Encyclopedia of Literary and Cinematic Monsters*. London, UK: Routledge. (Original work published 2014.)

Wilde, J. (1887). *Ancient Legends, Mystic Charms, and Superstitions of Ireland*. London, UK: Ticknor and Co.

DUNE: *The Faerie Dust Must Flow!*
James P. Nettles

I was ten or eleven years old when I received a copy of Frank Herbert's *Dune* as a gift. I started it several times, but it didn't grab me. A few years later in 1984, David Lynch 'awakened the sleeper' and brought his cinematically stunning, hot mess of an interpretation to the big screen. And I was hooked. As with many books made film, there was no way to show all *Dune*'s major plot points, much less the incredible details and nuances. The movie felt like it had been made solely for fans of the books, and I needed to understand. I ran through the novels as fast I could read. I think I even read *Dune* twice back to back.

Rabid fans of hardcore science fiction—and I am one of them—often fail to see the esoteric concepts from faerie myth and legend in this universe of spaceships and galactic battles. But they're there. *Dune* is, in fact, riddled with references to the unseen and magical realms. Fundamental aspects of the fae throughout time include esoteric knowledge; metaphysical and supernatural abilities; respect for and use of nature and their environment; an affinity for trickster behavior; alteration of perception; enchanted hospitality, food and drink; portals through time and space to unseen realms. What of the often nebulous but incontestable relationship between the Fair Folk and death? Longevity? We see the fae represented as immortals. In some stories, we see humans taken to the land of the fae and, if returned, many years or decades have passed. We even have ideas that the fae are the spirits of our dearly departed, connecting us to the realm of the dead. In *Dune*, we see all of these ideas represented.

If you remove the spaceships, both the books and the film could just as easily be an epic fantasy like *Game of Thrones*. In fact, *Dune* has often been compared to *The Lord of the Rings* for its influence on the science fiction genre, its significant length compared to novels in the genre at the time and in regard to many of the story elements.

Herbert is credited as influencing 'hard' science fiction by injecting a focus on psychology and sociology over technology, and with being the first to tackle ecology in the genre. These elements, however, are still seen as "scientific" rather than mythic. With such a focus on characters, culture, and worldbuilding, it is no wonder that humanity's common myths and themes would make their mark on the work.

When I recently caught *Dune* on TV, I put on my stillsuit, sat with a cup of spiced tea in hand, and settled in for an afternoon on Arrakis.

EMPIRES, HOUSES, & COURTS

In viewing the film, and even with some of the descriptions in the book, it can be hard to remember that even the most alien looking beings in *Dune* are, at their core origin, humans and descendants of Earth. Or at least they started that way.

As it is in *Dune*, nature is a critical key to all of faerie literature and myth. Within the film, the environment reflects the character's nature. We see the Antagonists—Emperor Shaddam IV in his throne room, even as it moves through space or lands on Dune, and Baron Harkonnen—only in industrial and technological settings. They represent power, greed, and the worst elements of destructive, polluting human nature. Contrast this against the living water planet Caladan, home of the protagonists, House Atreides. Even Arrakis, the seemingly dead locale giving the series its name (otherwise known as 'Dune'), is the battleground between the opposing forces of total dependence on excessive technology and living in balance with nature. Every House and group serves a purpose in the story. Even when we see the Bene Gesserit witches operating in the halls of power—initially appearing to be just a sidebar to power—it is to an end.

At the core of the story is Dune's major natural export, and the surface reason for the battle of House Harkonnen versus House Atreides and House Atreides versus the Galactic Emperor. The battle is about who controls the most valuable spice called '*melange*.' Without it, space travel is all but impossible and the universal economy would collapse. It is only known to come from one place, Arrakis, making an otherwise inhospitable desert planet in the middle of nowhere the most important planet in the universe. As Leto quotes, "He who controls the spice, controls the world."

The spice is infused into everything on Dune: the sand, the air, the meager aquifers inside the planet, and anything living on the planet for any length of time. From a fae perspective, if one considers melange a 'divine food,' this makes Arrakis a holy or magical place. The worth and the divine nature comes not from the commercial value; that is but a by-product. The real value is in the way it affects and transforms the humans who come in contact with it.

As with the touch of the fae (as an example of transformative experience, confirming that some element of the supernatural is real), the spice is addictive, and once a person is infused with it, they are forever changed. One cannot break the addiction and survive. There is a similar element in the German and Scandinavian legends of the Elle-Maid, an alluring faerie who offers food, drink and company to young men passing by. If the unsuspecting man consumes the offering, they will be driven mad, and eventually die if they are unable to consume it regularly.[326]

Despite the side-effects, one of the most sought after effects of melange is the properties of life extension into the hundreds, even thousands of years. It is both life and death in the one substance.

If the spice was merely a psychedelic, a magic mushroom or even something like *ayahuasca* that leads to mind-expanding and life-altering experiences, I would be of a different opinion. But melange creates extreme physical, psychological, and metaphysical changes in its users. The spice expands the consciousness of the user, grants mystical powers, extends life, and even allows for movement through space and time at the low, low cost of killing those who no longer partake of the divine and cursed sustenance. Once you have partaken of this 'faerie food'—as in the mythology of Western Europe—there is no going back. Part of you will 'always be in Fairyland' due to the dependence on the spice. And if you leave Arrakis, you must take some of it with you, and return often.

We meet the next players in this mystical tale, the Fremen. The Fremen are the indigenous peoples of Arrakis, their eyes a striking, near-glowing blue: the first visible sign of dependence on the spice. They are forever linked to, and dependent upon, the product of the sands. To these people, their blue eyes are a sign of pride and of their link to their home. To outsiders, it is denigrated as a visible sign of spice addiction, having crossed a threshold from which one cannot return. As we often see in legends of the fae, they may seem human, but that small detail—the blue eyes—tell us the Fremen are different: not us, not fully human. To me, they represent the fae as seen in mythology and popularized in Theosophy—caring about the planet, seeking to teach humanity hard lessons about trespassing and screwing with Mother Nature. Initially, it seems that they are in mortal conflict with the Emperor, the Houses, and the Bene Gesserit.

Another player in this drama are the Navigators. A select few chosen humans consume amounts of melange that would kill a village of Keith Richards's clones, eating it, drinking it, immersed in a gaseous orange cloud of it until they undergo extreme physical and mental transformations and take on an 'aquatic appearance,' as Herbert described it. Those who survive the transition gain the power of prescience, an ability to see possible futures, and become the prized Guild Navigators—the key to space travel. Through these Navigators, humanity has developed the ability to 'fold space' and travel among the stars.

One can compare this to stories of human midwives called to attend to a faerie birth where a salve or ointment must be applied to the newborn, and if the midwife rubs some of it onto her eyes, it wipes away the glamour that hides the true nature of the fae, and their home. Forever changed, the midwife may lose her vision, but will forever be given another kind of sight allowing the consumer to see what was hidden, or by opening doorways to other lands, other universes, even other dimensions. The Navigators 'see' where they want to be, then go there. In the film, the Navigator takes the form of a giant tadpole opening dimensional doorways. Like stepping into a faerie ring, the giant ships never seem to move, and yet they magically shift from one place to another.

The final major player in the story are the Bene Gesserit. A matriarchal religious and political order, the Bene Gesserit spend their lives blending physical and mental practices augmented by melange to become 'witch-like' in appearance, obtaining near magical abilities. For acolytes of the order to join their highest ranks, that of the Reverend Mothers, the spice is used in the 'waters of life.' In the advancement ritual, the candidate must use their innate disciplines to neutralize the toxic substance and unlock the Other Memory: gaining the genetic memories and egos of all their female ancestors.

It is in all of these dichotomies that we find connections with the fae. For humans 'fortunate' enough to sample faerie fare, it is reputed to be heavenly in taste and form, in some stories granting mystical powers, extending life, and opening the gateway to Fairyland—just like melange. What could go wrong?

In legends around the world, people are warned never to accept food from faeries, gods, or spirits. This comes from a belief that while human food sustains the body, faerie food will enhance or change any human who consumes it. It is deemed too powerful for mortal men, even if the revealed 'food' is nothing more than detritus—leaves, dirt, worms, etc.—cloaked in faerie 'glamour' to appear more appealing. In this idea, it is not the food itself, but the *essence* that is important. If a human dines at Tinker Bell's Café, the person undergoes a physical and metaphysical transformation. They are changed.[327] They may take on animalistic qualities including shapeshifting, they can lose their sense of time and space, their behavior may become erratic, and they will never again be fully sated by mere human food. They will no longer be fully human. Most importantly, the fortunate few that do manage to escape Fairyland have an eternal link to the other realm, and an insatiable pull to return. Or, in terms of Herbert's story, once you've taken the spice, you must forever take the spice.

Studying the various peoples comprising the *Dune* universe, the Fremen of Arrakis are most directly reminiscent of the fae. They live in balance with the harsh elements of the planet, and are changed from birth by melange. Every Fremen benefits from the spice's physical and metaphysical qualities. Though human in origin, the spice fueling their piercing blue eyes and tribal nature makes it clear they are no longer purely human.

Deeper study of their culture shows an intimate relationship with every aspect of the planet, making them feel much like stewards of the sands, reminiscent of the fae being guardians of the forests. As with portrayals of faeries, the denizens of Arrakis live with one foot walking the liminal path of death at all times. They cannot leave the planet without a consistent supply of melange, just as the faeries' existence is tethered to their environment, be it a lake, boulder field, or forest. They may be able to physically travel beyond the borders of their domain, but their identity and very being is intrinsically linked. Like the fae of folklore, their primary dwellings are underground.

The famed Arrakis sandworms are always looking for a meal, just as magical creatures threaten elf and faerie alike. In *Dune*, the harsh and unforgiving environment could take a Freman's life in an instant. And yet, like the fae, the Fremen have what seem to be vast magical abilities to avoid death's most certain arrow. They hold on to a secret desire concerning their homeworld, one which would forever change their ecosystem and way of life.

Their Spartan existence is exemplified by their stillsuit technology, clothing that is both life and death in one. Designed to absorb and recycle sweat and other bodily fluids into life-giving potable water, the stillsuit preserves and provides life for both the individual and the tribe. When a member dies, their water, their essence, is recovered and added back to the tribe's stores. In this way, the essence of *all* members of the tribe and their ancestors is a part of every member of the tribe. The inevitable return of water to water, dust to dust. Thinking of this in more esoteric terms, the Fremen live like fae exiled from earth but carrying on with their spiritual legacy, ever-mindful of their need to keep the balance in all things

If the Fremen are the 'common' fae in the story, the sisterhood of the Bene Gesserit and its Reverend Mothers are reminiscent of the faerie princesses and queens in their exotic beauty, sexual energy, and seductiveness; they outwardly appear to serve others, while in reality subversively manipulate circumstances to their own benefit. They can be compared to the Seelie Court of Scottish legend.[328] That court—led by Queen Titania, Irish warrior Queen Maeve, Queen Mab, or Lhiannan-Shee, depending on which legend you choose from which tradition—is well-represented by the Bene Gesserit. Recruited from the most noble houses to be schooled in their physical and mental arts, the Bene Gesserit acolytes are feared yet coveted for their abilities as consorts to those in power, especially the heads of imperial houses.

Dominated by strong, feminine energy, the Bene Gesserit outwardly seem to be working solely for the good of the different houses and of the empire. However, much as we see with the trickster motif, and as feminine energy has often been portrayed as subversive evil through time, Herbert portrays the Bene Gesserit as always working to their own agendas and using their wiles to achieve their aims.

Beyond the sexual energy, the members of the order are consistently shown to be strategic in their thinking, tactical in their actions, and cunning in their execution. The Weirding Way (their martial art) is a prized skill taught to men and women alike. Their seemingly mystical powers can warp minds as well as bodies, and we find multi-generational intrigue and plotting is their way of existence. While the film shows certain psychic and telekinetic abilities the original book does not bestow upon the order, later novels open up the possibilities shown so effectively onscreen.

One of the Bene Gesserit's greatest assets is that they have spent thousands of years seeding stories and mythologies into the different peoples and planets of the Empire. Much like the earthly myths of fae and monsters, they've seeded the rise and fall of prophets and the coming of wise women in various cultures. For the Bene Gesserit, this is often a convenient way of embedding a Reverend Mother in a position of power for that people. However, their most important story is an almost-universal myth, that of the Kwisatz Haderach.

The Bene Gesserit have worked for centuries to create their own, powerful messiah who will bring the Bene Gesserit order their just due. As they prepare to bring him forth, the order carefully crafts the mythology of Kwisatz Haderach, their coming messiah, to pave the way. One could even say they have created 'fairy tales' and spread them throughout the universe to pave their way to power.

There is an elegant beauty to the Bene Gesserit plan, for those in imperial power fail to recognize or understand how they are being steered and manipulated even as they demand and enjoy a Bene Gesserit-trained concubine or wife. To me, the Bene Gesserit echo the memories of Morgan la Fey ('the Fae') of Arthurian legend, especially with consideration to the Bene Gesserit mastery of the art of seduction.

It's worth noting that the inspiration for the order (as reflected in their wardrobe in the film) is the Catholic nuns who taught Herbert in his youth. The name "Gesserit" is derived from the Jesuits, an order called "God's Marines," famed for their political intrigue and dissent with the church leadership. Like the Bene Gesserit, Jesuits have a single-minded dedication to their mission, and a hard foundation in education and the sciences. They are also seen as an esoteric order protecting arcane knowledge, the sort of information that may be used in a far-flung future to create power or ascend to another level of existence.

While not fae in origin, this mythic Christian ethos of the Jesuit tradition also plays into *Dune*'s origins. Many convents in Herbert's time, especially the teachers, were Irish or of Irish descent. Stories of famed Christian saints and sinners from the Celtic peoples are adoptions of older cultural memories, and those worldviews can be seen in teachings surrounding figures like Saint Patrick or Saint Brigid.[329] These folk heroes of Celtic legend are interwoven not only with Pagan faiths but also faerie stories, which Christianity syncretized. One can easily imagine this working its way into Herbert's Bene Gesserit order, layered on top of the general structure and politics of the Catholic Church against which he rebelled. We cannot escape our cultural myths, our cultural history, even though we often do not know the origins when we look at their modern interpretations.

Despite all of their power, augmented by melange, the Bene Gesserit sisters have one significant weakness. Their prescient abilities are imperfect because they have no access to male memories (or the masculine energy). Hence, the primary aim of the Bene Gesserit is to bring about the birth of the Kwisatz Haderach, a male under their control who would have perfect prescience, and access to both male and female genetic memories. The balance of the divine feminine and masculine in one person. A messiah for the masses.

There are certainly mythic overtones to their aim. This has been the main effort of the order through a ten-thousand-year breeding program: creation of the tool by which the sisterhood would forever ensure their power, and ostensibly bring stability to the human race. Through their mental disciplines, they have developed physiological control to the point where they can determine the gender of their offspring. Through careful pairings and determinations of offspring among the wealthy, powerful, and those who have specific genetic advantages and traits, they seek to create this messianic being.

If we compare this ability to stories of faerie changelings—while manipulative breeding and gender selection are not equivalent to swapping a human infant with a sickly fae child—the results are much the same. Both the Bene Gesserit and the faeries seek to generate offspring with favorable traits to be raised under optimal circumstances. The removal of chance in gender and the deliberate ability to influence the child's genes are certainly a legacy of faerie legend.[330]

If the Bene Gesserit are the Seelie Court—inclined toward kindness, yet still dangerous—on the opposite side we have the Unseelie Court, inclined toward malice. According to certain interpretations, this court is predominantly male and regarded as the darker, even malevolent, side of the faeries. Here, we have two contenders for the role of Oberon, King of the Unseelie Court in some literature.[331]

Starting with the obvious candidates, consider Emperor Shaddam IV and Baron Harkonnen. The Emperor orchestrates the downfall of his perceived royal rival, Duke Leto Atreides, by using an ages-old rivalry with House Harkonnen. While only out for himself and his house, the Emperor's wife (a Bene Gesserit) has followed her training and borne him only daughters, guaranteeing he shall be the end of the line for his house. While not deeply explored in the film, this is all part of the Bene Gesserit's greater plan.

As we often see in faerie stories and legends involving Queen Titania and King Oberon, these surface feuds are petty jealousies and insecurities unbecoming a royal. The resulting plots tend to backfire on the Unseelie due to the differences of the nature of the two courts and the shortsighted-ed nature of their schemes. This is true in *Dune*, and as in the Unseelie Court, this petty shortsightedness is the Emperor's undoing.

Secondly, and more interesting, we have the Baron, Vladimir Harkon-nen. He embodies many of the traits described in stories featuring the dark faeries. Short-tempered, impetuous, and vengeful, like the dark fae, he is narcissistic and sinister. Both are fundamentally evil in nature and revel in it. However, the Baron fails the "fae" test in one important way: he cares not for the planet, but only for what it can give him.

In the film, musician and actor Sting's performance as Feyd-Rautha, the Baron's nephew and heir apparent, is frenetic yet deliberate, animalistic yet brilliant, the predator staring back at all times waiting for the first sign of weakness. I can easily see him as one of the rare male furies.

Studying the various peoples that make up the *Dune* universe, House Harkonnen represents something equally important to understand. In ad-dition to representing dark faeries, Harkonnens also represent the worst of humankind. The Seven Deadly Sins are wrapped up in the bloated and diseased form of the Baron: a dependence on technology and placing it above nature, absolute greed and gluttony, no regard for human (or any other) life not in his own family, and destructive narcissism. It is in this that the Baron reminds us of many stories from the evil side of faerie folklore. While not part of the 1984 film directly, these traits lead directly to the Baron's fall from power and death, a direct echo of a faerie curse.

A POST-APOCALYPTIC FAIRYLAND

In an attempt to collect Baron Harkonnen's genetics as a part of the Bene Gesserit breeding program, Reverend Mother Gaius Helen Mohiam blackmails him to father a child with her. That child turns out genetically undesirable and is killed. When Mohiam returns to the Baron for another attempt, Harkonnen drugs and rapes her. In retribution, she infects him with a disease that causes obesity and, as seen in the film, covers him in sores. She essentially curses him for not only his evil actions but for breaking their contract. A form of faerie blast, maybe?

In opposition to the evil of House Harkonnen, Duke Leto Atreides and his house gives balance to humanity's characterization, taking control of Arrakis with apparently more honorable intent on how to manage the planet and its inhabitants. We see the Duke rescue workers in lieu of saving a load of spice being harvested in the desert. Seen as noble and honorable like the knights of mythic stories, Leto gains too much power and popularity for the Emperor's liking and is marked for death. Leto's assassination sets up the transformation of his son.

Thus, we come to Paul Atreides, prince and heir to House Atreides, the pivot point of each of *Dune*'s complex story lines. He is the son of Duke Leto Atreides and his Bene Gesserit concubine, Lady Jessica. Though not detailed in the film, Lady Jessica was matched with Leto and commanded to produce a daughter, one that could then be wed to Feyd Rautha Harkonnen, and it was this conjunction that would produce the male child destined to become the Kwisatz Haderach.

However, love for Leto overrides Jessica's duty to the Bene Gesserit, and she instead produces a male child for the Duke, an heir to his house. Jessica's choice and Paul's birth inject the fae effect of chaos, free will, and chance into the mix even as it throws 10,000 years of Bene Gesserit planning and breeding into question.

Raised and trained in the Bene Gesserit disciplines of the 'Weirding Way' and 'enhanced observation' by his mother, and secretly enrolled by Leto in Mentat training of enhanced cognitive abilities, Paul Atriedes is unique. Weapons and combat training by his mentors Duncan Idaho and Gurney Halleck prepare him from childhood to be a formidable leader and ultimate heir to Leto.

The Bene Gesserit think otherwise. They are furious with Jessica for ignoring the plan. Reverend Mother Gaius Helen Mohiam puts Paul through the trial of the 'gom jabbar,' a painful test designed to weigh the person's 'humanity' versus their baser instincts. Paul, however, is far more complex and dangerous than anyone knows, having endured more pain than any other male who has ever taken the test. Reluctantly, Reverend Mother Mohiam sees in him the potential to salvage their breeding program and create their messiah—but only if he can be controlled. Once again, chaos and chance as the staples of mythic storytelling appear to disrupt the status quo.

In changeling mythology, human infants are taken often for their preferable traits, their humanity, or simple revenge and exchanged for sickly faerie babies. Parents feared that if they found their child ill, or the child showed unusual behavior, they might be a changeling.[332] The gom jabbar test is reminiscent of how parents in changeling stories tested infants with painful, if not deadly, trials to determine whether their child was human or faerie.

Considering both Jessica and Leto undertook to secretly train their child in certain arts, the child each parent expected was supplanted by something greater than the sum of each training regimen, something wholly unexpected and greater than the sum of his parts. Like any hero in a fairy tale, all Paul needed was the trigger that would force him to realize that potential. A spiritual awakening; facing the death of ego and of the self which unleashes the magic. One that allows him to survive the trial.

It is in Paul's multiple trials that we can consider how the greater society in the *Dune* universe has been subverted. In the opening monologue we are told that mankind surrendered itself to technology, apparently artificial intelligence (though not called that), for an extended period. In this newfound era, humanity still firmly embraces science but has reclaimed a form of mysticism in the Bene Gesserit, the Mentat, and the spice. Both Herbert's books and the film lead us to believe this 'magic' is nothing but enhanced science, training, and clever use of technology. For instance, the pain-inducing box in the gom jabbar test is simply an enhanced device causing the body to believe it is being grievously injured.

I could agree with this 'enhanced science' interpretation of *Dune*'s universe except for the talents and abilities that are seemingly augmented, if not granted, by the ingestion of melange. The ability to see the future; fold space and time; pass genetic memories. Maybe this future world is not so much about humanity reclaiming itself, but instead represents the echoes of Morgan La Fey's magical descendants resurfacing, reactivated by the spice?

Everything comes to a head in the story as Paul comes into focus. The next trigger in Paul's transformation occurs when House Harkonnen overthrows and assassinates Leto for control of Arrakis. Lady Jessica and Paul are taken to the desert to die, but using their training and abilities they escape. Falling from wealth and the status of a house powerful enough to potentially challenge the emperor, to be deposed and stranded in the desert, is not only near-physical death, but death of the ego as well. Paul must face his true self and his destiny.

After their crash in the desert, Paul comes to understand the potential of his power and denies the plans of the Bene Gesserit, refusing to be led by them. Lady Jessica once again steps outside her training and compulsion to realize that her son has a greater power than her order had hoped for, one far outside the control of the Bene Gesserit, if only he can realize and harness it. Knowing that "the sleeper must awaken," Jessica turns her back on her Bene Gesserit obligations and throws her lot in with her son and the murky, unknowable future, driven by chance.

Escaping deeper into the deserts, they confront a sandworm for the first time and are rescued by Fremen warriors. Having lost himself in the wilderness, Paul's transformation is just beginning; to parallel Arthurian legend, he has drawn the sword from the stone, putting Merlin, destiny, and magic in control. Paul and Jessica have entered the liminal state of Fairyland.

Though we have met a few of the Fremen in the capital city, viewers are now introduced to them in their natural environment of the desert. Dozens appear from the night and the sands in a flash of lightning, reminiscent of how faeries travel on the wind, invisible unless they wish to be seen.

If we consider the Fremen the rank and file 'warrior faeries,' then the cave system they call home is a post-apocalyptic Fairyland. It appears that long before humans arrived, Arrakis was a wet planet, but the evolution of an ecosystem in which sandworms are the apex predator, coupled with their tunneling behavior, terraformed the now-desert world.

The civilization Paul and his mother discover underground is like stepping into the land of the fae. It far exceeds anything the rest of the universe thought possible. On entering the underground network, the Fremen reveal their secret desire and mission to terraform the planet, using vast reservoirs of water they have been able to gather. They will make it again a living, breathing world.

The Fremen, typically not hospitable to unwelcome guests, have their own spiritual order complete with their own myths and legends and equivalent Reverend Mother, Sayyadina Ramallo. Jessica discovers she and Paul fit the Fremen's messianic prophecies (conveniently planted over millennia by the Bene Gesserit), the pair are welcomed into the sietch (tribe), and Paul takes his new name: Paul Muad'Dib. In this act, Paul Atreides echoes the creation myth as he dies in a sense and is reborn.

What's a hidden boy prince who has all of the esoteric combat training and faerie backing to do? Form an army, of course, teach them the fundamentals of war, including the Bene Gesserit martial art, and prepare the overthrow of House Harkonnen and the Empire.

One feature Lynch's cinematic version introduced to the *Dune* universe are the technology-based 'weirding modules' which Paul builds for the Fremen. For the time, it met the need to give 'ray guns' to 'the good guys,' largely as it was what audiences expected. Plus, to show the Fremen using nothing but enhanced Bene Gesserit martial arts would have made the big battle scenes look more like *Crouching Tiger, Hidden Dragon* in the desert against *Star Wars* stormtroopers, and Bruce Lee wasn't available to leap from a sandworm.

This does, however, allow us to explore the idea of technology empowering magic rather than opposing it. *Dune* is about balance and this is one way in which Paul's character introduces that balance into the story. The modules turn certain sounds into sonic beams of varying intensity. Paul selects a Fremen warrior to attack an obelisk of their hardest stone by hitting, kicking, and even trying to cut it, all to no avail. But using the Weirding Module with a word and a thought from Paul, the stone is shattered. We see the same principles applied in every mythic story of magic: intention, energy, and focus applied to create a desired result.

A TRUE NAME

As the warriors train, it is revealed that Paul's new surname, Muad'Dib, is one of the most powerful sounds that can be used through the Weirding weapons. Ultimately, we see Paul ascend to the point where he no longer

206 | FAIRY FILMS

needs the module to focus his voice as a weapon. This also speaks to the legendary idea that names have power; to know the true name of something is to have power over it. Among the Fremen, they have the name they are known by, and a secret name known only to those closest to them. A 'true name.'

The concept of a true name is found in religions and folklore around the world, and even in our legal system. Gaining one's true name is often seen as a rite of passage, a movement into maturity or a ritualized acceptance into a community. Returning to Herbert's Catholic teachings, a confirmation name would be an example.

It is also one's source and often describes the entity, their power, and their core identity. This is even found in the Greek concept of *logos*, which now lends its name and idea to every graphical representation for a brand. Knowing a being's true name can give another influence and even absolute control over it. Now a popular trope, we see this idea in the spiritual practice of knowing a demon's name to capture it, execute your will, or exorcise it. In Arthur C. Clarke's *The Nine Billion Names of God*, knowledge of all God's names destroys the universe.[333]

In Homer's *Odyssey*, when Odysseus is captured by the cyclops Polyphemus, he lies and uses a name that translates to "nobody." In his escape he blinds the cyclops, who then calls for help, screaming, "Nobody has blinded me!" Apparently cyclopes weren't a brilliant species. Once again unable to control himself, Odysseus reveals his true name in victory, and his conceit ultimately brings repercussions.

Returning to our fair folk: in *Rumpelstiltskin*, a miller's daughter is taken by the king and forced to magically spin a room full of straw into gold overnight, or be executed. Unable to perform such a feat, an imp appears to her and offers to fill the room in exchange for a necklace. The following morning the king, still unsatisfied, takes the miller's daughter to a second, larger room. Trading for a ring, our little friend fills the room again. The third day, the king offers marriage if she can fill another, still larger room. With nothing left to trade and no alternative solutions, the miller's daughter reluctantly promises Rumpelstiltskin her first born.

Leaping forward, the miller's daughter, now a queen expecting her first child, gets a visit from our story's namesake, looking to collect. Distraught, our queen tries every negotiation tactic before finally relenting, but only if she cannot guess the imp's true name within three days. (In some variations, she gets three guesses per day, exemplifying the magical rule of three.)

She, of course, fails on the first day (it seems to me 'Chad' would be an odd name for a goblin), and on the second day as well. Having failed twice, our Queen desperately tracks the wee lad into the forest, and over-hears him burst into a song that is some variant on, "Rumpelstiltskin is my name, taking babies is my game!"

On the third day the Queen plays coy, but finally uses the imp's name. Depending on the telling, Rumpelstiltskin is either magically banished, takes flight on a skillet out the window, or throws a temper tantrum that makes any preschool full of petulant two-year-old kids proud, stomping himself out of existence. Again, hubris is his undoing.

In *Dune*, Paul becomes known 'Usul,' meaning 'the base of the pillar.' 'Mua'Dib' is the name he uses to hide his royal identity and spread fear throughout the galaxy. Through his two names, we are told his public name is power and force, but privately he is the foundation for the Fremen people. It is only in the closing moments of the story that the Fremen warleader Mua'Dib is really Paul Atreides. The Fremen boogeyman of the desert is revealed to be the hidden prince, come to defeat the Emperor and the Baron and take his rightful place on the throne. Will this be Paul's downfall?

But before this can happen, two more critical transformations must take place.

THE SLEEPER HAS AWAKENED

When Lady Jessica escapes to the desert, she is pregnant with Leto's child—a daughter. Once welcomed into the tribe, she initiates the Water of Life ritual in order to take on the role as the Fremen's Reverend Mother from the aged Sayyadina Ramallo. In the ritual, the bile of a young drowned sandworm is given to Lady Jessica, and if she can convert the poison into the 'Waters of Life,' the past Reverend Mother will die and Jessica will become a full Reverend Mother for the Fremen.

In Lady Jessica's case, the process also triggers an early labor and her daughter Alia is born with all the powers and memories of a Reverend Mother. Seen as abominations by the Bene Gesserit, these children do not have a lifetime in which to develop their own personalities and sense of self, nor do they receive training and discipline before being subjected to the ancestral memories of past Reverend Mothers. The infant child has within them an old soul, one that is not quite human, and she will mature with abnormal and disturbing speed. It is a form of possession, and again reminiscent of the changeling: in addition to swapping out human children for faerie babies, sometimes the fae would instead substitute an elderly faerie in the infant's place. Moreover, faerie scholars from Lady Gregory through Evans Wentz alternatively suggested changelings may be evidence of 'soul-swapping,' wherein the consciousness of the recently deceased enters the body of the recently born.[334]

The second transformation, Paul's, is the apex of our story. After several years in the desert leading attacks against the Harkonnens and harvesting spice, Muad'Dib decides he must face his destiny as foretold in both the Fremen and Bene Gesserit prophecies and perform the 'Water of Life' ritual himself. In the movie, the voiceover reminds us that every man who has ever taken the waters has 'tried and died,' and many warn Paul to leave well enough alone.

Unfazed by the prospect of death, Paul steals into the desert with his lover Chiani and his most trusted guard. Taking the bile, we see Paul undergo a grueling trial. In a purely mythic moment, sandworms converge on the site, but do not attack. Instead, it seems they are there as witnesses as well.

Paul successfully transmutes the waters. His mind is opened. He is granted access to the 'other lives' and the masculine genetic memories, where the women of the Bene Gesserit cannot go. He has ascended. He is the Kwisatz Haderach. To quote Paul from the film—calling back to a scene where Leto proclaimed his son was asleep, and unaware of the greater world and his destiny—"Father, the sleeper has awakened." We have seen Paul pass through another process of death and rebirth. He has now left behind the body and concerns of man to become a god in the eyes of the Fremen and the Bene Gesserit. He has also truly ascended to his father's place as head of House Atreides.

About now, you may be thinking that these elements are present in most fantasy, but I would argue that you don't see them often in hard science fiction, which is how *Dune* was billed upon release. I consider this evidence as to how deeply our folklore and cultural history is embedded in our modern lives, our faith, our politics. I started early on with the statement that Frank Herbert's vision is epic fantasy wrapped in science fiction; so is *Star Wars*. Many of Lynch's movie interpretations and additions to *Dune*'s literary universe were directly attributable to the success of George Lucas' vision, from spice to weirding modules to psychic abilities.

RESTORATION

There's one other piece I haven't addressed, and the primary reason I argue Herbert's *Dune* universe as well as Lynch's interpretation are deeply rooted in faerie folklore. At the moment Paul awakens as the Kwisatz Haderach, he says, "The Worm is the Spice! The Spice is the Worm!" All of life is connected, intertwined, just as Paul's fate is intertwined with that of the universe.

We have looked at length how the melange spice is a divine (faerie) food, in a raw state, in a processed state, and as the Waters of Life. It is a product of the worms' life cycle, so how is it considered 'divine'? It imbues and enhances everything it touches with a form of magic.

I look at Arrakis's sandworms as elemental creatures; dragons sailing through the sands instead of the air, spreading a magical fire. Through most of the film, the worms are portrayed as apex predators, reacting on instinct alone, but the Fremen people worship them as mortal incarnations of the one God that created the universe. They call the worms '*Shai-Hulud,*' which has many meanings and interpretations, including 'Old Man of the Desert' and my favorite, 'Old Father Eternity.' Sandworms are the source of extended life, telepathic abilities, prescience, and controlling the folding of space and time at the cost of eternal consumption, or death. They are more than a simple giant worm waiting to be put on the hook.

I doubt *Tremors*'s graboids would be so inclined. Rolling into the big final battle, the Fremen use 'thumpers' to summon every sandworm in range. Paul, wondering if the sandworms were answering the call, results in the famous line, "... we have wormsign the likes of which even God has never seen." In the literal sense they have generated enough noise that any sandworm will be irresistibly drawn to the site—but another way to consider it is that elemental forces have answered the call of the fae warriors for the final battle. Timing the attack to coincide with the cycle of Coriolis storms on the planet, worms and their Fremen riders appear at the capital city in the midst of a great sandstorm (shades of the faerie blast, again) which covers their approach, and the elements work to the Fremen's advantage. The army of Muad'Dib, of Paul Atreides of House

Atreides, has come to confront the powers of evil, the Unseelie Courts of the Emperor and the Baron Harkonnen.

In the closing moments, Paul's young sister Alia has been captured. Ostensibly a hostage, she is dressed as a Reverend Mother and warns the Emperor of Paul's approach. Reverend Mother Mohiam calls her an 'Abomination' and demands her destruction, but Alia invades Mohiam's mind, removing her from the chessboard. The Emperor demands Baron Harkonnen eliminate the child. The curse Mohiam placed on the Baron comes to fruition in this scene, though it is never explained. Lady Jessica is the child of the rape of Mohiam by the Baron, thus Paul and Alia are the grandchildren of both Reverend Mother Mohiam and Baron Harkonnen. In the emptied room, Alia takes control of the Baron's mind, and strikes him with a gom jabbar needle, poisoning him. Though visually entertaining, the strike is not what kills the Baron in the film. Lynch instead chose to blow a hole through the wall, and Vladimir Harkonnen is sucked out to give a sandworm indigestion. Regardless, the loop is closed.

The Fremen ride the sandworms like giant living tanks, providing offensive and defensive capabilities much like Alexander the Great's elephants. Against the Emperor's elite Sardaukar forces and the Baron's troops, the fight definitively becomes a battle of Nature vs. Technology, Elves vs. Orcs.

With the capture of the capital of Arrakeen and the Emperor's throne room, the surviving leadership gather before Paul and his warriors. Mohiam tries to take control of Paul and complete the Bene Gesserit plan to create the Kwisatz Haderach, but instead she finds him more powerful than imagined and beyond their influence. Facing her challenge and harkening to the beginning of the story where she put him through the gom jabbar, Paul chastises her, saying, "Try looking into that place where you dare not look, and you'll find me there, staring back at you."

I find the *Dune* universe not necessarily a story of humanity trying to reclaim its agency over artificial intelligence, but instead a restoration of the natural order in balance with humanity and the forces beyond it. If we consider the idea that faerie energies may have been driven all but extinct by humanity's surrender to technology, could these energies be revived once humans reclaim their natural and supernatural abilities, something giving us the legendary powers of myth and legend?

In this, Paul as the Kwisatz Haderach is that restoration of balance: masculine and feminine energy; life and death; the natural and the supernatural. *Coincidentia oppositorum*. The extraordinary feminine energy of the Bene Gesserit may have subconsciously expressed the need to recreate this force in the universe, and by Lady Jessica bearing the male child instead of one to be bred with House Harkonnen, the trickster influence ensured that overwhelming order was disrupted, and the wildness of chance and life could be brought anew.

In the final battle, Paul faces off not against the Emperor but Feyd Rautha, the last surviving Harkonnen. The Emperor names Feyd his Champion, promising him his daughter's hand and his throne should he kill Paul. It is a meeting of destinies. Had Paul been born the female child as the Bene Gesserit commanded, Feyd would have been the father of their children, including the planned Kwisatz Haderach. Paul forever changes the plan, killing the genetic line driven only by technology and greed.

Instead Feyd, representing the madness of his house, the evil of the Unseelie Court, and the technology-dependent and destructive side of humanity, carries the emperor's metal blade into the ring of combat. Thus does the Emperor cede the battle's outcome, and the Empire, to the winner. Paul wields his Fremen crysknife, honed from the crystal tooth of a sandworm: a natural element versus the Emperor's blade. This is akin to a fight between the Unseelie and Seelie courts writ large on the screen. Evil versus good. Excessive, poisonous technology versus an ideal of humanity in perfect balance with his innate magic and the forces of nature.

In true Unseelie fashion, Feyd fights dirty and attempts to win with a treacherous, hidden, and poisoned blade in his stillsuit. Ultimately unharmed by Feyd's trick due to his extraordinary powers and abilities, Paul drives his blade into the Harkonnen's skull to the shock of the Emperor's court.

Rising over Feyd's body, Paul Muad'Dib grunts a killing word powerful enough to shatter Feyd's body and the floor underneath without a weirding module. Balance, nature's power, and magic coalesce in Paul Muad'Dib, Head of House Atriedes, Leader of the Fremen. His transformation is complete, and he takes his power as Kwisatz Haderach, and with it the throne of the Emperor.

Famously, Frank Herbert was not a fan of Lynch's interpretation. Had Lynch had a full miniseries or multi-film arc to tell the story, I believe he could have had a reasonable opportunity to explore the rich characters, culture, and intrigue of Herbert's *Dune*. Having to pack so much into a few short hours, even with the use of spectacular visual effects, over-the-top characterizations, and barely seasoning the story with the details of intrigue, Lynch still reveals an epic fantasy wrapped in science, giving us a chance to see the occulted themes buried in the story.

Many friends and colleagues will disagree with my postulation as presented here. In fact, some have called it a heresy. A heresy, damn you! *Dune* is Science Fiction! Yes and no.

Dune is an epic fantasy with spaceships, an early space opera, if you will. And if my idea is a heresy, it is fitting for the story. Everything within Herbert's universe is a heresy in some way if you are a hard science fiction fan: a post-AI civilization running on an exclusive drug both opening gateways and driving it mad; warrior nuns seducing the rich and powerful to birth a millennium-long planned messiah; all of it relying on a giant elemental earthworm whose product is both life and death to its users.

Utter madness and chaos. How, then, can you deny its roots in the fae?

Walt and the Fairies, 1922-1960

Dr. Simon Young

Introduction: Fairy Animation

The troll jumping up and down at the bus stop in *Totoro*; Aisling's disappearance and brief return in *The Secret of Kells*; the extraordinary fairy "raid"[335] at the end of *Tinker Bell and the Lost Treasure*... here are some of the great moments of fairy cinema. My interest in these scenes and the films that contain them is two-fold. I get goose bumps just putting them down here. First, as a father with three young daughters, many of my evenings have been enriched by these movies. Second, as a fairyist who writes about both fairy folklore and fairy experiences (sightings, interactions, etc.), I have come to believe that cinema and television are the most important ways that fairylore is transmitted to the general public. Images penetrate the human mind in a much more powerful way than words.[336] Frequently, when people write to me about their fairy encounters they will say that the fairy they saw looked like "Tinker bell" or some other fantastic entity that they saw on the big or small screen.[337]

The careful reader will have noted that all the scenes listed above are from cartoons. This is not accidental. Other contributors to this volume I know may disagree, but for me the most successful fairy films are animated. Live-action film just doesn't seem to be up to the job of portraying fairies, nor does it, in my modest experience, do a very good job of fantasy generally. (I gave up on *Game of Thrones* not because of the sex or violence but because of the sheer silliness of the dragons, the zombies, and the giants.)

Things that are powerful on the page or when drawn become ridiculous when acted out in the "real" world; perhaps their fascination lies in their unreality. Some claim that CGI has transformed matters. I am not so sure. Yes, we have gone beyond the "uncanny valley": Gollum or Aslan might pass muster in terms of how they move and their facial expressions. But we see, if anything, too much. Good horror, thinking of a parallel genre (*The Shining, Rosemary's Baby,* etc.) only works because the horror is glimpsed and hinted at rather than addressed directly.[338] In live-action fantasy, we have reality unwelcomingly lathered all over our faces.

I offer this rant by way of an explanation for my interest in the fairies of Walt Disney. Whether you love him or hate him—I, for the record, admire him—Disney was the most successful animator of the 20th century. He produced not just a series of influential films, but a characteristic way of seeing the world. In as much as Disney introduced fairies into his films these have become the filter through which westerners see fairies. Children in my generation (b. 1973) grew up with fairies in books, fairies in toy stores, and, most importantly, fairies in Disney films and their derivatives. This influence has been recognised by fairyists and folklorists who even talk of the "Disneyfication" of fairies.[339] Their idea is that the ghostly, beautiful, ambivalent, wingless, and often cruel fairy of folklore has been transformed by Hollywood. We now have, instead, a sugar-coated cherub who is more likely to be seen cuddling voles or polishing water lilies than stealing babies and killing cattle (its traditional activities).

As I'll try and show below, things are, where Disney is concerned, more complicated than this. In the next pages, I give an overview of the way that Disney used fairies in his productions. I look at his early animations (the first Disney fairy known to me appeared in 1922) and in his feature films to 1960. We are covering a period of about forty years with the *Laughograms,* the *Silly Symphonies, Snow White, Fantasia, Cinderella, Peter Pan, Sleeping Beauty,* and, the only live-action film I will refer to here, Disney's *Darby O' Gill and the Little People,* among others.

I am also interested in another question: did Walt Disney, in fact, believe in fairies? I ask because we have some strangely compelling British evidence from the 1950s that suggests just that. It will be best looked at after, rather than before, our survey of the Disney fairy.

Introducing Walt Disney

Walter Elias Disney was born in Chicago in 1901, but grew up on a farm in Marceline, Missouri, the Shangri-la of his youth: an interlude which ended at 11 when his family moved to a much tougher life in Kansas City.[340] Walt showed early promise as an artist and managed as a young adult to get involved in the burgeoning field of animation, eventually heading out to California, where he sold his cartoons. By the 1920s Disney was running animation companies (with his brother Roy's help) and Disney's name was burnt into film history in 1928 with the creation of Mickey Mouse. A decade later in 1937, Disney released the first film-length cartoon, *Snow White and the Seven Dwarfs*. Then, after a series of animated films, the studio broadened its production to include documentaries and live-action films. Disney had, following the war, taken an increasingly hands-off approach to the Disney cartoons and from the early 1950s began to plan the creation of Disneyland, which opened in July 1955. He died in 1966 of complications from lung cancer.

Walt Disney is at times described as an American genius who created some of the greatest works of art of the 20th century. Alternatively, he is presented as a reactionary, a racist, and a heartless "capitalist pig" guilty of destroying fantasy with excessive commercialisation. Such positions tell us, it is needless to say, more about his adulators and detractors than they tell us about Disney.

These contradictory opinions thrive, in part, because of the enigma around Disney's personality. Walt was, even to friends, opaque. Then, by the age of thirty, he was, in any case, so centred on his business that we lose the man in the bailouts and strikes and overseas deals that defined and shaped his art. Our best Disney biographers, Neal Gabler and Bob Thomas produce fascinating accounts, but both, in the end, tell us more about the kingdom than the king.

I have no special insight into what the hidden "essence" of Disney was. Disney was no "open book" and I wonder whether even his wife and children really understood him.

There are, though, occasional glimpses of a beating heart in his actions. For instance, Disney, the leader of a business empire, began to tinker compulsively in the late 1940s on the studio lot with trains.[341] He soon moved on to creating his own railway track. This fixation led, by Disney's own admission, to Disneyland. Disney clearly had an internal fantasy world, it is just that it only very rarely juts above water. Disney's life, Gabler claims, "would become an ongoing effort to devise what psychologists call a 'parcosm', an invented universe that he could control as he could not control reality."[342] This gets closer to Disney than any other sentence I know.

As to fairies... It is important to understand, first, the different kinds of fairies that were likely to be known to a little boy who grew up in Missouri and Kansas in the 1900s and 1910s.[343] Broadly speaking, we can make a distinction between two main strands that dominated fairy thinking in the early 20th century: folk fairies and Theosophic fairies.

Folk fairies were the traditional European fairies who, to some extent, crossed the Atlantic to the New World with colonists and immigrants, and who arrived in greater number later, confected in folk-story collections. These fairies were believed to live in communities in the wilderness beyond human settlements. Humans and fairies depended on each other and came into contact as humans begged favours from fairies (as gurus, wish-dispensers, and "godmothers"). Fairies stole human babies, got human women to nurse their children or even fell in love with humans. Most fairy stories (as opposed to fairy tales) are about the moments of contact, when the human and the fairy world collide, often with tragic consequences.

The other fairies were "Theosophic" fairies. From the mid-late 19th century spiritualists had tried to remap the universe: giving new places to the dead, to good and evil, and even to "elementals" (i.e. fairies). Theosophists (an intellectualised splinter of spiritualism) articulated the way that elementals governed the natural world: some were fire elementals, some plant-life elementals, some water elementals, some rock elementals.

The Theosophic vision of fairies drew on earlier ideas in European mysticism and they were taken up by other mystic traditions, for instance, anthroposophists (Rudolph Steiner and his ilk). But the idea also gradually leached out into the cultural mainstream. There are late nineteenth-century children's stories with fairies taking care of gardens, and we have the "Flower Fairies" Cicely Barker drew in the 1920s. The Cottingley Fairy photographs may have been faked with Theosophy in mind (I doubt it). They were certainly interpreted in Theosophic terms when they appeared before the public in the early 1920s. In fairy terms, the 20th century was one long battle between the Theosophic and the traditionalist fairies.[344]

Spoiler: the Theosophic fairies won.

From the *Laughograms* to the *Silly Symphonies*

Fairies had appeared in film from the earliest years of cinema. The first example I know of a fairy on celluloid is *La Fée aux Choux* (*The Cabbage Fairy, circa* 1895), a disturbing minute-long film in which a fairy plucks real life babies from cabbages. Fairies were natural choices for silent film. Their elegance gave the wardrobe department opportunities to shine as in Georges Méliès's *Le Royaume des Fées* (The Kingdom of the Fairies, 1903). In their dancing, they allowed directors to play with movement: a mania for the earliest film-makers as seen, for instance, in the court scenes in *Fairy of the Surf* (1909). There was spectacle: in an otherwise black and white film *La Fée Printemps* (1902), the fairy is coloured yellow and transforms winter to spring; the flowers are coloured as well. Directors could play with special effects of scale: in *Peter Pan* (1924), Peter sweeps up tiny living fairies ("I expect it is just those bothersome fairies again"). There was also a sexual charge with scantily-dressed ungovernable fairies flouting human rules. So in *The Nicotine Fairies* (1909), the human smoker—a moustached cad—and the miniature fairies openly flirt in a way that would have shocked and thrilled Edwardians.

Disney was not the first filmmaker to use fairies, but he may have been the first animator to do so. Fairies had already appeared on cinema screens before he was born. In his 1922 *Cinderella*, a seven-minute short in the *Laughograms* series (not to be confused with the 1950 Disney feature), we have, once the stepsisters leave Cinderella to go to the ball, a visit from the fairy godmother. This fairy helper has no wings and looks like a fifty-year-old woman with scoliosis. The only thing that marks her apart from the humans in the film is a crooked staff that she uses as a wand and her trick of levitating and vanishing.

There do not appear to have been any fairies in Disney's fifty-seven *Alice* films: a live-action girl mixed into a cartoon world; few survive. Nor were there any fairies in Disney's *Laughograms*, I think, with the exception given above. The series, though, introduced Disney's taste for folk-stories: titles included *Goldie Locks* and *Little Red Riding Hood*.

Fairies are much more in evidence in the *Silly Symphonies*, Disney's main product from 1929 to 1939. The *Silly Symphonies* were animated shorts, each lasting between five and eight minutes, which gave an important role to music in creating scenes and stories. These are the antecedents of *Fantasia*. About six were released annually through the 1930s, though numbers changed with production problems and shifts in distributors. Of the total seventy-five *Symphonies*, ten (about fifteen percent) include what could loosely be called fairies. In 1929 Disney released *The Merry Dwarfs*; there was *Playful Pan* in 1930 (if Pan can be taken as a fairy); *King Neptune* (1932, with mermaids) *Santa's Workshop* (1932, with gnomes); *Lullaby Land* (1933, bogey men and the sandman); *The China Shop* (1933, Billygoatlegs the satyr); *The Flying Mouse* in 1934; *The Goddess of Spring* (1935, again if a nature goddess can be taken as a fairy); *The Golden Touch* (1935); *Water Babies* (1935); and *Merbabies* (1938). Fairies or fairy-like figures were becoming part of Disney's repertoire. [345]

Disney, through the *Silly Symphonies*, carried on experimenting with simple folk stories: the most famous of these shorts is unquestionably *The Three Little Pigs* (1933). Fairies do not generally appear in these tales. Indeed, perhaps only two of the fairies listed above can be said to be part of a proper narrative. There is Goldy the Elf in *The Golden Touch* (the King Midas legend): Goldy provides the curse that teaches the king a well-needed lesson. Then in *The Flying Mouse*, a mouse rescues a butterfly. The butterfly turns into a winged fairy who, grateful, grants a wish and gives advice. The butterfly is, I think, the first winged Disney fairy and the first winged fairy known to me in cinema history, though I wait to be corrected.[346] She is sometimes said to be the prototype of the Blue Fairy in *Pinocchio*, and there is certainly a passing resemblance in character and appearance.

In the *Symphonies*, it is much more typical for fairies to appear as part of what might be termed a "natural ballet" where the story is non-existent or only of secondary importance, but where the dance represents a process in nature. For instance, in *Water Babies* and *Merbabies* the fairies dance in and on a marine element. In *Playful Pan*, Pan dances through the countryside eventually encountering a fire, which he manages to charm into a lake. In the *Goddess of Spring*, the eponymous character dances with flowers and birds until she comes into contact with a threat to the natural order, a devil who brings winter by kidnapping the goddess for a season. This is the story of Persephone. One could extend the fairy category to include such shorts as *Summer*, *Night*, *Spring* and *Frolicking Fish* where animals, plants and trees are shown dancing together with little or no storyline. These are not fairies *per se*, though when trees come alive and flowers do a jig, we approach the Theosophical views of the fey.

In the first Disney fairy phase, we see a bias towards Theosophic fairies. Fairies are not just found in the wilds, they *are* the wilds. They are depicted moving together and in their dances we get hints of natural or seasonal changes. Those who know Disney's output will recognise here, a theme present in the studio's later films: from the Nutcracker Suite in *Fantasia*, to *Bambi* (with its strong emphasis on the changing year), to the "Firebird" in *Fantasia 2000* (a scene that Disney had himself sponsored before he died).

Is it possible that Disney had come into contact with Theosophic ideas earlier in his life and that he was reproducing them here? Or are we just seeing a reflex of the kinds of animated films made in this period: short features strongly based around music?

From *Snow White* to *Fantasia*

In 1937, after three years of planning and work, Disney Studios made cinema history by releasing the first full-length animated film: *Snow White and the Seven Dwarfs*. It is impossible, I think, for anyone born after the war, to properly grasp the excitement that this film caused among cinema audiences when it was released. Perhaps the closest experience those in my generation have had were the first computer animated films in the mid and late 1990s. Disney achieved in *Snow White* two new things.

First, the film was long: 83 minutes. This was no longer a "short" with which audiences relaxed between features, a film-goer's *aperitivo* or *digestivo*. It was a feature length movie in its own right and tightly plotted as with all of Disney's early films.

Second, Disney had slowly been advancing the quality of his studio's animation in the previous decade, not least by using human and animal models. This progress is clear watching the changes in *Silly Symphonies* from the late 1920s to the late 1930s as jitters and "shimmying" become less frequent. *Snow White* marks a breakthrough in terms of the quality of animation.

Snow White was a huge hit and Disney followed his first feature up with some of his most famous films, though none were as financially successful as *Snow White*. In 1940 there were both *Pinocchio* and *Fantasia*. In 1941 came *Dumbo*, and then in 1942 *Bambi*.

Looking back at the first five Disney cartoons the most striking thing is their range. Though they all have certain recognisable Disney touches, they are actually very different. It goes without saying that Disney was no longer at the head of a ragged band of artists. To produce these pictures it had proved necessary to employ and train literally hundreds of staff and Disney could do no more than direct the efforts of others. But he dedicated all his energies to that end. He picked projects in consultation with his inner circle. He stalked down corridors where animators drew at his instructions: "Man is in the forest" was whispered from desk to desk whenever Disney drew near. He also managed meetings on plot developments and characterisation.[347]

The first three films are interesting in terms of fairy-lore. In *Snow White*, Disney took one of the most famous European folk stories and turned it into an animated film. We have witches, we have dwarfs, we have magic mirrors, we have poisoned apples and, a little awkwardly, we have some North American vultures in the fairy-tale forest.

The dwarfs are evidently "knockers": the fairies of mining. They have their own mine and famously whistle as they work. The Disney artists lovingly detailed their cottage with pseudo-Bavarian carving and kitchenware. The dwarfs are also each given their own personality, a contrast with the hive-like uniformity of Disney's *The Merry Dwarfs* (1929), less than a decade before. They retain something of a fairy "edge" too, in the characters of Doc and particularly Grumpy. They are not just sweet old men, though they proved too cute for J.R.R. Tolkien and C.S. Lewis who saw the film together in 1938.[348]

If these points take us back towards traditional European folklore fairies, other parts of the film recall Theosophical fairies. A crucial theme in Snow White is the relationship between the heroine and nature. Animals and birds flock to Snow White both before and during her exile in the forest. In her relationship with nature she recalls the *Goddess of Spring* from the *Silly Symphonies* who had a similar magnetic effect in the natural world.

But there is a remarkable scene in *Snow White*, as the heroine runs away from the woodsman, where this relationship is turned on its head. Snow White suffers from the cartoon version of a psychotic break and begins to construe objects around her as monsters: for instance, a twig catching at her dress becomes a monster's hands; a trunk with an owl becomes a grotesque Sylvan face ready to gobble her up.[349] This "fit," which lasts a long minute on the screen, marks the destruction of Snow White's world and reminds us of the diabolical side of nature.

Pinocchio is based on the 1883 book by Carlo Collodi: *Le avventure di Pinocchio: Storia di un burattino*. Collodi, a pen-name of the Tuscan writer Carlo Lorenzini, was not writing folklore proper. But Collodi borrowed freely from Italian folklore in composing *Pinocchio*.[350] The Disney film is very unlike the book and this is the reason it works so well. The Collodi original is an anarchic, directionless, and often bleak journey through a fairy-tale countryside: the very lack of coordinates is part of its power. It has proven difficult to make into a film, though many have tried: Pinocchio defeated even Roberto Benigni.

Disney's success here was based on simplification. He ruthlessly imposed a three-part structure on an impossible story, in cinematic terms. Even fairy-tale scholar Jack Zipes, who is unremittingly hostile to Disney, acknowledges that the "story was superbly condensed by Disney and his collaborators."[351]

Pinocchio has two main fairy parts: the Blue Fairy and Pleasure Isand (a kind of bogeyman's lair, where naughty boys are turned into donkeys). The Blue Fairy in Collodi's book is moody, irrational and sometimes downright vindictive: in short, a traditional fairy. Disney, instead, creates a "blonde, winged, middle-class, American mother" who descends from the sky.[352] Disney's sanitisation of the Blue Fairy is perhaps the most striking example of traditional fairylore being "tidied up" in Hollywood.

For traditionalists disappointed by Disney's treatment of the Blue Fairy he, in any case, makes up for this with Pleasure Island. The moments where Pinocchio and his friend are turned into donkeys catches the essence of Collodi's original like no other part of the film. It is perhaps the most disturbing scene in the entire Disney canon. Watch your kids' faces when the boy Alexander (just transformed into a donkey) is asked his name by the coachman. "You boys have had your fun, now pay for it!"

Fantasia, released later in 1940, is a very different film, a series of seven pieces of classical music with images and stories. In Walt's words: "we could do some very exciting entertaining and beautiful things with music and picture and color and things."[353] Typically, narratives are set to music. In *Fantasia*, music is set to narrative as the rises and falls of the orchestra are given corresponding images or tales.

Of the seven parts of *Fantasia*, several borrow from fairylore. This includes the weakest set, the Greek mythological scenes of Beethoven's *Pastoral Symphony*: where a cherub's round buttocks resolve themselves into a Valentine's heart, which must be the most ill-judged scene in the early Disney films. It also includes the strongest, Mussorgsky's *Night on Bald Mountain* where a Slavic pagan god, Chernobog, and his legions (ghosts, witches, bogies...) meet in a mountain top black Sabbath, only to be banished by the bells at dawn. In European folklore, church bells were often said to be able to magically drive away evil. Disney underlined this by rounding off the piece (and the film) with Schubert's *Ave Maria*. Walt: "There is still a lot of Christians in the world, in spite of Russia and some of the others."[354]

The most interesting segment of *Fantasia* in fairy terms is Tchaikovsky's *Nutcracker Suite*, which takes us through the seasons in a way that is reminiscent of several of the earlier *Silly Symphonies*. Enter Disney's "delicate art-deco fantasies resembling animated versions of 1930s book illustration."[355] In spring, diaphanous fairies with may-fly wings bring life to plants: opening blossoms and leaving dew on morning roses and spider webs. In autumn, fairies with dragon-fly wings cause the leaves to fall. Then in winter, fairies with frost-edged wings bring ice to the world just before the snow falls. Between these fairy scenes animals and plants—including gold-fish and "Chinese" mushrooms—dance their own way through the seasons.

The Nutcracker Suite is the most "Theosophical" scene in all of the early Disney films: fairies are very much portrayed as the caretakers of nature. This is taken as a given in contemporary cinematic fairylore. We too easily forget that Disney had been a pioneer in showing fairies on the screen in this way.

From the Strike to *Darby*

In the spring of 1941, Disney suffered one of the most devastating setbacks of his life: a strike by his workers against the company's pay and privilege inequities. What to someone else would have been an inconvenience or a business problem or even an ethical quandary, became for Disney a poisonous act of betrayal. In his own mind, the strike ruined the paradise that he had tried to create at his Burbank studios; a serious blow for a man who dealt in ideal worlds.

Then in December, Japan brought the United States into the war and Disney's attentions were directed to propaganda shorts and films. Disney never really returned to the job he had before the war. He managed the new films created by the studio, but in a more detached way, spreading his attention more thinly. The films of 1937-1942 are very much Walt's films: a collective effort directed by a single man. The films created in the later 1940s, the 1950s, and the 1960s were Disney Studio productions: collective efforts directed by a company ethos. From the 1950s Disney would give the best of himself instead to his new paradise, Disneyland.

Disney continued, however, in the war and its aftermath to approve films with fairies. Part of this was Disney's concentration on traditional folk stories. Disney would release *Cinderella* in 1950, and *Sleeping Beauty* in 1959. There was also Disney's long-standing obsession with Hans Christian Andersen's tales and a planned biographical film of Andersen's life which was essentially derailed by the war.[356] Another part of it was just the fact that fairies appear in children's classics: Disney brought out *Peter Pan* in 1953. There also seems to have been a curiosity about the fairy realm *per se*: "the Little People have always fascinated me," confessed Disney in the late 1950s.[357] In 1946, Disney gave instructions to open a file on a live-action film on Irish fairies, which would eventually come out in 1959 with the title *Darby O' Gill and the Little People*.[358]

There were other failed projects that point to his passion here. In 1942, Disney was contacted by Roald Dahl, a Royal Air Force lieutenant and, later, a celebrated British writer. Dahl was pushing an idea for a script about "gremlins," the malignant spirits held responsible for damaging planes. Disney was interested and for a year the Studio gnawed away at the story, trying to find a way to make it work. In the end, motive proved an insurmountable difficulty: "Dahl failed to give a logical reason or motive for the gremlins' behaviour." The best the studio could come up was that the gremlins were angry with the RAF not because the fairies were closet Nazis: it was because the RAF kept cutting down trees to make runways. That final detail is a very Disney touch and was resolved by giving the gremlins postage stamps: apparently the plane-wreckers were obsessed with philately.[359]

Let's turn back though to the films that were made. In *Cinderella* in 1950 Disney returned to a fairy he had introduced almost thirty years before in *Laughograms*: the Fairy Godmother. The contrast with the Blue Fairy in *Pinocchio* is notable. Here Cinderella's patron is a "comfortably padded,"[360] kind but bluff, no nonsense woman: "We have to hurry because even miracles take a little time," she tells her astounded understudy.

Cinderella's fairy godmother is human in appearance. Flora, Fauna, and Merryweather, the three fairy godmothers seen in *Sleeping Beauty* nine years later, are instead diminutive, winged and bumbling humanoids; note incidentally their Theosophic-style names. We have returned with this trio to the group humour of the seven dwarfs or even regressed back to the *Laughograms*. I am not sure that the three in Sleeping Beauty have individual characters. They are, certainly, an inadequate foil to perhaps the most interesting fairy in any cartoon in any genre, the evil Maleficent: the Darth Vader of the Disney universe. When critics accuse Disney of cloying floral fairies, they too easily forget the horned woman in black.

Peter Pan in 1953 also brought a notable fairy into the Disney family, Tinker Bell. Tinker Bell had always been a favourite in Barrie's play where she was represented on stage by a torch light. Disney took the courageous decision to give her a form. Incidentally, claims that her figure was based on Marilyn Monroe are untrue,[361] but there is a jarring unexpected sexuality in Tinker Bell's wiggles, posturing and pouting. Disney also gave full space to her wild-cat spitefulness. At one point, "Tink"—who occasionally glows red with anger—tries to kill Wendy by making her drop from the sky. When asked by Peter whether she had attempted murder, Tink joyfully nods.

Other members of the fairy kingdom in *Peter Pan* are scarcely better behaved. The mermaids roughhouse with Wendy and when one is berated, she complains, "But we were just trying to drown her."

I have kept Disney's Irish film, the live-action *Darby O' Gill and the Little People*, for last. *Darby* details a battle of wits between Darby O' Gill (a stage Irishman) and, on the one hand, his successor as estate caretaker, Michael McBride (played by a young Sean Connery), and, on the other hand, King Brian, the lord of the local leprechauns. There is much interest in scale differences between the knee-high Brian and the human-sized Darby: special effects that characterised some of the earliest fairy films.

Darby lacks the tight plotting of most Disney cartoons. There are bit appearances by a banshee, a death coach, and a pooka, none of which are entirely necessary. But the story winds down pleasantly enough. Michael, after seeing off a local bully, gets engaged to Darby's daughter Katie, and Darby, after a battle of wits, makes peace with Brian, the king under the mountain. Perhaps my own dislike of live-action fairy films has blinded me to the charms of *Darby*. Many Disney aficionados consider the film to be a neglected classic.

In one sense the film is a travesty of Irish fairylore. Leprechauns don't have "kings." They are solitary fairies. Disney had taken the best known Irish mythical character and forced him into the place of the *Sídhe*, the Irish fairies proper. This was a tactical decision that made commercial and, as we shall see, perhaps personal sense.

More generally, the writers took their fairy folklore homework very seriously. Small details of Irish fairylore are included: for instance, the idea that dirty water must not be allowed to fall on fairies when thrown out of windows.

Disney had visited Ireland with a team from the studios in November 1946 in preparation for the film.[362] While in Dublin he visited the Irish Folklore Commission. The Commission's director, then Séamus Delargy, took responsibility for sending Irish material to Disney and his team, including numerous books on Irish manners and legends. The final version of the film thirteen years later suggests that these books were read back in California and then used intelligently.

Disney gave his own description of the creation of *Darby* in an entertaining mockumentary: *I Captured the King of the Leprechauns*. Here Disney—who proves to be an exceptional dead-pan actor: "Well, could I carry [a leprechaun] back in a shoe box?"—visits Ireland and goes to the Irish Folklore Commission (where he is solemnly shown a leprechaun's suit of clothes). Disney talks of his grandfather describing leprechauns as being "knee high to a mortal." In the publicity for the film, meanwhile, we get this memory from Walt:

> Being half Irish myself, I learned about the Leprechauns of Ireland while I was still a small boy on our farm at Marceline, Missouri. I began to believe in Leprechauns, then, because some of my relatives had pretty convincing stories to tell about the magic powers of these Little People, and their tricks, and what they could do when angry. So, I promised myself that one day, after I had grown up, I would go to the land of the Leprechaun myself, and meet one in person.[363]

I have no idea whether leprechauns were a frequent topic of conversation in the Disney family; I am sceptical, in truth. But that Walt associated leprechauns with the happiest period of his childhood tells us something important. A good rule with Disney is that when Marceline is evoked, we are dealing with the animator's soul. For a moment, with his grandfather measuring leprechauns against his leg, we peep through the gates, wrought in five decades of iron, and back into Disney's lost Eden.

Did Disney Believe in Fairies?

I end this chapter with a Disney fairy mystery, one which is roughly con-temporary with *Darby* and one that is interesting because it might point to surprising Theosophic loyalties in the boy from Missouri. In June 1956, a photostatted newsletter was produced by a minor British association in Nottingham in the English midlands. The back of this newsletter showed a list of almost a hundred members of said association.

Reading these names today, the strongest impression is the contrast be-tween the famous and the utterly obscure. Important figures include Lord Dowding (head of fighter command in the Battle of Britain) and Alasdair Alpin MacGregor (a notable Scottish writer). Less well known are Daph-ne Charters (a minor English mystic) and June Kynaston, author of *Nude Dancing for Health*. The members are broken down by region, most being resident in Britain. There were also some members abroad including a member in Holland, a member in Italy, and a single member in the United States—Walt Disney.

And the organisation? This was the Fairy Investigation Society (FIS), a group of Theosophic fairy believers.

The FIS had been founded in London in 1927, when séances and psy-chic studies were fashionable in the United Kingdom. Its members might not have all described themselves as Theosophists, but they believed in the idea of the "natural" fairy of Theosophy. Early members included mystic artist Bernard Sleigh, medium Clare Cantlon, Estelle Stead (daugh-ter of famous Victorian journalist and psychic William Stead), and ra-dio-telegraph scientist Quentin Craufurd.

There is a very good chance that Arthur Conan Doyle, Sherlock Holmes' creator and the man who had publicised the Cottingley Fairies, was also a member. Doyle certainly corresponded with the organisation.

The FIS had fun in the capital in the years before the Great Depres-sion. There were meetings, magic lantern shows, discussions, attempts to contact marsh fairies by wireless, and the FIS brought out at least one newsletter in the late 1920s. The society fell, however, into quiescence in the 1930s. Craufurd refounded the organisation after the war and became its president. Then, in 1950, one Marjorie Johnson was made secretary.[364]

We know about the FIS in the 1950s thanks to Marjorie Johnson. First, there are a series of newsletters prepared by Johnson, sent out to members most years. Six of these survive, though there were certainly others; I have an incomplete set. Two of these newsletters contain membership lists and both of these lists have the name "Walt Disney" in the "USA."[365]

Second, there is a manuscript that Marjorie Johnson prepared and that was finally published posthumously in 2014 as *Seeing Fairies*. This manuscript was Marjorie Johnson's life mission, an attempt to prove the existence of fairies by giving literally hundreds of accounts of fairy encounters. In this work many FIS members sent accounts of their own experiences to Johnson for inclusion. Walt Disney does not appear in this book. At least he does not under his own name.[366]

What does Disney's appearance in the FIS membership list mean? We can, I think, assume that this is *the* Walt Disney. But other than that, I am uncertain. Taken at face value, it could mean that Walt Disney had contacted the FIS and had asked to become a member, at which time his name had been put down. Let us call this "scenario one."

Did Disney understand what the FIS was? Did he realise that it was an organisation of fairy believers? Or for Disney was it perhaps just a folklore society interested in "the Little People"?

Then there is "scenario two." Had Marjorie Johnson taken the first step and contacted Disney, offering to bring him into the magic circle? Perhaps she had seen fairies in his films and had decided to reach out to the great man: I can imagine her sitting spellbound through *Fantasia*. In this second scenario, we must suppose that Disney replied, in any case, in the affirmative.

"Scenario three" is that Marjorie Johnson added Disney's name unilaterally, deciding that it gave the FIS prestige. This I would reject out of hand. Johnson was painfully honest and "proper."

Lacking more FIS documentation—Johnson's letter collection was thrown out at her death in 2012—and also lacking any insights from the Disney archives, I can only speculate.[367] But this, for what it is worth, is my guess.

In 1947, Disney visited Ireland to prepare the way for *Darby O' Gill and the Little People*. In this period, Disney was keen to find as much material as possible on fairies. At some point then or in the next years—while the project was "live"—the name of the FIS crossed his desk. The best bet is that this was in 1955, when Marjorie Johnson appealed through tens of newspapers (in Britain and abroad) looking for fairy encounters for *Seeing*

Fairies.[368] Disney, according to this hypothesis, sent an inquiry or asked for membership. Doubtlessly thrilled, Marjorie Johnson replied.

If this scenario is correct, I suspect that membership was for Disney a little like ordering folklore books through the Irish Folklore Commission. It was not a statement of fairy belief so much as an act of research and adventure. However, Disney had an unusual imagination. I suspect he was the kind of man who found it quite easy to believe and to not believe simultaneously.

Disney's Fairy Legacy

As we saw at the beginning of this chapter Disney has often been accused of the "Disneyfication" of fairies: the replacement of "the people of the hills" by bouncing nature-loving fairies in tutus. I hope my overview of Disney's film-making in the early and mid 20th century show the injustice of this charge. What is most striking to me is the variety of Disney fairy forms: a variety comparable to what was found in the traditional realm of fairy.

Yes, there are the necessarily simple seasonal fairies in *Fantasia* and their equivalents in the *Silly Symphonies*: dancing ciphers of the changing year. But there is also: wild Tink; the chattering godmothers of *Sleeping Beauty*; charismatic Maleficent; the quarrelling but well-meaning dwarfs; Cinderella's to-the-point guardian; a witty leprechaun king; homicidal mermaids; the blood-chilling banshee; and the maternal Blue Fairy who lets us wish upon a star.

On this evidence Disney did not have a doctrinaire view of what fairies should be. Rather, fairies were moulded to the needs of the individual film. Disney was many things—artist, innovator, filmmaker, voice actor, musician, businessman—but he was also an extraordinary story-teller.

In this essay, I have insisted on a division between folklore and Theosophical fairies. It goes without saying that the crowds that went to see Disney shorts or films in the 1930s did not point at the screen saying "folklore" or "Theosophical" every time a fairy popped up. But for us looking back at films made nearly a century ago, I hope the division has proven useful. It is not in the least surprising that Disney inherited folklore fairies from his childhood: from books, from the radio, from his grandfather and, yes, from the cinema.

What I find anomalous is Disney's use of the Theosophic fairy: the fairy as the guardian or personification of nature. As noted above, in modern fairy films this is the norm. In fact, there has been, in the cartoon films of the last three decades, the full triumph of the Theosophic fairy as they marched through the institutions. Take *Fern Gully*, the *Tinker Bell* cycle, or *Epic*. The Green consciousness, which has characterised the West for fifty years, has done more to "Disney-ify" fairies than Walt.

But the fact remains that Disney is something of a cinematic pioneer here. The Theosophic fairies of the *Silly Symphonies, Snow White and the Seven Dwarfs*, and *The Nutcracker Suite* in *Fantasia* were not commonplace on the screen: in fact, I only know of one very partial antecedent, *La Fée Printemps* (1902). The easiest explanation is that Disney and his animators absorbed these ideas in their early years from various sources, though Disney's later membership in the FIS opens up other possibilities. Theosophical notions also, it must be said, plugged into certain mental habits of the cinema industry. Early filmmakers, particularly those of the silent era, were obsessed with movement. The pastoral ballets of Disney provided not just movement but movement through the seasons, movements through time bringing change.

But there is something else. Early Disney films (and, indeed, many later ones) have "a thing" for nature.[369] They go beyond simple dances: *Bambi* is the most striking example, a pastoral ballet that becomes a narrative. The hunters are not part of the cycle—they disturb and break the natural order.[370] For all Disney's faux-pioneer and bluff mid-western values, he evidently had an ecological streak.

The Theosophic fairies would have approved. The folklore fairies, I suspect, would have rolled their eyes.

Acknowledgements

I'd like to thanks to Josh Cutchin, Davide Ermacora, and Chris Woodyard for help with this essay.

DEEP: An examination of the faerie themes in Takashi Shimizu's film Marebito

Wren Collier

When considering films that contain Western pulp science fiction and faerie story themes, Japanese cinema might be overlooked. Japanese cinema—especially the subgenre dubbed "J-horror" in the West—has a strong tradition of depicting supernatural horror, particularly ghost stories and the Japanese equivalent of faeries, known as *yokai*. However, these movies typically draw from the folklore of Japan and the animist traditions of religions like Shinto.

One film that starts with uniquely Western narratives as its base is the haunting direct-to-video, low budget 2004 film *Marebito* (稀人) by director Takashi Shimuzu. If we open up *Marebito* and look within, we find a rich and unique utilization of Western sci-fi and fantasy tropes, reflected through the context of early 2000s Japanese culture and politics. More to the topic of this essay, we see a deconstruction of one of the most common and enduring faerie story narratives: the changeling child.

The name of the film, *Marebito*, is a word meaning "rare person or spirit." It is used to describe supernatural visitors from afar who bring gifts of knowledge. Iwai Hiroshi, in his "Encyclopedia of Shinto," speculates that the tradition of *marebito* is the basis for all folk religions in Japan. The *marebito* are visitors from the Otherworld, and despite the fact that they inspire dread and fear, nevertheless carry enlightenment to bestow upon others.[371] The titular *marebito* of the film, discussed later in this essay, carries with her this intermingled gift of fear and knowledge of what fear itself truly is.

"I want to see what he saw then," says Masuoka, the protagonist of the film. Masuoka (played by celebrated Japanese director Shinya Tsukamoto) is an unemployed amateur video photographer who is fascinated with capturing the look of fear on other people's faces. He is watching a tape he filmed earlier of a man named Arei Kuroki piercing his own eye with a knife in a subway station. Masuoka is obsessed with what sort of fear Kuroki experienced that would cause him to gouge out his own eye rather than continue to face it. Masuoka begins to obsess over the very concept of fear itself.

Alienated by the society he lives in, Masuoka feels there is a world of the unknown just under the surface of the mundane day-to-day life he leads. He describes capturing images of UFOs and ghosts, but considers these banal because they have already been described as strange by others. He says that these things merely cause anxiety in others, but nothing like the absolute fear he observed in Kuroki's fixed gaze. He wishes to find *true horror*. Even watching what appears to be a snuff film, Masuoka laments the fact that it does not seem quite real. He cannot find that otherworldly, absolute horror he so desires to know, and expresses a willingness to go to inhuman lengths to obtain it. In a line that will come back to haunt us later, Masuoka declares that he would even "imitate" a psychopath, murdering someone so that he may record their terror on his retinas. He is willing to sacrifice his own humanity in pursuit of knowledge.

"By looking at her through my lens, I believe that I've salvaged her soul," Masuoka declares as he voyeuristically observes a woman who has barricaded herself in her apartment, windows covered in cardboard and debris to block out the light. Not only alienated by his own culture and society, Masuoka further self-alienates by only viewing the world through his camera lens, always filming as he walks the streets of Tokyo, creating a wall of observation and detachment in his interactions with his surroundings.

Revisiting the scene of Kuroki's suicide, Masuoka dejectedly declares that it seemed more real when he watched the recording he captured played back on the evening news. Thus, the film intentionally starts questioning the separation between reality and unreality, blurring the line between the two.

While in the subway station, he catches a fleeting glimpse of a strange creature scurrying into a side passage. Following this strange apparition, Masuoka descends into the labyrinthian bowels of Tokyo, down spiral staircases and steam tunnels, past maintenance shafts and enormous cables which run through the metropolis like the veins of a great animal or the corpse of a dead god.

THE UNDERWORLD

Eventually, Masuoka reaches a section abandoned since World War II, where a homeless vagrant living in the tunnels warns him about the "Dero." Masuoka is cautioned that, should the Dero find him, they will devour him. Travelling even further into this subterranean maze of crumbling Imperial wartime architecture, Masuoka determines that he's crossed the boundary of the Netherworld. Accordingly, he encounters the ghost of Kuroki, who leads him onwards with an oil lamp, like Virgil leading Dante into Hell.

It is here that we get our first correlation to faerie legends, with Kuroki describing how people think of the Netherworld—traditionally the land of the dead—as being underground, because they do not know what lies beneath their feet. The inability to truly know what's beyond the veil of death places the Underworld beneath us, characterized by ultimate darkness, a place where our knowledge only extends to the boundary.

Indeed, in faerie lore across the world, the fae are imagined as a subterranean people inhabiting underground kingdoms. As Joshua Cutchin points out in his book *Thieves in the Night*, Germanic and Scandinavian folklore is clear about the relationship between the subterranean and the fae, naming them the "underground people."[372] In Portugal, the *mouras* are said to live under the earth, specifically in a world called Mourama that is said explicitly to be the land of the dead.[373] In Susan B. Martinez's *The Lost History of the Little People*, she writes that Iberian and Russian folklore are both direct in equating the fae with the dead, especially the prematurely deceased and the spirits of venerated ancestors. She quotes author Katherine Briggs, who states, "It is a common thing for underground fairies to live under human dwellings. It may be that they were the spirits of former inhabitants."[374]

In the context of *Marebito*, this rings especially true. What greater underworld could there be than the subterranean kingdom lurking beneath the streets of Tokyo, one of humanity's largest and most densely populated metropolises? *Marebito* evokes Martinez regarding the premature dead in the ghost of Kuroki, who as a recent suicide, haunts this rhizomatic undergrowth lying just below the feet of millions. Kuroki even says out-right to Masuoka that entrances to the Underworld are present in popu-lated areas the world over. The Underworld exists where people exist, a shadow cast by our own civilization. However, there is an unreality to this underworld that is difficult for the modern person to conceptualize, due to our Materialist dualism.

Humanity at one time understood the Underworld was both quite liter-ally under the ground, but was simultaneously an Otherworld, not bound by the material laws and forces we take for granted on the surface. The Underworld is both a physical location *and* the world of spirits and the dead. Indeed, in ancient Greece, certain caves and rivers were thought to be actual physical entrances to Hades; the dead were as close to them as the still pools of water in those caves, pools that the Greeks stared into in order to speak with them. In our haste to separate the real from the imaginal, we lose this nuance and dual understanding of the Underworld.

Leading Masuoka deeper, he and Kuroki discuss the Hollow Earth the-ory, with Kuroki listing off several entrances to the underworld, such as Brussels and beneath the Patala Shrine in Tibet. Kuroki states that there are at least two main Hollow Earth theories: one, that the Earth is hollow like an enormous egg, and the other, that Earth is honeycombed with vast underground complexes and cave systems. He brings up Agar-tha, the legendary—and fictional—underground capital first described by French occultist Alexandre Saint-Yves d'Alveydre in 1910.[375] In relation to Agartha, he makes reference to Madame Helena P. Blavatsky, co-founder of the Theosophical Society. In Theosophy—a syncretic esoteric religion combining elements of European philosophies such as Neoplatonism and Asian philosophies such as Buddhism and Hinduism—Agartha was imagined as a vast subterranean city complex inhabited by evil sorcerers and demons.[376]

Masuoka and Kuroki's discussion turns to the Shaver Mystery, the se-quence of stories written by author Ray Palmer, based on letters received from Richard Sharpe Shaver in 1943 and published in the science fiction magazine *Amazing Stories*. Kuroki warns Masuoka about the Deros, or "Detrimental Robots," that Shaver described in his letters: degenerate hu-manoids that were abandoned underground in the ancient past by their progenitor race as they fled Earth to escape some manner of cataclysm. The Dero were equal parts sadistic and brutal, kidnapping surface dwell-ers for food and torturous entertainment, and were the cause of any number of maladies, from accidental injury to major catastrophes like natural disasters.[377]

The fae are similarly described in folklore, guilty of kidnapping innocents and sometimes abusing them for their own amusement, as well as causing a vast array of broader problems for households, crops, and livestock. There are other parallels between Shaver's Dero and the fae: the Dero made use of invisible ray guns to beam negative and paranoid thoughts into the minds of people on the surface with the intent to drive them mad; parallels with elf-shot (the faerie ability to shoot invisible arrows at people to cause both physical and mental ailments) are immediately apparent. This ability of the fae to invisibly affect humans at a distance is found as far and wide as the legends of the indigenous American Shoshone peoples of Montana, as referenced in Cutchin's *Thieves in the Night*.[378]

It is unknown if Shaver himself was familiar with the legends of the fae or if anything he wrote about truly existed in the first place, perhaps being just the manifestations of a profoundly unwell mind. Ray Palmer himself went back and forth on whether or not Shaver's accounts were fiction, culminating in a young Harlan Ellison famously calling him out for his duplicity.[379] However, what is abundantly clear is that the mythopoetic narratives of Shaver's Dero closely mirror faerie legends known to cultures throughout history.

Kuroki, now accepting the fact that he truly is dead, extinguishes his lantern and abandons Masuoka in the darkness of the depths. Masuoka faints, regaining consciousness after an undetermined amount of time. Waking, now having journeyed successfully into the Underworld, Masuoka observes a literal light at the end of a tunnel and emerges into a vast subterranean complex of ruins and mountains that he refers to as "The Mountains of Madness," a reference to the H.P. Lovecraft novella. This allusion is pertinent to the film's meditation on the Shaver Mystery, given how much of Lovecraft's "Cthulhu Mythos" revolves around similar ancient and lost extraterrestrial civilizations here on Earth, sometimes lurking in dreamlike hibernation underground or beneath the ocean, their subterranean megastructures inhabited by twisted and horrific creations of the alien races who built them. In particular, *shoggoths*—enormous protoplasmic monstrosities genetically engineered by the Great Old Ones— haunt the halls of the titular "Mountains of Madness," embedded deep beneath the Antarctic ice.[380] Like Lovecraft's *shoggoths*, *Marebito's* scuttling Dero cry out with haunting, high-pitched piping vocalizations.

F

Descending into the crumbling and impossibly ancient subterranean ruins, Masuoka discovers a young woman, pale and bruised, chained naked within a recess in the wall. He touches her face and she awakens, leading into the main plot of *Marebito* and what makes the film so interesting in the lens of faerie lore: *Marebito* as an inversion and subversion of the changeling narrative. Instead of a faerie kidnapping a child from the human world and raising it in the Underworld so that it may become a faerie as well, *Marebito* tells the story of a human descending into the Underworld and kidnapping one of the fae's children, and attempting to raise it as a human.

Naming the girl "F," Masuoka takes her back to his apartment. F is feral and animalistic, hiding under his computer desk like a scared dog. She will neither eat nor drink. She is pale and sickly, characteristic hallmarks of the pitiful changeling. Most disturbingly, F sports enormous and sharp canines, making her appear even more bestial and predatory. A typical feral child, she is unable to speak or communicate normally. Masuoka even calls her "my little Kasper Hauser," referencing the famous story of the German boy who claimed to have spent the entirety of his youth in the captivity of a darkened cell, completely isolated from human contact.[381]

More aptly, F is reminiscent of The Green Children of Woolpit, two mysterious youngsters found in a wolf pit in 12th century England. These children boasted green skin, spoke no English, and would only eat broad beans. Both were sickly; one of them died, but the other survived and learned to speak, later claiming that she and her brother were from a lightless, subterranean kingdom called Saint Martin's Land inhabited by similarly green-skinned people.[382]

In further parallels to changeling lore, F barely walks, sleeps nearly all day, and is only observed moving around with purpose when Masuoka is out of the apartment, as he discovers when watching surveillance footage secretly taken of her when he's gone. Similar behavior is described by writer Thomas Keightley in *The Fairy Mythology*, who discusses a changeling boy that "ran up the walls like a cat" when no one was at home, but when accompanied by others "sat dozing at the end of the table."[383]

While buying garments for F in a women's clothing store, Masuoka is approached by a store attendant who asks if he is shopping for his daughter, something he quickly denies. Masuoka continues observing F surreptitiously through the tiny screen of his cellphone, noticing that, disturbingly, she seems to be talking to someone in the room with her, slightly off-camera. As he ponders whom F is talking to, Masuoka is confronted by a prototypical Man-in-Black (MIB) in the mall who stares him down menacingly, but says nothing. Escaping through a side door, Masuoka notices that he's also being followed by a mysterious woman. He avoids her and returns home.

Perhaps unintentionally, perhaps not, Shimizu brings in an element of classic Ufology—the ubiquitous MIB—to his faerie story. The close parallels between faerie lore and Ufology have been documented by numerous authors, most prominently by Ufologist and scientist Jacques Vallée in his monumental work *Passport to Magonia*.[384] Given Shimizu's familiarity with the Shaver Mystery and brief mention of UFOs earlier in the film, it is likely that the MIB reference is intentional. Interpreting this MIB as a psychopomp manifestation of the figure of Death again links to the association between the fae and the dead. Death incarnated is a liminal figure, able to travel between the worlds of the living and the dead in order to carry out the transmigration of human souls; in *Marebito*, this spectre of Death is an emissary from the Underworld, as we soon discover.

Returning home, Masuoka discovers an emaciated and obviously unwell F having a seizure on the floor. He attempts to force her to drink a glass of milk that she immediately vomits all over herself. In a situation typical of MIB narratives, Masuoka gets a call from a mysterious and foreboding stranger with a distorted robotic voice, who tells Masuoka that he is in trouble, that there is someone with him that "shouldn't be" and that "she can't survive." Masuoka is warned that, in attempting to save F's life, he's actually killing her. However, the MIB doesn't explain how F can be helped before hanging up.

The next day Masuoka is severely beaten by a man on the street for filming him, and returns home to F with his hand cut and bleeding. F stares, transfixed by the blood. When Masuoka offers his bloody finger to F, she greedily starts lapping up his blood in a disturbing parody of eroticism. Realizing that F needs blood to survive, Masuoka slices his hand with a boxcutter, spilling his blood onto the floor which F licks up like an animal. Intercut are disturbing images of F's blood-covered fangs and her biting into animals that Masuoka has killed and brought for her to feed on. However, he notes that nothing makes her truly content but human blood. F's blood-drinking brings to mind the folklore surrounding vampires, especially in the figures of the *strigoi*, mythical woodland creatures closely associated with owls that were said to descend upon travelers in the night and feed on their blood. In Jewish folklore, the figure of Lilith and her children (the *lilin*) existed as predatory spirits of the night that drank the blood of children and were also closely related to owls—the word *"lilin"* is even translated in the King James version of the Bible as "screech owl."[385] In a more critical interpretation of F's hematophagy, Jay McRoy writes in *Nightmare Japan: Contemporary Japanese Horror Cinema*:

> The correlation between 'F''s blood consumption and her increased (though by no means complete) acclimation to human society is not simply a convenient plot device. Masuoka literally feeds 'F' blood and carnage to sustain her most vital systems, but is this not what humans do figuratively everyday in a media(ted) culture saturated with, and ideologically buttressed by, images of corporeal trauma?[386]

While uncommon for fairies themselves to have an interest in human blood, it is not unknown. Folklore describes how fairies in the Isle of Man, if denied offerings, would extract human blood to make cakes,[387] and speaks of a faerie mistress that fed her children on the blood of humans.[388] In this sense, the fae require blood to reproduce—but oftentimes this need is more closely concerned with human genetics and bloodlines, rather than literal blood.

F's consumption of blood seems to make her more humanlike, as Masuoka observes while spying on her with his surveillance cameras. Pondering F's nature, Masuoka concludes that she must have been raised on blood, rather than breast milk, and speculates that she must have been reared by the Dero from birth. By adopting F and taking care of her, Masuoka has taken on the role of the so-called "Faerie Nurse" present in some changeling narratives. Again, Cutchin details this aspect of changeling lore in *Thieves in the Night*, describing multiple stories in which women are coerced into providing food and care for faerie children, sometimes being rewarded for their service, other times punished direly for seemingly minor transgressions.[389] In a similar vein to *Marebito*'s inversion of the changeling narrative, so is Masuoka's role as nursemaid inverting his traditional gender role. He is a man and therefore cannot provide breastmilk, but he can offer his blood and the blood of others. While he should be a paternal figure, he is relegated to a maternal role in a perverse parody of childcare.

At this point, the film throws the reality of previous events into question when the same mysterious lady who stalked Masuoka at the mall confronts him outside his apartment. She claims to know him. Masuoka denies knowing who she is and in response she demands to know what happened to "Fuyumi." Again Masuoka claims ignorance, but the woman then exclaims that she is his wife and "Fuyumi" his daughter.

Throwing her off, Masuoka retreats to his apartment only to find F missing. Distraught, he scours Tokyo for F, terrified that she's been kidnapped. Searching late into the evening, Masuoka once again comes face-to-face with the MIB. Masuoka demands to know whether F has returned to the Underworld; the MIB telepathically tells Masuoka that he has failed and that he had hoped Masuoka would be the one to "tame" F. Despite this admonition, Masuoka finds F soundly asleep on the floor of his apartment when he returns.

"DEEP"

The next day, the woman once again confronts Masuoka as he leaves his apartment. She follows him as he walks around Tokyo, demanding that he acknowledge her and provide answers. In a scene marking a jarring change in tone for the film and equal parts surreal and disturbing, Masuoka removes his camera from his bag and calmly films himself stabbing the woman to death.

It is here that we see Masuoka fully embrace his threat from earlier in the film, to become a psychopath and kill other people in order to truly know and understand what lies beyond the realm of humanity. Once his victim dies, he mechanically drains her blood into a plastic trash bag in broad daylight as people walk by in the foreground, oblivious—willingly perhaps—to the butchery happening meters away from them. Masuoka has given up his own humanity in an attempt to make F more human. He detachedly records F drinking what is possibly her own mother's blood from a baby bottle as she writhes on the floor, making his role as faerie nurse even more explicit.

We next see Masuoka leading a teenage schoolgirl into a park from the perspective of the LCD viewfinder on his camera. The girl assumes that Masuoka is a run-of-the-mill pervert and simply wants to pay her to make pornography. In a sequence reminiscent of the 1960 Michael Powell horror film *Peeping Tom*—in which a serial killer uses a portable film camera to record himself murdering women—we watch Masuoka continue filming as he slashes the girl's throat. Through the voyeuristic perspective of Masuoka's camera, we observe the horrified expression of his victim as blood pours from her neck. His desire to see fear taken to its utmost end, Masuoka dejectedly admits that while the look of someone in fear "is beautiful," "if that fear is the fear of death, it is mediocre." We see the girl reaching her hand helplessly through a hole in the wall that's blocking them from view, with the word "DEEP" graffitied on the wall. This graffiti is emblematic of Masuoka's journey in *Marebito*: he has truly gone as *deep* as he possibly can. Not deep in a directional or subterranean sense, but he has plunged beneath the surface of his own humanity, sacrificing himself, becoming like the Dero he so wants to believe exist. The camera turns as we watch Masuoka, expressionless, from the girl's perspective. He remarks that he no longer recognizes himself.

In this sequence, Shimizu makes his commentary on horror films as a genre. He wordlessly asks the viewer what they gain from watching scenes of depravity and brutality, even fictionalized. As McRoy elaborated upon in his essay on *Marebito*, does this ingestion of fictional blood somehow sustain us as humans, as the blood of others sustains F? Is being witness to this violence necessary to sate some natural bloodlust we feel, that we desire in our most animalistic tendencies?[390]

In a meta-commentary on Japanese horror in particular, Shimizu evokes the spectre of the infamous *Guinea Pig* series of exploitation films, starting with Satoru Ogura's 1985 film *The Devil's Experiment*. This faux snuff film, recorded in a found footage style, depicts a group of men kidnapping and torturing a girl to death. The fact that serial child murderer Tsutomu Miyazaki had a copy of the sixth entry in the *Guinea Pig* series (*Devil Woman Doctor*) created a moral panic in Japan parallel in scope to the United States of America's "Satanic Panic" of the 1980s. It is telling as well that the violence in these films is largely misogynistic in nature. Women are almost exclusively the victims of the torture depicted. Indeed, in *Marebito* all of Masuoka's victims are women; it appears as though he never considers using a man's blood to feed F.

Further reinforcing this commentary on the viewing of horror films, *Marebito* constantly shifts perspectives in a dizzying manner. Sometimes we watch through the grainy distortion of Masuoka's camera, other times we observe Masuoka as *he* films *us*. The line between viewer and viewed blurs, Masuoka existing in a liminal state between the imaginal and the real. McRoy remarks on this shift in point-of-view (POV) and perspective, writing:

> Consistently conflating Masuoka's POV with the image on his digital camera's LCD screen until the perspectives become not only interchangeable but indistinguishable, Shimizu posits Masuoka's POV as a product of technological mediation. In other words, Masuoka's camera becomes a prosthetic eye that at once enriches and circumscribes his vision.[391]

By circumscribing this vision of what is occurring, the viewer has no choice but to go along for the ride, trusting Masuoka's point-of-view, since it is also presented as our own, despite all the hints laid throughout the film that he is insane. Much like the Shaver Mystery itself, we have no choice but to approach the contents of the story phenomenologically, throwing aside any question if the storyteller is providing an accurate account of the events as they perceived them. We must leave our suspicions at the door. In a similar vein, a common aspect of faerie lore is that the fae can completely control whether or not humans can see them, appearing or disappearing on a whim. We must therefore assume that what the Fae allow us to see is that which they have carefully constructed and allowed. Our vision of the anomalous is circumscribed by the phenomenon itself.

BROKEN PERSPECTIVES

As Masuoka watches F feed on the blood he's freshly procured for her, he dials the payphone from where the MIB called him earlier in the film. He says that F is now "content," and, acting as emissary of the fae, the MIB tells him that *"they"* are satisfied with how he's raising their changeling. However, the film finally breaks perspective to show us something outside of Masuoka's point-of-view, erasing the circumscription that he has carefully constructed for us. The pay phone has no one on the other line. Masuoka is talking to himself.

Returning to the scene where he murdered the schoolgirl the night before, Masuoka tapes a segment for the local news station. Perhaps he realizes that his carefully constructed fiction is collapsing; depressed, he sits and speculates that humans are a degenerate species, and that in the ancient past they could see creatures from different dimensions. Masuoka's nostalgic musings on ancient humanity evoke the concept that modern industry and society have killed the faeries and our relationship with them, causing them to retreat from all but the most remote parts of the planet. Out of touch with nature and the Otherworld, humans no longer interact with the fae, despite the occasional witness who is written off immediately as a crank, lying, or both. Masuoka wishes to live in an en-spirited world, instead of the disenchanted and alienated neon wasteland he currently inhabits.

But given the monsters that also inhabit this hypothetical enchanted world—such as the Dero—is it such a good idea to wish for a return? *Marebito* asks those who are interested in the anomalous: what horrors are you willing to endure—and possibly perpetrate—to catch a glimpse of the truly unknown? As researcher John Keel noted, for many Ufologists, this desire to know "the truth" can lead to obsession, paranoia, and mad-ness. Albert K. Bender, father of the modern Men-in-Black mythos, was driven half-insane by the beings he willingly invited into his life, becoming so gripped with paranoia that he gave up his entire interest in UFOs and escaped, never looking back. Bender was lucky. Perhaps maintaining a detached irony and sense of humor about the phenomenon, like author Gray Barker, is the only way to approach the paranormal safely. If not, we may end up like John Keel in 1967, paranoid and holed up in a West Virginia hotel room awaiting robotic phone calls from spectral entities promising tantalizing glimpses of future events.[392]

Perhaps desiring desperately to return to the human world, Masuoka dresses F and takes her out into the streets of Tokyo. She marvels at the outside world, staring wide-eyed at shopping mall window displays filled with girls' clothing. Weak and barely able to walk, she stumbles along, handcuffed to Masuoka. He takes her to a karaoke bar and offers his own wrist for her to feed on. Feeling successful in his return to civilization, Masuoka abandons F in the bar, taking a train to an unknown destination. On a rocky beach he wonders if he should just settle down in the nearby village and live a normal life. However, he is met once again by the ghost of Kuroki, who reminds Masuoka that "we come from the depths of the ocean," mirroring Masuoka's musings about the abilities of ancient man to perceive the supernatural world. Kuroki puts forth the idea that we were wiser back then, when we were able to perceive and interact with spirits, when we existed "deeper" than we do currently.

One shouldn't mistake wisdom for happiness though, as this whole sequence evokes the Lovecraftian sense of "Starry Wisdom," a knowledge from beyond existence that brings with it equal parts madness and enlightenment. Nostalgia for a world once again enspirited carries with it great risk, as modern humanity has no framework with which to engage with those spirits that inhabit the Otherworld. In the past we had shamans, whose purpose was to mediate the interactions with the spirit world, to bargain, beg, and banish on our behalf. Humanity thrust back into that world without the helping hand of the shaman could only result in madness. We see this repeated again and again in modern encounters with the anomalous: dealings with the fae, confrontations with Sasquatch, and contact with UFOs are invariably traumatic for those unable to integrate those experiences into their normal life. Desire for this contact is often a proverbial Monkey's Paw, carrying unforeseen consequences. The desire to know the terror that Kuroki knew in the subway is reiterated by Masuoka, and Kuroki clarifies that Masuoka desires that terror because it is synonymous with the unknown. Once again echoing the concept of Lovecraft's Starry Wisdom, Kuroki states that terror is actually a kind of ancient knowledge in its own right.

Finally, Masuoka accepts the fact that this fantasy he created was a fiction all along. Simply desiring to know the unknown through true terror, he killed his own wife and treated his daughter like an animal. He failed to drive himself truly insane, to gain the Starry Wisdom he desperately wants to acquire.

Or has he? Wandering the streets, he encounters two Dero scrambling into a nearby alley. Chasing them, he finds and answers a ringing cell phone. We cannot hear what the person on the other end of the line says, only the piping Dero vocalizations heard earlier, when Masuoka first spotted one in the subway tunnels. We can only observe a swelling of fear on Masuoka's face as he drops the phone with the realization that F is still in his apartment. On the dropped phone we see a photo of Masuoka himself on the screen, his face gripped in an expression of true horror.

Running back to his apartment, he takes an elevator in which appears the ghost of the first woman he murdered, the one who claimed to be his wife. He ignores her. When the elevator reaches his floor, her ghost is gone, representing Masuoka's descent back into the Underworld and full embrace of his original fiction. He finds F on the floor of his apartment, barely alive. In what is perhaps a reference to Park Chan-wook's 2003 film *Oldboy*, Masuoka uses a boxcutter to sever his own tongue and feed the blood to F in a disturbing, incestual, vampiric kiss. A smiling, bloody-mouthed F leads Masuoka back into the labyrinths below Tokyo, descending once again into the Underworld. Masuoka expresses that he will no longer speak because he no longer has any need for human words. He has obtained his gnosis, his knowledge of true terror, his Starry Wisdom, and that gnosis can never be expressed through language.

The film ends with him returning to the realm of the fae, to the same spot in those mysterious ruins where he found F, her filming his horrified expression as he observes something that the audience cannot see. He finally knows what Kuroki saw in the subway, but the answer to that question remains hidden to the viewer, only known to Masuoka now, unable to be communicated. That terror must be *experienced* by the individual; it cannot be described.

KATABASIS

Marebito's subject matter, whether intentionally referencing faerie lore or not, is unique among contemporary movies in its utilization of Western science fiction narratives and folklore. Japan has its own cultural faeries in the form of the *yokai*, a varied assortment of nature spirits, goblins, and monsters that act in a similar capacity to the fae of Europe and the British Isles. Dissemination of similar folklore across a wide array of cultures speaks to the shared cultural reality of these creatures. One such example is the similarity between a *yokai* called the *kappa*—a man-eating combination of human, frog, and turtle that lives near water—and the Slavic *vodyanoy*, a frogman who similarly drowns and devours those who stray too close to the water's edge.[393] Much like other Japanese media such as the *Dark Souls* video game series (which takes Western fantasy tropes and tabletop RPGs and recontextualizes them from a distinctly animist and Buddhist perspective), *Marebito* takes faerie lore, pulp sci-fi, and occult theories like the Hollow Earth and recasts them from the Japanese perspective of modern urban alienation.

Masuoka is himself a commentary on this alienation, loneliness, isolation, and nihilism brewed by Japan's ten-year-long economic recession, referred to as "The Lost Decade." As described by an article in the *Financial Times*, following the collapse of the Japanese "bubble economy" in 1991, the Lost Decade helped to erode Japan's sense of social unity and led to a suicide rate 60% higher than the rest of the developed world.[394] Masuoka is one such casualty of this period, so alienated from his fellow humans that he desires otherworldly knowledge in an attempt to escape the crushing weight of mundane reality. His fellow citizens are so alienated from him that they scarcely recognize the killer in their midst, not even seeing him as he drains a woman of blood in broad daylight. Thus it makes sense the film uses the Shaver Mystery's Dero as a central plot element: Dero is short for "Detrimental Robot," but this does not imply they are mechanical in nature. "Robot" refers to the robotic, inhuman way they carry out their tortures and depravity, their humanity and empathy bred out of them from eons spent underground. In a similar fashion, Masuoka has become a Dero due to his own alienation from other human beings.

As much as *Marebito* is a film presenting an inversion of the changeling narrative, it is also a film about "*katabasis*," a Greek word meaning "descent." The descent into the underworld is a common narrative found in a diverse number of mythologies around the world, with a hero or deity journeying into the Underworld or land of the dead in search of a loved one or enlightenment. Perhaps most famously known in Western culture is the descent of Orpheus to bring his lover Eurydice back to the land of the living, a task in which he notably fails by transgressing and looking back at her as they climb out.[395]

Japanese mythology even has its own very similar legend in the myth of Izanagi and Izanami. The goddess Izanami dies in childbirth, and her husband-brother Izanagi descends into the underworld of Yomi to see her again. However, she warns him not to look at her. Ignoring her pleas, he lights a torch only to see her rotting, maggot-eaten corpse. Enraged and ashamed, she sets the Hags of Yomi—analogous to the Greek Furies—after Izanagi, who is forced to flee and seal the entrance to Yomi.[396]

This narrative is also found much farther back in history. Perhaps the first of such tales is the descent of the Mesopotamian goddess Inanna into the underworld of Kur in an attempt to overthrow her sister, Ereshkigal. For her hubris, Inanna is stripped of her divine status and killed, only able to return after the god Enki rescues her. However, Ereshkigal's guardians, the *galla*, take Inanna's husband Dumuzid in her stead, only permitting him to leave one half of the year while his sister Geshtinanna replaces him in Kur, thus resulting in the mythological basis for seasons in the upper world.[397]

Anyone familiar with Greek mythology will see immediate parallels to the myth of Persephone and Demeter, the former of which is kidnapped and raped by Hades. She eats several pomegranate seeds while in the Underworld and, due to tasting the food of the Underworld, must return there part of the year, even after Hades is forced to return Persephone due to Demeter's petition to Zeus.[398]

This is paralleled in faerie folklore, where there are many prescriptions against accepting food offered by the fae, lest the person who partakes be trapped in Faerie forever. In a metaphorical sense, it is a statement about how wisdom, once gained, is irreversible. Once knowledge of the beyond is gained, it can never be lost; it can only fail to be integrated.[399]

Masuoka's story is one of katabasis. His is a quest for knowledge of the unknown. He is like the Finnish folk-hero demigod Väinämöinen, who travels into the underworld in search of knowledge and occult wisdom. Väinämöinen's gateway to the Underworld is the belly of a long-dead giant.[400] Masuoka similarly descends through the bowels of Tokyo, itself a living creature like all metropolises, veined with natural gas pipes and fiber optic cables. The underworlds of various cultures are often described as containing multiple layers—usually nine. The Underworld of Tokyo in *Marebito* is no different, with Masuoka passing through the layers of maintenance tunnels, down into abandoned WWII bomb shelters, and finally into the vast and alien "Mountains of Madness." Like Dante, he is provided a guide in the guise of Kuroki, someone who inhabits this Underworld after his suicide.

In Norse mythology, the god Odin sacrifices himself *to* himself, self-crucifying upon the World Tree Yggdrasil, bringing back knowledge of magic and the Runes when he returns from the Underworld. Like Odin, Masuoka's quest for gnosis requires sacrificing himself—or more aptly, his humanity—through murder and depravity. Only by descent into the Underworld and journeying back does the hero prove their mastery over both realms and establish proof that they are more than human.

This idea of "Crossing the Abyss" in pursuit of true gnosis is also found in modern initiatory practice of Thelema, where the aspirant attempts to cross the Abyss, described by British occultist Aleister Crowley as such:

> This doctrine is extremely difficult to explain; but it corresponds more or less to the gap in thought between the Real, which is ideal, and the Unreal, which is actual. In the Abyss all things exist, indeed, at least in posse, but are without any possible meaning; for they lack the substratum of spiritual Reality. They are appearances without Law. They are thus Insane Delusions. Now the Abyss being thus the great storehouse of Phenomena, it is the source of all impressions.[401]

Thus is the Abyss analogous to the liminal spaces between the upper and lower worlds, the place that must be traversed to gain the knowledge of the depths. The Abyss contains all things, but also contains nothing but delusion. There are guardians, known as The Dweller on the Threshold, and failure of the aspirant to successfully overcome this Dweller—and their own ego—results in the destruction of the traveler. They are bound to remain there forever, trapped in the Underworld.[402]

Crowley called this guardian "Choronzon," but Masuoka knows her name as "F." While Masuoka thinks he has achieved his true gnosis by the end of his journey, he has in reality failed to do so successfully and cannot communicate the knowledge he has gained.

Richard Shaver spent his final years painstakingly documenting "rock books," hidden knowledge of the ancients allegedly contained in cross-sections of rocks he found on his farm. Despite Shaver's insistence otherwise, anyone looking at images of these "rock books" could not see what Shaver said they contained. Driven into the depths of his own Abyss, he was unable to communicate what he found there to others, trapping this knowledge in his own mind. Similarly unable to integrate this wisdom he has gained, Masuoka is dragged back into the Abyss by his Dweller on the Threshold, doomed to remain there forever. Masuoka's story is an examination of the dangers in dealing with the fae, or with the anomalous in general. These entities can provide great gifts or just as easily eat the unwary who are unable to resist their glamour. Like F, they hide sharp fangs behind beautiful faces. They can provide wisdom, but at a price that is often not understood until it is too late.

F takes the role of the titular *marebito*, coming from the underworld to the surface to provide Masuoka with the eldritch gnosis he desires. As an essentially Lovecraftian story, *Marebito* is a cautionary tale of desiring to know truth in regards to the unknowable. It warns us all that by going too deep, we may never find the light of the surface world again.

BIOGRAPHIES

1) Jack Hunter - *Through a Crystal Darkly: Cultural, Experiential and Ontological Reflections on Faerie*

Jack Hunter, PhD, is an Honorary Research Fellow with the Alister Hardy Religious Experience Research Centre, and a tutor with the Sophia Centre for the Study of Cosmology in Culture, University of Wales Trinity Saint

David. There, he is lead tutor on the MA in Ecology and Spirituality and teaches on the MA in Cultural Astronomy and Astrology. He also teaches on the Alef Trust's MSc in Consciousness, Spirituality and Transpersonal Psychology.

Jack is the author of *Manifesting Spirits: An Anthropological Study of Mediumship and the Paranormal* (2020) and *Spirits, Gods and Magic: An Introduction to the Anthropology of the Supernatural* (2020). He is the editor of *Deep Weird: The Varieties of High Strangeness Experience* (2023) and *Greening the Paranormal: Exploring the Ecology of Extraordinary Experience* (2019).

He is also is co-editor with Dr. Rachael Ironside of *Folklore, People and Place: International Perspectives on Tourism and Tradition in Storied Places* (2023), and with Dr. Diana Espirito Santo of *Mattering the Invisible: Technologies, Bodies and the Realm of the Spectral* (2021). He is also a musician and lives in the hills of mid-Wales with his family.

2) Joshua Cutchin - *"I Am—We Are": Decoding the Faerie Motifs of Alex van Warmerdam's* Borgman

Joshua has appeared on countless paranormal programs discussing his work. He is the author of several books: 2015's *A Trojan Feast: The Food and Drink Offerings of Aliens, Faeries, and Sasquatch* (translated into Spanish as *Banquete Troyano*); 2016's *The Brimstone Deceit: An In-Depth Examination of Supernatural Scents, Otherworldly Odors, & Monstrous Miasmas*; 2018's *Thieves in the Night: A Brief History of Supernatural Child Abductions*; and 2020's *Where the Footprints End: High Strangeness and the Bigfoot Phenomenon*, Volumes I & II, with coauthor Timothy Renner. 2022 saw the release of his two-part masterwork *Ecology of Souls: A New Mythology of Death and the Paranormal.*

Joshua is also a regular contributor to Fortean essay collections, with excerpts of his work appearing in *Fortean Times* and *Edge Science*. Cutchin has been featured on the hit History Channel television show *Ancient Aliens*, and is a recurring roundtable guest on the "Where Did the Road Go?" podcast. Joshua has been invited to speak at a variety of paranormal conferences throughout the United States.

He can be found online at joshuacutchin.com.

3) Mark Anthony Wyatt - *"More wind please!": The Magic, Myth, and Mystery of* Twin Peaks

In recent years, Mark Anthony Wyatt's interest in folklore and the supernatural has combined with his passion for the literary arts, especially weird fiction. Much of his current research is centered around how creative artists/free-thinkers—people like David Herbert Lawrence, Aldous Huxley, and Aleister Crowley—were all closely linked and how they and others inspired and conspired to shape our modern world. He is interested in the concepts of *genus loci* and blood-consciousness, the emergence of communes in the early years of the 20th century, and, tying into all of that, the surprisingly large part that tiny Cornwall has played in hosting and inspiring creatives of all kinds.

Mark has published three books to date: *Wyatt's Weird World* and *The Spirit of Cornwall: A Haunted Legacy*, Volumes 1 & 2. He's currently writing a memoir of his gardening and surfing days, *Surf 'n' Turf*, scheduled for publication in early 2023. More recently, he created "The Cuckoo Town" podcast, focused on High Strangeness and the cultural arts. Mark is a frequent podcast guest and has given talks on both sides of the Atlantic.

When he's not reading, writing, or digging into research, Mark enjoys restoring old properties to their former glories, usually while listening to paranormal/cultural podcasts.

Mark can be reached via e-mail at markawyatt1960@zoho.com.

4) Neil Rushton - *Handmaidens of the Eternal: Consciousness and Death in* Photographing Fairies

Neil Rushton is a freelance writer who has published on a wide variety of topics, from archaeology to folklore, in academic journals (*Archaeological Journal, Journal of Interdisciplinary History,* et al.), online (Ancient Origins, Beyond Science, Sott), and print magazines/books (*New Dawn, The Daily Grail*). He also co-authored a guidebook to Mont Orgueil Castle, Jersey.

Neil's first novel is 2016's *Set the Controls for the Heart of the Sun,* and explores the confluence between consciousness, insanity, and reality in a drug-fueled contemporary setting. His second novel, *Dead but Dreaming,* was published in July 2020 and tells the story of a young folklorist who travels into rural England in 1970 in search of faerie traditions. Neil also produces a blog site, deadbutdreaming, which investigates the faeries in both their folkloric and metaphysical guises.

Neil received a PhD from Trinity College, University of Cambridge, in 2003. The thesis investigates aspects of monastic poor relief in medieval England. Neil also co-hosts a podcast channel with Kate Ray, called *Hare in the Hawthorn,* which investigates all aspects of the faerie phenomenon and includes regular guest appearances by aficionados of the subject.

He maintains an active web presence at deadbutdreaming.wordpress.com.

5) Susan Demeter - *You Are Not My Son! Revealing the Changeling in* The Hole in the Ground

Susan Demeter is an author, artist, magical practitioner, and an experient of High Strangeness. The themes of her writing, research, art, and magical practice incorporate her keen interest in exceptional human experiences, UFOs, social history, mysteries, and cosmic magic.

Susan has carried out scholarly research on behalf of the Defence Studies Department of the Canadian Armed Forces College in Toronto, Canada on the topic of UFOs, and for the The Koestler Parapsychology Unit at the University of Edinburgh. For three decades, she has conducted in-person and online outreach to those who have had spontaneous and deliberate extraordinary encounters. Her approach is phenomenological: acceptance of the reality of the experience without judgement on its nature.

Susan's first solo book, *Cosmic Witch*, was published in both English and Italian in August 2020. She is also a co-creator and occult consultant for the Ufology Tarot deck. This tarot uses the 22 Major Arcana cards for learning and personal reflection based on the historical figures of Ufology.

Susan lives in the Apennine Mountains near Bologna, Italy, with her husband, astrophysicist and electronic musician Massimo Teodorani, and their two cats, Pixie and Merry. Her home studio faces a mountain peak that was in ancient times considered to be a holy place by Celts, Etruscans and early Christians. And it is there that the ultra-terrestrials give her inspiration.

Susan can be found on the web at susandemeter.com.

6) Patrick Dugan - *You Can't Spell Frank-N-Furter Without F-A-E: Fairy Lore of* The Rocky Horror Picture Show

Patrick is the author of the award-winning Darkest Storm Series published by Falstaff Books. Other titles include Never Steal From Dragons, The Shadow Blade series, and Watchers of Astaria series from Distracted Dragon Press. Other publications include Fairy Films: Wee Folk on the Big Screen, a collection of fairy essays. Patrick is a member of SFWA.

An avid gadget user, Patrick is also the Director of Technology Services for Author's Essentials LLC providing solutions and advice for writing professionals. Patrick writings delve into software, hardware, social media, and all things web-related. The primary focus of Author's Essentials is how and when to employ technology to enhance your writing process.

Patrick resides in Charlotte, NC with his wife, two children and their spunky Cavalier King Charles, Blaze. In his spare time, he's a PC gamer, homebrewer, 3D printer enthusiast, and DIYer. You can usually find him in the Hearthstone Tavern or wandering Azeroth as a Blood Elf Warlock in the evenings.

You can find out more at https://linktr.ee/patrickdugan

7) David Floyd - Close Encounters of the Third Kind: *A Faerie Story of Liminality and Individuation*

David Floyd is an Associate Professor of English at Charleston Southern University, specializing in 19th-century British fiction and culture. He has presented on literature and folklore in England, Scotland, and the United States, including the Ohio Bigfoot Conference (2015), the Virginia Bigfoot Conference (2016), the International Bigfoot Conference (2017), and the History Channel's *AlienCon* (2018). He has also appeared in Bilco's *Cultured Bigfoot* (2018) as well as Small Town Monsters' *The Bray Road Beast* (2018), *On the Trail of Bigfoot* (2019), and *On the Trail of Bigfoot 2: The Journey* (2021).

8) Allison Jornlin - *Scary Fairies: Bogeymen of Yore*

Allison Jornlin has been investigating strange phenomena for more than 20 years. She developed Milwaukee's first haunted history tour in 2008. Since then, Allison has led numerous tours and presented talks on a variety of Fortean topics—poltergeists, fairies, UFOs, cryptids, demonic possession, etc. Allison currently works as a professional weirdo, writing articles for a variety of publications, developing haunted history tours for AmericanGhostWalks.com, and awaiting the birth of her first book.

9) James P. Nettles: DUNE: *The Faerie Dust Must Flow!*

James Nettles has a 30-year career consulting for clients from startups to Fortune 100s and as a media contributor, speaker on the IOT, privacy, business continuity and disaster recovery, futurism, and coming disruptive technologies and their impact on businesses and individual daily lives. He teaches workshops on Intellectual Property, Marketing and Branding,

Social Media, book development and publication, and the business of creativity.

Leveraging his background in technology, game theory, anthropology, and sociology, he is the author of four novels, multiple novellas, and over a hundred short stories in science fiction, fantasy, horror, steampunk, and contemporary genres.

He is the founder of Author Essentials, a company dedicated to the education of authors and author services. His latest release is *Business Essentials for Writers: How to make money in an ever-changing industry*, with 2020 releases in book marketing and tools and technologies for authors.

He is also the host of "Books and Beer," of the "Creating Pros" podcast under the Author Essentials brand, and one of the founders and technical director for "ConTinual: The Never Ending Convention."

10) Simon Young - *Walt and the Fairies, 1922-1960*

Simon Young trained as a medievalist and, after several years living in Spain, completed his doctorate at the University of Florence in 2006. His early written work concerned Irish ecclesiastical influence on the continent and British settlement in northwestern Spain. In 2005 and 2006 he brought out two historical novels with Weidenfeld and Nicolson (one of which sold well...).

In 2006, Simon began teaching American university students in Florence. This was the best thing, professionally-speaking, that has happened to him and something that he has continued to do with enthusiasm ever since. He usually teaches on contemporary Italian, religious, and food history.

In the early 2010s, he changed his focus of study and decided to write about supernatural beliefs, putting together scores of articles on the subject since. His eighth and ninth books are *The Boggart: Folklore, History, Placenames and Dialect* (Exeter University Press, 2022) and *The Nail in the Skull and Other Victorian Urban Legends* (Mississippi University Press, 2022). *The Boggart* was runner up for the Katharine Briggs Prize and was given Honorable Mention for the Wayland Hand Prize.

Simon is co-editor (with Davide Ermacora) of the monograph series Exeter New Approaches to Legend, Folklore and Popular Beliefs. He believes passionately in viewpoint diversity in academia and, to that end, he is a member of the Heterodox Academy.

252 | FAIRY FILMS

11) Wren Collier - *DEEP: An Examination of the Faerie Themes in Takashi Shimizu's film* Marebito

Wren Collier is a researcher, author, magician, and alchemist who has had a deep interest in the paranormal since childhood. He has been a frequent guest on a number of podcasts such as "Where Did the Road Go?", "Conspirinormal," "Agitator," and "What Magic is This?"

Originally from Alabama, Wren currently lives in Minneapolis, Minnesota, with his partner Isabel and their wonderful dog Sadie. Wren is a practicing occultist with a specialty in Renaissance magic and Early Modern cunning craft. He is active in the occult community in Minneapolis (affectionately referred to as "Paganistan" by the natives) and is a member of the Leaping Laughter Lodge in the Ordo Templi Orientis.

Wren is currently working on *Cthonia*, a book examining katabasis narratives, the Hollow Earth, and deep underground base mythology, and how they intersect with magic and pop culture. In partnership with Alynne Keith, he co-created the New Aeon English Qabalah calculator, available at naeq.io, that was featured in the documentary series *Hellier*. Wren is also the co-founder and admin of the Lunar Cry online occult community, and in his spare time he crafts fine occult material for sale under his label Atelier Argent. He can be contacted via his blog, Liminal Room, at liminalroom.com.

ENDNOTES

1   This chapter is related to two others that I have contributed to different volumes that also deal with the interplay of popular culture and extraordinary experience. The first 'The Dark Knight Rises: Shamanic Transformations in Gotham City' (2019) deals with the shamanistic undercurrents of the Batman mythos, and the second 'Mysterium Horrendum: Exploring Otto's Concept of the Numinous in Stoker, Machen and Lovecraft' (2020) tackles the power of horror fiction and movies, and weird fiction in particular, to invoke a sense of the numinous in the reader/viewer.

2   Young 2019

3   Ibid.

4   Ibid.

5   Lynch 2005, p. 41.

6   Evans Wentz 1911.

7   McAra 2013, p. 103.

8   For an in-depth exploration of this motif see Cutchin 2018.

9   Who also made some unique musical contributions to the film (Giuffre, 2012).

10   Cutchin 2015.

11   Bullard 1989; Jarrell 2016.

12   Bullard 1989, pp. 154-155.

13   Bonafin 2009.

14   Cutchin 2015.

15   A complete exploration of the influence of popular faerie 'natural history' books like Froud and Lee's—and those of other artists and writers (see for example, Poortvliet & Huygen, 1977; Day, 1979; Macnamara & Anderson, 1999), on real-life faerie encounters exceeds the limits of this chapter, though I think it would be a fruitful area for future research. It certainly seems as though they had an influence on my experiences.

16   Jones 2015.

17   Wood 2006, p. 285.

18   Bane 2013, p. 5.

19   Roth 1997.

20   Mkhize 1996.

21   Foster 2015.

22   Hutton 2014, p. 1137.

23   De Rosario Martinez 2010, p. 67.

24   Hall 2004.

25   Hutton 2014.

26   Hall 2004, p. 1.

27   Evans Wentz 1911.

28   Lamb 2000, p. 307.

29   Forsberg 2015.

30   Silver 1986.

31   Cooper 1997.

32   Although there is almost unanimous agreement that the Cottingley photographs are fake—owing in no small part to the confessions of both girls involved in the affair—I still feel that there is room to dream with the Cottingley photographs. There is one photograph of a little 'gnome' that neither of the girls ever declared as fake, and which also features an unusual anomaly—the girl in the photograph has a weirdly elongated hand (Cooper, 1997). Furthermore, as we will later see, it is interesting to note how two-dimensional the entities I encountered appeared to be, almost like cardboard cutouts.

33   Warner 2006, p. 234.

34   Davis *et al.* 2020.

35   Letcher 2001.

36   St. John 2015, p. 342.

37   Strassman 2001; Tramacchi 2006; Davis *et al.* 2020.

38   Hunter in Young 2018, pp. 142-143.

39   Bullard 1989, p. 155.

40   Kripal 2011.

41   Luke & Friedman 2010.

42   Evans 1987, p. 75.

43   Rojcewicz 1986, p. 138.

44   Wilson 1988, pp. 80-81.

45   Hunter 2020.

46   Hyams, R. (May 20, 2013). Dutch film Borgman by Alex Van Warmerdam intrigues Cannes audience. Retrieved April 10, 2020 from http://www.rfi.fr/en/culture/20130520-borgman-alex-van-warmerdam

47   Rosser, M. (September 13, 2013). Netherlands enters Borgman into Oscar race. Retrieved April 10, 2020 from https://www.screendaily.com/news/netherlands-enters-borgman-into-oscar-race/5060416.article?blocktitle=LATEST-FILM-NEWS&contentID=40562#

48   Tallerico, B. (June 6, 2014). Review: Borgman. Retrieved April 10, 2020 from https://www.rogerebert.com/reviews/borgman-2014

49   Badt, K. (December 6, 2017). Creepy Film at Cannes: Alex van Warmerdam's Borgman. Retrieved April 27, 2020 from https://www.huffpost.com/entry/creepy-film-at-cannes-ale_b_3312721

50   Rooney, D. (Mat 19, 2013). Borgman: Cannes Review. Retrieved April 27, 2020 from https://www.hollywoodreporter.com/review/borgman-cannes-review-525208

51   Dillard, C. (June 2, 2014). Review: *Borgman*. Reterieved April 27, 2020 from https://www.slantmagazine.com/film/borgman/

52   D'Angelo, M. (June 5, 2014). The Dutch Curiosity *Borgman* Strains Too Hard for Instant Cult Appeal. Retrieved May 12, 2020 from https://film.avclub.com/the-dutch-curiosity-borgman-strains-too-hard-for-instan-1798180798

53   Wilde, J. (1887). *Ancient Legends, Mystic Charms, and Superstitions of Ireland*. London, UK: Ticknor and Co.

54   Handler, J. (March 6, 2014). An Interview with Alex van Warmerdam, Director of BORGMAN. Retrieved April 10, 2020 from http://roboapocalypse.blogspot.com/2014/03/an-interview-with-alex-van-warmerdam.html

55   Gallagher, P. (June 5, 2014). DM INTERVIEWS ALEX VAN WARMERDAM, DIRECTOR OF THE SURREAL THRILLER 'BORGMAN'. Retrieved April 10, 2020 from https://dangerousminds.net/comments/dm_interviews_alex_van_Warmerdam_director_of_the_surreal_thriller_borgman

56   Handler 2014.

57   Daimler, M. (2017). *Fairies: A Guide to the Celtic Fair Folk*. Station Approach, UK: Moon Books.

58   Jenkins, R.P. (1997). Witches and Fairies: Supernatural Aggression and Deviance Among the Irish Peasantry. In P. Narváez (Ed.), *The Good People: New Fairylore Essays* (pp. 302-335). Lexington, KY: The University Press of Kentucky.

59   Ashliman, D.L. (December 22, 2012). The Origin of Underground People. Retrieved November 30, 2018 from http://www.pitt.edu/~dash/originunder.html

60   Briggs, K. (1976). *An Encyclopedia of Fairies: Hobgoblins, Brownies, Bogies, and Other Supernatural Creatures.* New York, NY: Pantheon Books.

61   Beachcombing. (2011, October 26). Eggs, Mermaids and Fairies. Retrieved July 3, 2017 from http://www.strangehistory.net/2011/10/26/eggs-mermaids-and-fairies/

62   Hyde, L. (1998). *Trickster Makes This World.* New York, NY: Farrar, Traus and Ciroux.

63   Buffinga, J.O. (2015). Alex van Warmerdam's *Borgman* (2013) as a study in visual contrasts. *Can. J. of Netherlandic Studies/Rev. can. d'études néerlandaises, 36*(1), 1-20.

64   Ibid.

65   Lecouteux, C. (2013). *The Tradition of Household Spirits.* (J.E. Graham, Trans.). Rochester, VT: Inner Traditions. (Original work published 2000)

66   Green, R.F. (2016). *Elf Queens and Holy Friars: Fairy Beliefs and the Medieval Church.* Philadelphia, PA: University of Pennsylvania Press.

67   Buffinga 2015.

68   Astoria, D. (1997). *The Name Book: Over 10,000 Names—Their Meanings, Origins, and Spiritual Significance.* Minneapolis, MN: Bethany House Publishers.

69   Andrén, A. (2014). *Tracing Old Norse Cosmology.* Lund, SE: Nordic Academic Press.

70   Bane, T. (2013). *Encyclopedia of Fairies in World Folklore and Mythology.* Jefferson, NC: McFarland & Company, Inc.

71   Evans Wentz, W.Y. (1911). *The Fairy-Faith in Celtic Countries.* London, UK: Henry Frowde.

72   Munro, J.U. (1997). The Invisible Made Visible: The Fairy Changeling as a Folk Articulation of Failure to Thrive in Infants and Children. In P. Narváez (Ed.), *The Good People: New Fairylore Essays* (pp. 251-283). Lexington, KY: The University Press of Kentucky.

73   Evans Wentz, W.Y. (1911). *The Fairy-Faith in Celtic Countries.* London, UK: Henry Frowde.

74   Ibid.

75   Guiney, L.I. (1888). *Brownies and Bogles.* Boston, MA: D. Lothrop Company.

76   Bane 2013.

77   Lecouteux 2013.

78   Ibid.

79   Silver, C.G. (1999). *Strange and Secret Peoples: Fairies and Victorian Consciousness.* New York, NY: Oxford University Press, Inc.

80   Lecouteux 2013.

81 Yeats, W.B. (Ed.). (1890). *Fairy and Folk Tales of the Irish Peasantry.* New York, NY: The Walter Scott Publishing Co., Ltd.

82 Evans Wentz 1911.

83 Briggs 1976.

84 Evans Wentz 1911.

85 WordSense.eu. (n.d.). Alb (German). Retrieved April 14, 2020 from https://www.wordsense.eu/Alb/#German

86 Lecouteux 2013.

87 Daimler, M. (April 12, 2018). Possession by Fairies or Elves. Retrieved April 20, 2020 from https://lairbhan.blogspot.com/2018/04/possession-by-fairies-or-elves.html

88 Briggs 1976.

89 Daimler, M. (2020). *A New Dictionary of Fairies: A 21st Century Exploration of Celtic and Related Western European Fairies.* Alresford, UK: Moon Books.

90 Arrowsmith, N. & Moorse, G. (1977). *A Field Guide to the Little People.* New York, NY: Farrar Straus & Giroux.

91 Lindow, J. (1978). *Swedish Legends and Folktales.* Berkeley and Los Angeles, CA: University of California Press.

92 Bane 2013.

93 Verstraten, P. (March 2014). Middle-of-the-Road Absurdism: The Cinema of Dutch Director Alex van Warmerdam. Retrieved April 16, 2020 from http://sensesofcinema.com/2014/feature-articles/middle-of-the-road-absurdism-the-cinema-of-dutch-director-alex-van-warmerdam/

94 Lecouteux, C. (2015). *Demons and Spirits of the Land.* (J.E. Graham, Trans.). Rochester, VT: Inner Traditions. (Original work published 1995)

95 Daimler 2018.

96 Hunt, R. (1903). *Popular Romances of the West of England: The Drolls, Traditions, and Superstitions of Old Cornwall.* London, UK: Chatto and Windus (3rd ed.).

97 Verstraten 2014.

98 Evans Wentz 1911.

99 Daimler 2018.

100 Evans Wentz 1911.

101 Kramer, G.M. (June 13, 2014). Interview: Hadewych Minis, *Borgman.* Retrieved April 13, 2020 from http://cinedelphia.com/interview-hadewych-minis-borgman/

102 Wilde 1887.

103 Briggs 1976.

104 Evans Wentz 1911.

105 Yeats 1890.

106 Cutchin, J. (2018). *Thieves in the Night: A Brief History of Supernatural Child Abductions*. San Antonio, TX: Anomalist Books.

107 Narváez, P. (1997). Newfoundland Berry Pickers "In the Fairies." In P. Narváez (Ed.), *The Good People: New Fairylore Essays* (pp. 336-368). Lexington, KY: The University Press of Kentucky.

108 Ibid.

109 Ibid.

110 Daimler 2020

111 Narváez, P. (1997). Physical Disorders: Changelings and the Blast. In P. Narváez (Ed.), *The Good People: New Fairylore Essays* (pp. 225-226). Lexington, KY: The University Press of Kentucky.

112 Evans Wentz 1911.

113 Bane 2013.

114 Evans Wentz 1911.

115 Silver 1999.

116 Bain, F. (2012). The Binding of the Fairies:: Four Spells. *Preternature: Critical and Historical Studies on the Preternatural 1*(2), pp. 323-354.

117 Why would a civilization, having harnessed the ability to traverse the galaxy, rely upon invasive procedures—methods akin to vivisection, or the infamous "anal probe"—to gather genetic samples? Why would a simple chicken farmer in Eagle River, Wisconsin, be involved in an exchange of water for bizarre "alien pancakes" in 1961?

118 Puhvel, M. (1978). Snow and Mist in "Sir Gawain and the Green Knight": Portents of the Otherworld? *Folklore 89*(2), pp. 224-228.

119 Evans Wentz 1911.

120 Ibid.

121 Hunt, B. (1912). *Folk Tales of Breffny*. London, UK: Macmillan.

122 Kramer 2014.

123 Maltin, L. (2014). Leonard Maltin's 2015 Movie Guide. New York, NY: Penguin Publishing Group.

124 Handler 2014.

125 uInterview. (May 24, 2013). Alex Van Warmerdam's 'Borgman' Confounds And Delights At Cannes. Retrieved April 27, 2020 from https://uinterview.com/special-event/cannes-2013/alex-van-warmerdams-borgman-confounds-and-delights-at-cannes/

126 Buffinga 2015.

127 Raup, J. (June 10, 2014). 'Borgman' Director Alex van Warmerdam Discusses Influences, Religion, and the Seriousness of Michael Haneke. Retrieved May 12, 2020 from https://thefilmstage.com/borgman-director-alex-van-Warmerdam-discusses-influences-religion-and-the-seriousness-of-michael-haneke/

128 Handler 2014.

129 Stone, S. (May 19, 2013). Cannes Review: 'Borgman' Makes No Sense – in a Good Way. Retrieved May 12, 2020 from https://www.thewrap.com/cannes-review-borgman-makes-no-sense-and-thats-good-92571/

130 Teitelbaum, J. (July 18, 2014) Borgman (2013). Reterieved May 12, 2020 from http://filmint.nu/?p=12780

131 Zacharek, S. (June 4, 2014). Borgman Invades a Home — and Maybe Your Dreams. Retrieved May 12, 2020 from https://www.villagevoice.com/2014/06/04/borgman-invades-a-home-and-maybe-your-dreams/

132 Buffinga 2015.

133 AFC. (May 21, 2013). Cinematographer Tom Erisman, NSC, discusses his work on "Borgman", directed by Alex van Warmerdam. Retrieved May 12, 2020 from https://www.afcinema.com/Cinematographer-Tom-Erisman-NSC-discusses-his-work-on-Borgman-directed-by-Alex-van-Warmerdam.html?lang=fr

134 Lecouteux 2015.

135 Perretta, D. (April 9, 2014). Film Analysis: Interpreting Alex van Warmerdam's Borgman (2013) or Die Trying. Retrieved May 12, 2020 from https://black-iswhiteblog.wordpress.com/2014/04/09/film-analysis-interpreting-alex-van-Warmerdams-borgman-2013-or-die-trying/

136 Father Gore. (June 19, 2018). *BORGMAN:* Kabbalah and Marx in the Garden of Eden. Retrieved May 12, 2020 from https://fathersonholygore.com/2018/06/19/borgman-kabbalah-and-marx-in-the-garden-of-eden/

137 Buccola, R. (2006). *Fairies, Fractious Women, and the Old Faith: Fairy Lore in Early Modern British Drama and Culture.* Selinsgrove, PA: Susquehanna University Press.

138 Szilagyi, S. (1992). *Photographing Fairies.* New York, NY: Ballantine Books.

139 IMBd. (n.d.). *Photographing Fairies.* Retrieved May 3, 2020 from https://www.imdb.com/title/tt0119893/?ref_=ttfc_fc_tt

140 Lavole, J.D. (2012). *The Theosophical Society: The History of a Spiritualist Movement.* Boca Raton, FL: Brown Walker Press.

141 Lachman, G. (2007). *Rudolf Steiner: An Introduction to his Life and Work.* Edinburgh, UK: Floris Books.

142 Rushton, N. (2019). *Paracelsus, nature spirits and faeries.* Retrieved May 5, 2020 from https://deadbutdreaming.wordpress.com/2019/11/17/paracelsus-na-ture-spirits-and-faeries/

143 Simaneck, D. (n.d.). *The Case of the Cottingley fairies.* Retrieved May 5, 2020 from https://www.lockhaven.edu/~dsimanek/cooper.htm

144 Beach Combing. (2017). *In search of the earliest fairy wings.* Retrieved May 6, 2020 from http://www.strangehistory.net/2016/12/17/search-earliest-fairy-wings/ ; Rushton, N. (2017). *The art of faerie.* Retrieved May 6, 2020 from https://deadbutdreaming.wordpress.com/2017/06/22/the-art-of-faerie/ ; Lancelyn Green, R. (1954) *Fifty years of Peter Pan.* London, UK: Peter Davies Publishing.

145 Froud, B. and Lee, A. (1978) *Faeries.* New York, NY: Harry N. Abrams, Inc.

146 Rushton, N. (2017). *Altered states of consciousness and the faeries.* Retrieved May 7, 2020 from https://deadbutdreaming.wordpress.com/2017/02/03/altered-states-of-consciousness-and-the-faeries/

147 Hancock, G. (2007). *Supernatural.* New York, NY: The Disinformation Company, Ltd.

148 Eliade, M. (2004). *Shamanism: Archaic Techniques of Ecstasy.* Princeton, NJ: Princeton University Press. (Original work first published 1951)

149 Lewis-Williams, D. & Dowson, T. (1988). The signs of all times: Entoptic phenomena in upper Palaeolithic art. *Current Anthropology 29*(2), pp. 201-45.

150 Peake, A. (2019). *The Hidden Universe: An Investigation into Non-Human Intelligences.* London, UK: Watkins.

151 Ginzburg, C. (2004). *Ecstasies: Deciphering the witches' sabbath.* Chicago, IL: University of Chicago Press; Wilby, E. (2005). *Cunning folk and familiar spirits: Shamanistic Visionary Traditions in Early Modern British Witchcraft and Magic.* East Sussex, UK: Sussex Academic Press.

152 Briggs, K. (1967). *The Fairies in Tradition and Literature.* London, UK: Routledge & Kegan Paul Ltd.

153 Rushton, N. (2017). *The faerie abduction of Anne Jefferies.* Retrieved May 10, 2020 from https://deadbutdreaming.wordpress.com/2017/09/23/the-faerie-ab-duction-of-anne-jefferies/

154 Ginzburg; Wilby. Op. cit.

155 Young, S. (2017). The Fairy Investigation Society: Fairy census 2014-2017. Retrieved May 11, 2020 from http://www.fairyist.com/wp-content/up-loads/2014/10/The-Fairy-Census-2014-2017-1.pdf

156 Hanna, J. (2012). *Aliens, insectoids, and elves! oh, my!* Retrieved May 11, 2020 from https://www.erowid.org/chemicals/dmt/dmt_article3.shtml

157 Strassman, R. (2001). *DMT: The Spirit Molecule.* Rochester, VT: Park Street Press.

158   Luke, D. (2017). *Otherworlds: Psychedelics and Exceptional Human Experience*. London, UK: Muswell Hill Press.

159   Bottrell, W. (1873). *Traditions and hearthside stories of West Cornwall, Vol. 2*. Penzance, UK: Beare and Son.

160   Evans Wentz, W.Y. (1911). *The Fairy-Faith in Celtic Countries*. London, UK: London, UK: Henry Frowde.

161   Evans Wentz Ibid.

162   Evans Wentz Ibid.

163   Luke, D. (2011). Discarnate entities and dimethyltryptamine (DMT): Psychopharmacology, phenomenology and ontology. *Journal of the Society for Psychical Research 75*(902), pp. 26-42.

164   Kastrup, B., Stapp, H.P., & Kafatos, M.C. (2018). *Coming to grips with the implications of quantum mechanics*. Retrieved May 12, 2020 from https://blogs.scientificamerican.com/observations/coming-to-grips-with-the-implications-of-quantum-mechanics/

165   Strieber, W., & Kripal, J.J. (2016). *The Super Natural*. New York, NY: Jeremy P. Tarcher.

166   Rennicks, R. (2014). The Banshee of the O'Neills. Retrieved April 15, 2020 from http://atriptoireland.com/2013/06/12/the-banshee-of-the-oneills

167   Buccola, R. (2006). *Fairies, Fractious Women, and the Old Faith: Fairy Lore in Early Modern British Drama and Culture*. Selinsgrove, PA: Susquehanna University Press.

168   Sandwell, I. (2019). New Horror Movie The Hole In The Ground Inspired By A Real-Life Tragedy. Retrieved May 1, 2020 from https://www.digitalspy.com/movies/a26571275/hole-in-the-ground-movie-plot-origin

169   Parry-Jones, D. (1953). *Welsh Legends and Fairy Lore*. London, UK: Batford.

170   Ingersoll, E. (1923). *Birds in Legend, Fable and Folklore*. New York, NY: Longmans, Green and Co.

171   Lysaght, P. (1997). Fairylore from the Midlands of Ireland. In P. Narváez (Ed.), *The Good People: New Fairylore Essays* (pp. 22-46). Lexington, KY: The University Press of Kentucky.

172   Rushton, N. (2016). Swapping Babies: The Disturbing Faerie Changeling Phenomenon. Retrieved May 5, 2020 from https://www.ancient-origins.net/myths-legends/swapping-babies-disturbing-faerie-changeling-phenomenon-007261

173   Meredith, D. (2002, July). Hazards in the Bog: Real and Imagined. *Geographical Review 92*(3), pp. 319-332.

174   Kim, M. (2018). This strange syndrome causes people to think their loved ones have been replaced by identical impostors. Retrieved May 10, 2020 from

https://www.washingtonpost.com/national/health-science/this-strange-syn-drome-causes-people-to-think-their-loved-ones-have-been-replaced-by-identi-cal-impostors/2018/04/06/0091f168-1be6-11e8-9de1-147dd2df3829_story.html

175   Evans Wentz, W.Y. (1911). *The Fairy-Faith in Celtic Countries*. London, UK: Henry Frowde.

176   Topel, F. (2019). 'The Hole in the Ground' Used Little CGI and a Finnish Contortionist for the Monster [Interview]. Retrieved May 20, 2020 from https://bloody-disgusting.com/interviews/3543797/sundance-finnish-contortion-ist-played-hole-grounds-monster-exclusive/

177   McGrath, T. (1982, Summer). Fairy Faith and Changelings: The Burning of Bridget Cleary in 1895. *Studies: An Irish Quarterly Review 71*(282), pp. 178-184.

178   Croker, T.C. (1862). *Fairy Legends and Traditions of the South of Ireland*. T. Wright (Ed.). London, UK: William Tegg.

179   Salto, C. (2019). Morag and the Kelpie. Retrieved May 20, 2020 from https://terreceltiche.altervista.org/morag-and-the-kelpie/

180   Basile, G. (1927). *Il Pentamerone*. New York, NY: Boni & Liveright. (Original work published 1634.)

181   Cutchin, J. (2022). *Ecology of Souls: A New Mythology of Death & the Paranormal – Volume 1*. Marietta, GA: Horse & Barrel.

182   Roberts, J. (2010). *Japanese Mythology A-Z*. New York, NY: Chelsea House. (2nd ed).

183   Lecouteux, C. (2013). *The Tradition of Household Spirits*. (J.E. Graham, Trans.). Rochester, VT: Inner Traditions. (Original work published 2000.)

184   Kirby, W.F. (1895). *The Hero of Estonia – Volume 1*. London, UK: John C. Nimmo.

185   Rocky Horror Wiki. (n.d.). Phantoms. Retrieved February 6, 2023 from https://rockyhorror.fandom.com/wiki/Phantoms

186   Daimler, M. (2017). *Fairies: A Guide to the Celtic Fair Folk*. Alresford, UK: Moon Books.

187   Yeats, W.B. (Ed.). (1890). *Fairy and Folk Tales of the Irish Peasantry*. New York, NY: The Walter Scott Publishing Co., Ltd.

188   Connor. (December 10, 2019). The Dullahan of Celtic Mythology. Retrieved February 6, 2023 from https://www.theirishplace.com/heritage/the-dullah-an/

189   Guiney, L.I. (1888). *Brownies and Bogles*. Boston, MA: D. Lothrop Company.

190   Geoffrey of Monmouth. (2011). *Vita Merlini*. USA: ReadaClassic.com. (Original work published c. 1150.)

191   Yeats 1890.

192   Curtin, J. (1890). *Myths and Folk-lore of Ireland*. Boston, MA: Little, Brown, and Company.

193   Bros. Grimm. (December 10, 2022). The Elves and The Shoemaker. Retrieved February 6, 2023 from https://americanliterature.com/author/the-brothers-grimm/fairy-tale/the-elves-and-the-shoemaker (Original work published 1812.)

194   Marlowe, C. (November 3, 2009). *The Tragical History of Dr. Faustus*. (A. Dyce, Ed.). Retrieved February 6, 2023 from https://www.gutenberg.org/files/779/779-h/779-h.htm (Original work published c. 1592.)

195   Cutchin, J. (2018). *Thieves in the Night: A Brief History of Supernatural Child Abductions*. San Antonio, TX: Anomalist Books.

196   Evans Wentz, W.Y. (1911). *The Fairy-Faith in Celtic Countries*. London, UK: Henry Frowde.

197   Cutchin 2018.

198   Rossetti, C. (1862). *Goblin Market and Other Poems*. London, UK: Macmillan.

199   Briggs, K. (1976). *An Encyclopedia of Fairies: Hobgoblins, Brownies, Bogies, and Other Supernatural Creatures*. New York, NY: Pantheon Books.

200   Campbell, J.G. (1900). *Superstitions of the Highlands and Islands of Scotland*. Glasgow, UK: James MacLehose & Sons.

201   Evans Wentz 1911.

202   Sherman, J. (2015). *World Folklore for Storytellers*. London, UK: Routledge. (Original work published 2009.)

203   Cutchin 2022.

204   Defining *science-fiction*, as well as what qualifies to be regarded as such, is another topic for another time.

205   Gordon 298, where he furthermore states, "To watch 30-year old Richard Dreyfuss play with his mashed potatoes is appalling."

206   The resurgence during this period of interest in J. R. R. Tolkien's *Lord of the Rings*, for instance, should not go unnoticed.

207   Even Jungian analysts are unable to agree as to the definition of *individuation*. Within the confines of this chapter, individuation may be regarded as becoming what one was created to be, only after the attainment of which one may fully contribute to the world with his or her particular gifts. The "higher self" frequently alluded to in considerations of this process should be understood not as a collapse into narcissism or self-indulgence, but rather as a kind of sacrifice to something greater than oneself.

208   Jung regarded such "symbolic folkisms" as phylogenetically inherited, or evolutionarily developed, as "a collective, genetic element in the human psyche" (Clarke 36). Experimental psychologists have deferred to Jung's regard of folk-

lore as "a manifestation of the nature and workings of the human psyche" (Georges and Jones 235) and a product of "dynamic mental processes" (Jones 90). While Jung's ideas have been incredibly influential among creative circles and various psychoanalytical schools, there is opposition to what Weston La Barre termed a "demonstrably false psychology" (La Barre 383). In contrast to Jung's phylogenic mechanisms, La Barre stressed ontological, or social, inheritance. Jung's assertions have also been faulted for their ethnocentrism and gender bias. This hardly discounts their demonstrative universality in the West.

209 See pages 207-254 of *The Archetypes and the Collective Unconscious.*

210 Traditionally, heroic narratives have been male-centric, an inclination somewhat modified upon the advent of late-twentieth-century feminist movements. The use of male pronouns here is a convenience.

211 Thus, in *The Empire Strikes Back* (1980), Luke Skywalker must endure the daunting swamplands of Dagobah to meet with Yoda, whose baffling syntax is used even to answer the simplest of inquiries. Similarly, in Disney's *Pocahontas* (1995), the titular character journeys into the forest to consult with the oracular tree entity, Grandmother Willow.

212 They also indicate the arrival at a place of notable difference, as epitomized by Dorothy Gale's iconic phrase in *The Wizard of Oz* (1939), "Toto, I have a feeling we're not in Kansas anymore." Likewise, Luke and Ben Kenobi's entrance into Mos Eisley spaceport dramatically indicates a shift from the former's mundane domestic context to the perilous undertaking before him.

213 Thus, as Luke warily scans the cantina, a thuggish criminal warns him, "You just watch yourself."

214 Platt 16-2; Musgrave 271. This notion has both positive and negative possibilities. On one hand, such self-authorizing as that of the vampire, is contingent upon the contagion of vampirism, which not simply kills but reinvents its victim. On the other hand, as in Roy's case, the intrusion of the entities into his existence contributes to an arguably more desirable transformation, even if the process is fraught with trial.

215 Cirlot 96.

216 Jung 32 and 215.

217 Hutton 1138, 1139, 1145, and 1149.

218 Baughman 232. Pixies were also known to lead people astray (Sedgewick 78).

219 Hand 141.

220 Wilde 135.

221 Wilde 142.

222 Enright 240.

223 Yeats 81.

224 Pickering 100.

225 Pickering 100.

226 Enright 240.

227 Saunders 179-206; Hutton 1140 and 1142.

228 Hutton 1138.

229 Hutton 1142.

230 N. Williams 457-478.

231 Hutton 1140, 1148, and 1155. A more specific demonstrative of the varieties of appellations applied to faeries, for instance, is the example of the boggart, a notably amorphous being of the faerie realm, appearing in various incarnations and with diverse purposes, but typically of an antagonistic nature. Citing the term as a Lancashire provincialism referring to the "the Bocker," in their 1873 work, *Lancashire Legends,* John Harlan and T. T. Wilkinson refer to the boggart as an "undefined sprite" (Harlan and Wilkinson 141 and 142, where they also address the Lancashire game known as barley-brake, related to the "Gothic celebration" of blindman's bluff as well as the Lancashire boggart (*Lancashire Legends,* 141). The later-middle-age *bug* specified an especially terrifying "entity of the night" (Hutton 1142). In his 1837 glossary, William Thornber simply defined the creature as "a ghost" (Thornber 332), while James McKay, in 1888, described it as "a spirit, a ghost, a soul released from the flesh" (McKay 125). Numerous accounts conflate the boggart with other faerie beings like brownies and goblins. The "half-faeries" of the Isle of Man were known as *buganees,* while the "half-ghosts" of the Scottish Lowlands were called *ogles* or *bogeys* (McKay 15). Etymologically similar terms are the English puck, the Scottish bogie or bogle, the French goblin, the German kobold, the Greek khobalus, the gobelinus of the Middle Ages, and the Cymric bwg, associated with "bug," "bugbear," or "hobgoblin" (Hardwick 127, 128, and 139; McKay 123).

232 That Roy amuses himself by toying with an artificial landscape not only seems to foreshadow his construction of Devils Tower in his living room, but too may allude to the opening lines of H. G. Wells' invasion fantasy, *War of the Worlds* (1897), which state, "No one would have believed in the last years of the nineteenth century that this world was being watched keenly and closely by intelligences greater than man's and yet as mortal as his own; that as men busied themselves about their various concerns they were scrutinised and studied, perhaps almost as narrowly as a man with a microscope might scrutinise the transient creatures that swarm and multiply in a drop of water" (Wells 11).

233 The moral question emerging from Roy's abandoning his wife and children is less important here than the archetypes with which these characters are associated. His domestic situation serves as his former life, mired in earthly, distracting, and potentially soul-killing detritus of modernity. The moral implications of the married Roy's kiss with Jillian, too, should be read similarly. Their kiss is not of a sexual nature, but an emblem of the union brought about by their

shared quest, what Jung would regard as the union of the anima and animus requisite of the process of individuation.

234 Jung 276, 278 and 279.

235 Campbell 53.

236 Campbell 186.

237 Orange is also the primary color of light attempting to penetrate Jillian's home the night of Barry's abduction.

238 Pickering 70 and 292; Achen 33 and 34, where he notes that, for some Classical cultures, because of its relation to the sun, yellow was regarded more positively, associated as it was with divinity, royalty, and wisdom.

239 The pilots, unable to identify the "traffic" with which they are engaged, refuse to file a report, one of them claiming, "I wouldn't know what kind of report to file."

240 Baughman 209.

241 Wilde 135.

242 Named after its creator, Zoltan Kodály, regarded for his novel pedagogical methods for teaching music, this is a method providing a visual aid used during singing exercises.

243 That the entities choose to communicate through music further entrenches their analogue to the fey, as music is, in Hand's terms, "a talent expected" of the fey (Hand 143, where he furthermore comments that those who are capable of hearing fey music often experience "the loss of reason.")

244 Collis, C. (October 24, 2017). Close Encounters of the Third Kind: 7 Rare Behind-the-Scenes Images. Retrieved February 4, 2023 from https://ew.com/movies/close-encounters-of-the-third-kind-photos/

245 Gordon 298.

246 Jewell 10.

247 Thornber 332.

248 Baughman 230.

249 Harlan and Wilkinson 16.

250 Thornber 100.

251 Harlan and Wilkinson 51.

252 Kirk 6.

253 Waugh 221.

254 Feitchte 59.

255 Baughman 112.

256 Monomania, introduced by the French psychiatrist Etienne Esquirol, "denoted a condition in which a break in the psyche—a separation of the faculties of emotion, reason, and will—produced a singular fixation, or aberration, within a mind that was otherwise rational" (Vrettos 76). Jillian similarly has visions of the structure, which she obsessively sketches. In addition to playing the iconic five-note tonal phrase on his xylophone, Barry too constructs the monolith in a glob of mud. The shared vision also compels a dozen other individuals to journey to Devils Tower on the day of the entities' arrival. The use of Devils Tower as the object of precognitive phenomena may reference the ubiquitous monolith of Stanley Kubrick's seminal 1968 film, *2001: A Space Odyssey.*

257 Campbell 5, 6, 12 and 280. This notion may be why Roy's meeting of the entities and the fruition of his search take place at night.

258 Pickering 288.

259 Noel 21 and 24.

260 Jillian's lack of a partner, as well as Barry's apparent fatherlessness, further entrenches the notion of the home's vulnerability.

261 Hardwick 139.

262 Harlan and Wilkinson 54; Hardwick 128.

263 Hardwick 129.

264 Rogers 22.

265 Wrigley 16.

266 Weeks 26 and 27.

267 Hutton 1146 n. 48.

268 Baughman 209 and 211.

269 Caldwell 77.

270 Waugh 217.

271 Sedgwick 69 and 78. There is a Lancashire superstition that rivers and fords are the habitation of beings who endeavor to drown travelers-by, and furthermore, on the occasion of someone drowning, that "The river spirit expects his annual victim but prefers an innocent child" (Weeks 29).

272 Scott 122.

273 Sedgwick 11. The boggart of Well Hall was rumored to appear at time with a child walking beside it (Weeks 33).

274 Baughman 229 and 230.

275 Waugh 217.

276 Weeks 33.

277 Weeks 33.

278 Bram Stoker's well-documented insistence on accurate references to folkloric beliefs throughout his seminal *Dracula* (1897) includes the vampire's inability to cross a threshold without an invitation (garlic is also an effective deterrent). There are also similar assertions that faeries are unable to cross running water and are repelled by iron and the sound of church bells.

279 Though a product of Britain, *Beowulf,* for instance, was inspired by the tales of Germanic peoples who believed in the existence of monsters on the verge of society. The unexplored areas on ancient maps notably feature dragons and other monstrous figures indicative of the unknown and contrastive with civilized spaces. Monstrous beings also populate the boundaries of architectural structures as well as the marginalia of illustrated manuscripts (Bildhauer and Mills 8 and 9).

280 So as not to relegate the presence of the fey exclusively to earthly sites, Hand includes "the airy expanse" (141).

281 Harlan and Wilkinson 52.

282 C. A. James 337.

283 McKay

284 McKay 114.

285 Harlan and Wilkinson 50.

286 Waugh 198. *Feeorin* refers to "fearful things."

287 Waugh 199. *Shippon* refers to a "cow barn or cow shed."

288 Harris 19.

289 Killeen 29.

290 Hume 286; Pritchard 435; Spencer 200.

291 Baughman 205.

292 The gate is somewhat inauspiciously emblazoned with a worn poster of a bullfighter engaged with the beast. Campbell notes that one's entrance into a place of worship represents a kind of self-denial of which not all are capable. Engagement with the entities requires, if not the self-denial of worship, at least openness to other possibilities that may adjust one's self-perception. Temple entrances, therefore, are often populated by intimidating figures such as dragons, gargoyles, monsters, and, yes, bulls (Campbell 77). Additionally, while a notably complex symbol bearing numerous meanings according to the respective culture, it should not go unnoticed that the bull represents the communication between heaven and earth (Cirlot 33). Perhaps notable, too, is the interference with cows, horses, and other domesticated beasts that is a preoccupation of the fey, especially dwarves, cluricauns, and fairies, who are fond of riding or even tormenting such animals.

293 Gordon 298.

294 Cirlot 96. That the pilots have not aged over the time they were missing finds similarities in faerie lore, as referenced in Baughman's F377—F377(d), which allude to supernatural lapses of time while in fairyland (Baughman 221, where he reports that the period of time it takes to dance with the fairies may actually be weeks, months, or even years. Other accounts include a boy who falls asleep on a hill, awakes in fairyland, where he spends half a day that is really three weeks, and one where King Herla visits the fairy king for a day which turns out to be two hundred years.)

295 Baughman 387.

296 English 45.

297 Campbell 43.

298 Woods 196.

299 Pickering 76.

300 During a subsequent argument with his wife, a poster emblazoned with the word "Help" hangs next to Roy's head.

301 Cirlot 210.

302 Farmer 252. The establishment of a specific faerie kingdom interestingly arises in tandem with French literary influences on English literature, exemplified by literary accounts of Arthurian legend. Initially a simpler Welsh military leader holding off Roman forces, Arthur was reimagined by the French as the better known monarch of Camelot, reigning over the Knights of the Round Table, in regal trappings comparable to the late-medieval romance depictions of faeries as aristocratic or royal beings that led privileged lives of leisure and opulence.

303 Baughman 204. Not until the sixteenth century had a cohesive pan-British literary concept of a faerie kingdom become codified, as attested to in English, Scottish, and Welsh sources (Hutton 1144 and 1151). The faerie kingdom ranged from leisure and opulence to indulgent hedonism.

304 Wilde 142.

305 Baughman 203.

306 Noel 8.

307 Cirlot 209.

308 Cirlot 208.

309 Jung 219 n. 14.

310 Teillard qtd. in Cirlot 208.

311 Guenon qtd. in Cirlot 210.

312 Jung 239.

313 Jung 239.

314 Jung 217.

315 Jung 215 and 216.

316 The wise old man appears "in the guise of a magician, doctor, priest, teacher, professor, grandfather, or any other person possessing authority" (Jung 216).

317 It is notably Lacombe who is the one to communicate through hand gestures to what one may assume is the lead entity.

318 Campbell 125.

319 If Jillian serves this vital function, Ronnie represents the temptress, the feminine figure who attempts to lure the hero from his journey. Again, consideration of archetypes necessitates not viewing characters in a literal sense, but taking them out of the personalized, local, particular context. That Ronnie is Roy's wife does not mean she cannot be the temptress, any more than Roy's relationship with Jillian should be read as adulterous. In Ronnie's case, her lure is less sexual and more characterized by assertions of logic and practicality, frameworks within which Roy's visions are unwelcome. It is notable, however, that when Roy takes his family out to wait for the return of the unidentified crafts, she attempts to distract him with a somewhat overzealous, rather socially inappropriate kiss.

320 Campbell 97.

321 Why does Jillian not join Roy on the mothership? This is connected to the archetype of the child, here represented by Barry. The child figure represents the emergence of a new paradigm. While Roy's journey involves his departure from earth, Barry's arguably is to reveal what he has seen to the world. As his mother, Jillian's role is to nurture her son, preparing him for his eventual role as teacher to the world. Hers and Barry's departure with Roy would undermine the role of the child archetype and divest him of his purpose.

322 Zipes ix.

323 Zipes 93.

324 Kluckhohn 168.

325 Lévi-Strauss 428.

326 Keightley, T. (1828). *The Fairy Mythology*. London, UK: William Harrison Ainsworth.

327 Cutchin, J. (2015). *A Trojan Feast*. San Antonio, TX: Anomalist Books.

328 Daimler, M. (2017). *Fairies: A Guide to the Celtic Fair Folk*. Alresford, UK: Moon Books.

329 Daimler, M. (2016). *Brigid: Meeting the Celtic Goddess of Poetry, Forge, and Healing Well*. Alresford, UK: Moon Books.

330 Cutchin, J. (2018). *Thieves in the Night: A Brief History of Supernatural Child Abductions*. San Antonio, TX: Anomalist Books.

331 Daimler 2017.

332 Cutchin 2018.

333 Guiney, L.I. (1888). *Brownies and Bogles*. Boston, MA: D. Lothrop Company.

334 Evans Wentz, W.Y. (1911). *The Fairy-Faith in Celtic Countries*. London, UK: Henry Frowde.

335 Put your own music on, because the script is terrible.

336 I have argued this in relation to the development of fairy wings, "When did fairies get wings?", *The Paranormal and Popular Culture*, (ed.) John W. Morehead and Darryl Caterine (London: Routledge, 2019), 253-274 at 273-274.

337 This begs the question of whether the screen image inspires the vision (or at least the form it takes), or whether it is a simple point of reference—see further Young, "Children Who See Fairies", *Journal for the Study of Religious Experience 4* (2017), 81-98 at 86.

338 Maria Beville, *The Unnameable Monster in Literature and Film* (London: Routledge, 2014).

339 e.g. Jenny Butler, "Fairy Forts and the Sídhe: Ireland", *Magical Folk: British and Irish Fairies at Home and Overseas*, (ed.) Simon Young and Ceri Houlbrook (London: Gibson Square, 2018), 95-107 at 107; note that I have also certainly used this expression!

340 Neal Gabler, *Walt Disney: The Biography* (London: Aurum Press, 2007), 10.

341 Gabler, *Walt Disney*, 465-468.

342 *Walt Disney*, xiv and Gabler continues, "From Mickey Mouse, through *Snow White and the Seven Dwarfs*, though Disneyland, through EPCOT, he kept attempting to remake the world in the image of his own imagination."

343 On children in Kansas and Missouri Chris Woodyard writes me: "the first thing I thought of was Arthur Stilwell of Kansas City, Missouri, whose articles about brownies were published in 1921. I don't know if there are earlier writings of his about Brownies—he made no secret of his belief."

344 Simon Young, "A History of the Fairy Investigation Society, 1927-1960", *Folklore 124*, 139-156 at 139. Theosophic fairies deserve a book-length study. Traditional fairies, note, had previously been associated, in a very allusive way, with nature, occasionally even with fertility, but not so clearly with natural production.

345 For this section on the *Silly Symphonies* I relied overwhelmingly on Russell Merritt and J. B. Kaufman's brilliant *Walt Disney's Silly Symphonies: A Companion to the Classic Cartoon Series* (Glendale: Disney Books, 2016).

346 Having a long-standing interest in the history of fairy wings, I'm fascinated by the way that fairies in early silent films did not have wings. Theatre storerooms and costume shops had fairy wings on offer. Why did early directors not use

them? My best guess is that they felt that putting wings on fairies would have obliged them to have fairies fly.

347 Gabler, *Walt Disney*, 328.

348 Trish Lambert, "Snow White and Bilbo Baggins: Divergences and Convergences Between Disney and Tolkien", helpfully republished at http://alasnotme.blogspot.com/2017/05/guest-post-trish-lambert-snow-white-and.html [accessed 11 Aug 2020]. Lewis wrote of "bad originality in the bloated, drunken, low comedy faces of the dwarfs. Neither the wisdom, the avarice, nor the earthiness of true dwarfs were there, but an imbecility of arbitrary invention."

349 David Whitley, *The Idea of Nature in Disney Animation* (Aldershot: Ashgate, 2008), 21 offers analysis.

350 *Interni e dintorni del Pinocchio: folkloristi italiani del tempo del Collodi* (ed.) Pietro Clemente and Mariano Fresta (Pescia: del Grifo, 1986), 187-295.

351 Jack Zipes, *The Enchanted Screen: The Unknown History of Fairy-Tale Films* (London: Routledge, 2011), 306.

352 Richard Sugg, *Fairies: A Dangerous History* (London: Reaktion, 2018), 232.

353 Kathy Merlock Jackson (ed.), *Walt Disney: Conversations* (Jackson: University of Mississippi Press, 2006), 109.

354 Gabler, *Walt Disney*, 339, though ever the business man Disney thought that the end could be snipped off for any market that might disapprove of the Christian message!

355 Juliette Wood, "Filming Fairies: Popular Film, Audience Response and Meaning in Contemporary Fairy Lore", *Folklore 117* (2006), 279-296 at 285.

356 Charles Solomon's brilliant *The Disney That Never Was* (New York: Hyperion 1995), 66-77.

357 Disney in *I Captured the King of the Leprechauns* (publicity film for *Darby*).

358 Tony Tracy, "When Disney Met Delargy: 'Darby O'Gill' and the Irish Folklore Commission", *Béaloideas 78* (2010), 44-60.

359 Gabler, *Walt Disney*, 395-396 and Solomon *The Disney That Never Was*, 106-114.

360 Wood, 'Filming Fairies', 285.

361 https://www.snopes.com/fact-check/tinker-bell/ [accessed 11 Aug 2020]. One Margaret Kerry was actually the model for Tink. Watching the film Margaret excitedly pointed out Tinker Bell to her husband who replied: "Margaret, I'd recognize those thighs anywhere."

362 See https://www.irishcentral.com/culture/entertainment/walt-disney-asked-to-meet-eamon-de-valera-while-researching-leprechauns [accessed 18 January, 2023].

363 See http://thehistoryofdisney.blogspot.com/2011/04/how-i-met-king-of-leprechauns-by-walt.html [accessed 11 Aug 2020].

364 Simon Young, "A History of the Fairy Investigation Society, 1927-1960."

365 Young, "A History of the Fairy Investigation Society, 1927-1960," 151-153. Note that I have Xerox copies of the original.

366 Marjorie T. Johnson, *Seeing Fairies: From the Lost Archives of the Fairy Investigation Society, Authentic Reports of Fairies in Modern Times* (San Antonio: Anomalist Books, 2014).

367 I emailed the archives during the Covid 19 lockdown of 2020 but got no satisfying reply. I suspect work in said archives would resolve this question.

368 Simon Young, "A History of the Fairy Investigation Society, 1927-1960," 145-146.

369 Whitley, *The Idea of Nature in Disney Animation*, 13.

370 In fact, Disney originally wanted the fire at the end of the film to kill the hunters (John Culhane, *Walt Disney's Fantasia* [New York: Abradale, 1983], 57) and even asked his animators to draw their dead bodies, leading to this question from an animator: "How do you want the bodies drawn, Walt?... medium, rare or well done."

371 Hiroshi, I. (2005). Encyclopedia of Shinto. Retrieved February 4, 2023 from https://www2.kokugakuin.ac.jp/e-shinto/?entryID=231

372 Cutchin, J. (2018). *Thieves in the Night: A Brief History of Supernatural Child Abductions*. San Antonio. TX: Anomalist Books.

373 Lindström, H.R. (October 2014). *Casas das Mouras Encantadas – A Study of dolmens in Portuguese archaeology and folklore*. (Master's thesis.) University of Helsinki, Helsinki, FI.

374 Martinez, S.B. (2013). *The Lost History of the Little People*. Rochester, VT: Bear & Company.

375 d'Alveydre, A.S.Y. (2008). *The Kingdom of Agarttha: A Journey into the Hollow Earth*. (J.E. Graham, Trans.) Rochester, VT: Inner Traditions. (Original work published 1886.)

376 Lachman, G. (2012). *Madame Blavatsky: The Mother of Modern Spirituality*. New York, NY: Tarcher.

377 Story, R.D. (Ed.). (2001). *The Mammoth Encyclopedia of Extraterrestrial Encounters*. London, UK: Constable & Robinson Ltd.

378 Cutchin 2018.

379 Toronto, R. (2013). *War Over Lemuria*. Jefferson, NC: McFarland & Company, Inc.

380 Lovecraft, H.P. (2005). *At the Mountains of Madness*. New York, NY: Modern Library. (Original work published 1936.)

381 Wilson, C. & Wilson, D. (2000). *The Mammoth Encyclopedia of the Unsolved*. New York, NY: Carroll & Graf Publishers, Inc.

382 Clark, J. (2013). *Unexplained! Strange Sightings, Incredible Occurrences, and Puzzling Physical Phenomena* (3rd ed.). Canton, MI: Visible Ink Press.

383 Keightley, T. (1828). *The Fairy Mythology*. London, UK: William Harrison Ainsworth.

384 Vallee, J. (1993). *Passport to Magonia*. Chicago, IL: Contemporary Books. (Original work published 1969.)

385 de Haza, S.C. (2008). *The Modern Vampire*. Morrisville, NC: Lulu.

386 McRoy, J. (2008). *Nightmare Japan: Contemporary Japanese Horror Cinema*. Amsterdam, NL: Editions Rodopi.

387 Evans Wentz, W.Y. (1911). *The Fairy-Faith in Celtic Countries*. London, UK: Henry Frowde.

388 Silver, C.G. (1999). *Strange and Secret Peoples: Fairies and Victorian Consciousness*. New York, NY: Oxford University Press, Inc.

389 Cutchin 2018.

390 McRoy 2008.

391 Ibid.

392 Keel, J. A. (1976). *The Eighth Tower: On Ultraterrestrials and the Superspectrum*. New York, NY: E.P. Dutton & Co. Inc.; Keel, J. (1976). *The Mothman Prophecies*. New York, NY: Signet Books.

393 Bane, T. (2013). *Encyclopedia of Fairies in World Folklore and Mythology*. Jefferson, NC: McFarland & Company, Inc.

394 Kaji, S. (March 9, 2015). The unseen casualties of Japan's lost decades suffer in silence. Retrieved February 4, 2023 from https://www.ft.com/content/042a592e-c283-11e4-ad89-00144feab7de

395 Ogden, D. (2001). *Greek and Roman Necromancy*. Princeton, NJ: Princeton University Press.

396 Willis, R. (Ed.) (1993). *World Mythology*. New York, NY: Henry Holt and Company, LLC.

397 Ibid.

398 Ibid.

399 Cutchin, J. (2015). *A Trojan Feast*. San Antonio, TX: Anomalist Books.

400 Lönnrot, E. (2021). *Kalevala*. (E. Friberg, Trans.) London, UK: Penguin Classics.

401 Crowley, A. (1996). *Little Essays Toward Truth*. Los Angeles, CA: New Falcon Publications.

402 Lachman, G. (2014). *Aleister Crowley: Magick, Rock and roll, and the Wickedest Man in the World*. New York, NY: Tarcher.